Once Upon a Time in Bollywood

The Global Swing in Hindi Cinema

Edited by

Gurbir Jolly
Zenia Wadhwani
Deborah Barretto

TSAR

We acknowledge the support of the Canada Council for the Arts for our publishing program. We also acknowledge support from the Government of Ontario through the Ontario Arts Council.

Canada Council for the Arts Conseil des Arts du Canada

ONTARIO ARTS COUNCIL
CONSEIL DES ARTS DE L'ONTARIO

Cover designed by Gurbir Jolly

Library and Archives Canada Cataloguing in Publication

Once upon a time in Bollywood : the global swing in Hindi cinema / edited by Gurbir Jolly, Zenia Wadhwani, Deborah Barretto.

Includes bibliographical references and index.
ISBN 978-1-894770-40-8

1. Motion pictures--India. 2. Motion pictures--Social aspects--India.
I. Jolly, Gurbir Singh, 1972- II. Wadhwani, Zenia B., 1971-
III. Barretto, Deborah

PN1993.5.I8O53 2007 791.430954 C2007-904919-2

Printed in Canada by Coach House Printing

TSAR Publications
P. O. Box 6996, Station A
Toronto, Ontario M5W 1X7
Canada

www.tsarbooks.com

Contents

Dedicated to all the Bollywood heroines, heroes, vamps, and villains
—on the big screen and off.

Introduction
Globalization: The Musical

GURBIR JOLLY

This collection examines how India's march towards globalization, or economic "liberalization," affects the aesthetics, production, and consumption of popular commercial Hindi cinema—affectionately called Bollywood. Since the early 1990s, various Indian governments have steadily distanced themselves from "socialist" policies that had characterized India since Independence, while increasingly committing themselves to free-market friendly policies which are the lifeblood of globalization. These policies, far from being all that *global* in their outlook, involve relaxing state restrictions over moving certain kinds of capital, disinvesting from public services, and conceding to the discipline, and whims, of transnational markets driven by wealthier communities in the Anglosphere (that is, the United Kingdom and the white settler colonies of its former empire, including the United States, Canada, and Australia). This economic trajectory, along with its radical social implications, has invited fierce criticism and support from across India's rich and checkered political spectrum. *Once Upon a Time in Bollywood* explores the often conflicting pressures and possibilities, if not fears and desires, that riddle Bollywood's stories of globalization.

Bollywood's well-crafted, lyrically lush responses to globalization are capable of staggering flair, in part because Bollywood has long been a site where Indians have negotiated their "global" affiliations. Based in Bombay (now Mumbai), a coastal city with colonial-era roots, Bollywood emerged out of a remarkable, albeit often uneasy, fusion of cultural movements, traditions, and innovations. Critically-minded connoisseurs of Bollywood have recognized, in Bollywood's hybrid origins, the resonance of epic Indian modes of storytelling, right alongside the influence of Parsi theater (which itself drew generously from

European sources), as well as the prominence of Muslim and Anglo-Indian actors. Engaging this kaleidoscopic range of steadily intensifying influences always risks pushing the envelope of sensory and imaginary overload, which is why watching Bollywood films, with their grand, spiraling, rollercoaster-like narratives, so often make you feel like you are spinning in some hypervivid dream. This robust, almost oversaturated hybridity allows Bollywood to demystify and remystify issues of political economy relying on dialogue, music, choreography, and characterization capable of being, at once, stirringly subtle and jarringly garish.

Our collection begins with Susan Dewey's "Doing Bombay Darsan: The IMF, Structural Adjustment and National Identity in the Hindi Film Industry." Delivered in the personal, self-reflective, visually fecund style of much contemporary ethnographic writing, Dewey's critical analysis of India's swing towards a neoliberal economy emerges from her months of research gathered while working in a Bombay film house. How has adjusting to "international standards" of commerce pressured Bollywood to reevaluate domestic standards for cinematic production, profitability, popularity, innovation, and excellence? These questions, Dewey reminds us, draw attention to a base uncertainty that underlies globalization: when is it "no longer clear where domination stops and agency begins?" Dewey's enterprising treatment of this question blends feminist critiques of cinema within her investigation into the cunning commerce of film production.

Monika Mehta's "Globalizing Bombay Cinema: Reproducing the Indian State and Family" considers the emergence and appeal of 90s-era blockbuster "family films." As Mehta details, these movies present quaint, yet politically charged narratives which champion "traditional" (read, stereotypical) Indian wholesomeness alongside "the pleasures of consumerism" in an attempt to weave "a happy marriage between Indian 'traditions' and the global market." Diasporic characters, primarily post-Independence émigrés, figure large in a number of these films, serving as convenient and potent symbols of "globalized Indians" who manifest, and usually triumph over, anxieties that attend globalization. Mehta begins her exploration of this cinematic phenomenon by considering the Indian state's unusual move, in 1998, to recognize the film industry *officially*—recognition that came with benefits, and strings. Now, doesn't globalization usually entail *de*regulation? Mehta untangles this irony for us by presenting an eye-opening portrait of the disparate and shifting channels of financing that keep Bollywood going. In these "family films," which blossomed under economic liberalization, Bollywood filmmakers presented a simulacrum of the Indian family and nation that shrewdly appealed to lucrative diasporic audiences beset with nostalgia, as well to domestic audiences facing massive, internationally-impelled economic reorientation.

Radhika Desai's "Imagi Nation: The Reconfiguration of National Identity in Bombay Cinema in the 1990s" presents another fresh, critical telling of India's economic reformation and Bollywood's rendition of this gospel of globalization. Beneath some of the key trends that signaled Bollywood's "global" turn—such as increasing state influence in production, and films that prominently featured diasporic characters who propagated narrow ideals of "traditional" Indian values—Desai identifies more sinister, upper-caste prejudices and sectarian discourses of Hindutva (a right-wing, fundamentalist movement, politically ascendant when most of the films discussed in this collection were made, premised on the doctrine that Hindus are the most legitimate Indians). Desai demonstrates how these family-friendly blockbusters, which are often love stories stretched across global locales, are the cinematic kin of another genre which thrived as India globalized: militaristic, jingoistic films which valorized the vision of a distinctly and aggressively bordered nation. One of the most intriguing features of Bollywood's story of globalization, as Desai accounts, are the compelling tensions and surprisingly deep parallels between the myth of pure-and-portable Indianness in love stories (where tradition is tenacious enough to blossom in any global setting), and the suspicious, us-and-them, the-border-stops-here posture of 90s-era action movies. Desai challenges us to consider how the symbolic schema of globalized Bollywood predicates each genre's cinematic sensibility, and success, on the other's.

Nitin Deckha's inquiry into the "anxieties about national identity and belonging" that can accompany globalization centres on constructions of masculinity in three smash-hit films made a decade after India began liberalizing its economy: *Dil Chaata Hai* (2001), *Salaam Namaste* (2005), and *Parineeta* (2005). Deckha, in "From Artist-as-Hero to the Creative Young Man: Bollywood and the Aestheticization of Indian Masculinity," clarifies how these films are aimed at "the burgeoning South Asian consuming classes," and how their characterizations of masculinity emerge from "a cultural politics of a late, globalized, hybrid Indian modernity." Deckha, nevertheless, contends that these films' leading men problematize simplistic formulations of either "tradition" or "progress"—two of the most fervent tropes in globalized Bollywood! "At a time when the urban young Indian male risks being stereotyped as a faceless technology worker," notes Deckha, "Bollywood is creating heroes whose inclinations and ambitions seem decidedly antitechnological." Deckha's analysis does not simply rest on his detailed reading of these films' narratives; he invites us to recognize how the politics of aesthetics represents an order of power in which globalized Indian masculinity struggles to reconstitute itself.

Jenny Sharpe's "Gender, Nation, and Globalization in Mira Nair's *Monsoon Wedding* (2001) and Aditya Chopra's *Dilwale Dulhania Le Jayenge*"(1995) contrasts and deconstructs these watershed films' shared central symbol for the apprehension and appeal of globalization: a young bride-to-be, wrestling with her misgivings over her marriage that has been arranged across the diaspora, all the while being genuinely drawn to "tradition" despite being less "traditional" than her family realizes. Chopra's film operates comfortably in the aesthetically calescent, fantastical, nonrealist narrative mode which is Bollywood standard-fare. Nair, a New York-based filmmaker, shot her film using a handheld Super 16 camera, typical of American documentary style. Although Nair certainly seems inspired by Bollywood's hybrid bravado, her departures from key Bollywood conventions—using street language, addressing taboo sex—gave her a different kind of latitude to explore "the contradictions of everyday life that opening India to globalization has produced." Nevertheless, as Sharpe details, *Monsoon Wedding* may be more like its Bollywood doppelganger, *Dilwale Dulhania Le Jayenge,* than we might initially appreciate. Both films harbour a complicated affection for the tenacity of the traditions they problematize, and both lay bare how globalization—far from being a dry issue of transnational political economy—catalyzes the fragmentation of intensely intimate desires.

Ravinder Kaur opens "Viewing the West Through Bollywood: A Celluloid Occident in the Making" with an avid and nimble defense of nonrealist popular film as an important stage upon which India's globalized middle class fictionalizes and fetishizes the West. Rather than trying to "correct" various cinematic distortions, Kaur draws our attention to one of the sustaining ironies of globalized Bollywood's plastic Occident. On the one hand, these films are littered with an overabundance of gaudy American and European brand-name logos—the veneration of corporate iconography going hand-in-hand with an endemic reverence for the fruits of Western consumerism. On the other hand, Euro-American characters, once restricted to playing British colonizers, international gangsters, or background dancers, are rendered in globalized Bollywood as "rude, aggressive wives, seductresses, crafty businessmen, hostile bus drivers, or greedy doctors who refuse to treat the patient until they get paid." What continues to fuel this fabricated Occident and continues to give its contradictions currency, argues Kaur, is its role in reflecting and sustaining a conflicted longing for some mythic "authentic Indianness" that can retain its purity in a globalized world where cultures mix promiscuously.

Usamah Ansari also explores Bollywood and the lure of authenticity, albeit using a very different set of discursive tools and strategies. Ansari's introspective, "Tempting Sights and Seven Seas: The Diasporic-Self, Bollywood, and the Gendered Politics of National Longing" draws on visual anthropology to examine the displacement, if not absence, of Muslims in Bollywood's fictions of homeland and diaspora. How does this mediate *his* longing for "home," as a diasporic Indian Muslim? Ansari considers Bollywood's role in nurturing Indian nationalism, then investigates how transnational audiences—wooed by Bollywood—can critically and imaginatively engage such "filmy" nationalism. Noting that his nostalgia for "home" has never been satisfied by his stays in India, Ansari proposes that Bollywood offers a "diasporic imaginary," that is, "something beyond the bound nation-state: the possibility of a point of departure; an originary home that may not exist in geographic terms." As a diasporic subject, with tangled ties to India, Ansari's analysis evinces how films pushing nationalist agendas, despite having serious transnational commitments, can constitute "home" within the landscape of the imagination.

Sonia Benjamin's study of Mani Ratnam's *Roja* (1992) takes up this motif of the Muslim "other" while judiciously demonstrating how the dynamics of otherness operates very, very differently in the original Tamil version of the film than in the later, "national," Hindi version. Benjamin's gutsy and imaginative take on *Roja* does not attempt to redeem a film which, nationally, was widely derided as a cinematic endorsement for the reactionary Hindu Right. Rather, "How I Stopped Worrying and Learned to Love *Roja*" spells out how large-screen others, when viewed from a regional vantage, can be radically recontextualized and reformulated. Proposing that *Roja*, as a Tamil movie, can be read "as a film of loss and mourning—the loss of beloved ideals and [the] mourning of lost humanity," Benjamin highlights the dangers of trivializing regional concerns when discussing how Bollywood appropriates regional cinema to test the nervous and alluring threshold between the nation and the world.

Ahmad Saidullah's "Western Receptions: Bollywood and Indian

Cinema at the Toronto International Film Festival (1994)" questions why avant-garde, socially progressive Indian films were lukewarmly dismissed at this festival while hallmark films of globalized Bollywood—including *Roja*—attracted considerably more interest. Saidullah suggests the "prevailing taste of North American festival-goers" was obsessed with "filmness," "fronting techniques," and "devices of disruption and discontinuity"—which is why Bollywood films, especially globalized Bollywood films, can so satisfy audiences seeking "experimental" deviations from dominant Western conventions of linear/realist cinema. Mani Ratnam's cinematic innovations notwithstanding, Saidullah questions how India's populist, popcorn-munching films can morph into Western, festivalesque exemplars of alternative cinema. Although Saidullah stresses differences between films dealing "with the problems of daily living faced by ordinary people in India" and Bollywood blockbusters oft-characterized by surging middle-class consumerism and acerbic nationalism, he cautions against pigeonholing films as either blockbuster pop or art-house progressive. He does this by drawing our attention to a fiercely controversial film, Shekhar Kapur's *Bandit Queen*, also screened at that year's festival, which tells the "true" story of Phoolan Devi (despite Phoolan's explicit concerns and objections about the film), a low-caste woman who slaughtered the high-caste men who had gang-raped her. Saidullah's article includes the full text of Phoolan's open letter to the Director of the Toronto Film Festival, a public statement from the Director, a press statement from BBC Channel 4 (which funded the film) defending itself against Phoolan's "allegations," and an interview between Saidullah and Kapur. Unlike *Roja*, a huge national hit, *Bandit Queen* had modest domestic success, for a number of reasons, despite much international acclaim. Because major Western film festivals, like TIFF, provide a glimpse into the politics of cinematic ambassadorship in an era of liberalizing international markets, festival audiences would benefit tremendously from Saidullah's exhortations to investigate how their engagement with *Roja*, with its over-the-top nationalism, affects their engagement with *Bandit Queen*, in which the brutalization of a low-caste, non-globalized Indian is cinematically figured for globalized audiences.

Jennifer Thomas's "Bollywood's Female Fantasies of Resistance: Online Fan Discourse and Modern Indian Identity" introduces us to the nascent but lively fan discourse streaming through globalization's digital nervous system, the Internet. Since online fan forums are often "anonymous, uninhibited, and not accountable to the authority of the film industry or government officials," they can provide a candid glimpse into how tech-savvy fans contest and reify globalized Bollywood's gendered codifications of "tradition" and "modernity." Considering the grand transnational forces that drive globalization, Thomas audaciously underscores the possibilities for interpretive agency among women audiences' "active use of star personas in their identity construction, as well the more general social spectator's active use of fan discourse to shape, control, and contain those star personas." Thomas focuses her discussion of fan responses to the on-screen roles and off-screen rumours that have significantly shaped the careers of Rani Mukherjee and Preity Zinta, two actors whose divergent bodies of work are ripe with emblematic, though often uneven, fantasies of female resistance. Resisting patriarchy might suggest abandoning tradition and embracing modernity (indeed, a number of films and fan discourses fall into this trap), but Thomas entreats us to consider how traditional and modern patriarchy collude and collide within globalized Bollywood.

Our collection concludes with Florian Stadtler's study of the ghosts of Bollywood past in Salman Rushdie's *The Moor's Last Sigh*, a novel which bears witness to the violent globalizing of Bombay. Rushdie's narrative unfolds in the mid-90s, emphasizes Stadtler, "when it became increasingly evident that Bombay had become a divided city not only between Hindus and Muslims, but also between those who gained from the changed economic environment and those who have been excluded." The precarious perseverance of classical Bollywood characters that Stadtler details in "Nargis and Aurora Zogoiby: Imaging Mother and Nation in Mehboob Khan's *Mother India* and Salman Rushdie's *The Moor's Last Sigh*" seems especially remarkable considering how alien these characters—vaguely socialist, Nehruvian idealists—might be in today's glitzy, globalized Bollywood. Stadtler teases the irony out of Rusdhie's trenchant use of the "golden-era" Bollywood mythos of "Mother India" by showing us how Rushdie metaphorically transforms Bollywood from a story-telling medium into a player cast in *his* story, set during India's early, turbulent years of globalization. As globalization threatens economic disjuncture, social dislocation, and political polarization, Stadtler's reading of the Bollywood mother imagery in *The Moor's Last Sigh* attests to the appeal, continuity, and elasticity of India's complex, populist, cinematic consciousness, transfigured from celluloid to ink.

Once Upon a Time in Bollywood explores Bollywood's stories of globalization, as well as stories of Bollywood's globalization. Bollywood films of this era have often glamourized India's global swing, but Bollywood has hardly been a predictable propaganda machine pimping economic liberalization. The deep ironies that punctuate globalized Bollywood need to be reckoned with because they speak to fundamental questions surrounding globalization. Does globalization constitute an invitation to be one of the big boys in the Anglosphere, or has "globalizing" India become a troubling euphemism for "civilizing" India? Supporters of globalization, often citing the steady and impressive expansion of India's Gross National Product, argue that these reforms help generate wealth, which holds the promise of India's graduation into the First World. Critics wonder if this comes at the too-high human cost of grossly exacerbating existing economic, political, and social inequalities—in effect, riding India to the First World on the backs of the most vulnerable. What invigorates globalized Bollywood, as *Once Upon a Time in Bollywood* showcases, are its volatile mixtures of conflicting predilections. The promise of market-driven prosperity confronts the presence of gross economic disparity. The desire for culture so expansive it blends and borrows easily confronts the fear of a culture so essential it cannot be eroded. And all this happens within borders imagined to be so porous they cannot contain Indianness, yet so policed they demand dangerously narrow definitions of authentic "insiders."

Doing Bombay Darshan: The IMF, Structural Adjustment and National Identity in the Hindi Film Industry

SUSAN DEWEY

The Visual Economy of a Neoliberal Bollywood

The advent of neoliberalism in Bombay brought not only a flood of images, products, and ideas from the United States and Europe but also a broader dialogue which pushed the question of "standards" to the fore. These "standards" were a synecdoche for ways of living and thinking that are largely European and American in character, ranging from business practices in the Hindi film industry to new ways of thinking about what it means to be Indian. This in turn created a visual economy in which imported "standards" became privileged over local ones in ways which raised questions of both identity and quality. Using the Hindi film industry as a specific lens through which to examine the vast socio-economic changes which have taken place in Bombay since the implementation of structural adjustment policies in 1991, this article will discuss how meaning is ascribed to European and American social and economic systems which directly impact India.

Theories of the gaze help to illustrate how individuals make sense of life in a world which is undergoing vast structural changes, as well as how power is embedded in the dialogical process of seeing and being seen. The gaze implicitly employs Foucault's (1975) notion of surveillance just as it draws upon the anthropology of class, power, and colonialism in order to address multiple ways of looking. Discussions of difference (Mulvey 1989), sexuality (Mulvey 1996), the self (Silverman 1996), and colonialism (Kaplan 1997) in feminist theory further underscore the power of the gaze to mold not only the image onscreen, but the spectator her or himself. Indeed, theories of the gaze are deeply indebted to broader feminist theoretical discussions about dominance and the distinction between subject and object. Part of the versatility of such analysis lies in their ability to collapse complex social realities into discussions of power structures that highlight the gendered nature of everyday life. Central to the conception of seeing and being seen in feminist theory is the idea of the male gaze, which posits that female identity and behavior are both structured and inhibited by the abstract but nonetheless dominating conflation of masculinity and authority.

Gender is an intersectional reality of life that cannot be separated from either the articulation of power or the practices of everyday life. As such, analyzing what it means to do "Bombay Darshan" is necessarily informed by gendered social identities, as is the implementation of "international standards." Feminist theoretical tools such as the gaze are of exceptional interest to the analysis of a country in which film stars command extraordinary power (Dwyer 2000; Virdi 2002) in their ability to mobilize individuals for political and social causes (Dickey 1993) or to serve as barometers of urban India's openness to "foreign" ideas. Above all, such tools allow for an analysis which transcends simplistic dichotomies and makes way for an understanding of the intersections of power in an increasingly interconnected world.

The anthropology of globalization has tended to frame its discussions around two poles of orientation until fairly recently as a "tension between cultural homogenization and cultural heterogenization" (Appadurai 1996:32). This notion of two extremes pitted against one another has been challenged by numerous ethnographies on the media (Ganti 2000; Gillespie 1995; Goodwin 1992; Gupta 1998; Hutnyk 2000; Mankekar 1999) that underscore the ways in which both individual and national identity is open to negotiation with broader global economic changes.

Structural Adjustment, Media, and National Identity

The neoliberal economy is a little more than a decade old in Bombay, which means that individuals are still coming to terms with the enormous expansion in media images and commodities that the open economy brought with it. Structural adjustment policies altered the lives of nearly everyone in Bombay, whether they were laborers who lost their jobs when "sick" industries such as cloth mills were closed in the interests of reducing government subsidies or film producers who sought to become famous with audiences in the United States and Europe. Even the landscape of the city itself was altered as areas formerly occupied by cloth mills and tenement housing for mill workers were cleared to make way for the construction of shopping malls, discotheques, and sleek apartments built along what were glossed as the "international standards" used in the United States.

The culture of consumption that arose following the implementation of structural adjustment policies was a great contradiction to postindependence India's economic policies of austerity aimed at reducing poverty and supporting national industries. Jawaharlal Nehru, India's first prime minister, placed a heavy emphasis on developing Indian industries, especially in the fields of science and engineering, while his daughter, Prime Minister Indira Gandhi became a strong ally of Soviet socialism prior to her assassination in 1984. Her son, Prime Minister Rajiv Gandhi, prompted a major shift following his election in 1984 by strengthening ties with the United States and taking steps towards a free market economy. This was reflected in the annual sales of packaged consumer goods, which rose 220% to 2.2 billion dollars per year by the late 1980s. Rajiv Gandhi's legacy of economic reform ensured that the Indian economy was more or less open to foreign investment by 1991, when the International Monetary Fund's structural adjustment policies were implemented in response to India's balance of payments crisis (Sharma 1996:308).

Structural adjustment programs have been introduced in over seventy countries around the world with significant debt to the International Monetary Fund (IMF). The IMF was formed in 1944 to establish a framework for economic cooperation and development, and provides policy advice, technical assistance, and short-term loans in order to remedy balance of payments crises (Kocchar et. al. 2002:16). Structural adjustment consists of two phases, both of which are aimed at reducing account deficits: short-term macro-economic stabilization and the implementation of structural reforms deemed necessary by the IMF (Rangarajan et. al. 1994).

In India these reforms amounted to the devaluation of the rupee by twenty-three percent, the introduction of a new industrial policy that was more conducive to foreign investment, government disinvestment in potentially profitable public sector areas, the closure of unproductive public sector units, the introduction of private banks, a liberalized import/export policy, cuts in social spending to reduce fiscal deficits, and amendments in laws to support all of these reforms (Chopra et. al. 1995). These policies deeply disadvantaged Bombay's poor, most notably in the closure of cloth mills deemed unproductive state ventures by the IMF (D'Monte 2000).

As a result, garment manufacturers relocated to regions in North India where real-estate and labour costs were comparatively low. Following a pattern noticeable in most countries where structural adjustment has been implemented, the poor were also victimized by deteriorating public health care (Qadeer et. al. 2001:3) and a general government shift away from social services (Nayar 2001:65). Conversely, those who benefited the most from structural adjustment were corporate investors with ties to multinational corporations involved in foreign direct investment (FDI), who were often the same families who profited from the economic restructuring which took place following independence in 1947.

Neoliberal economic policies also welcomed major international media corporations to India, thus allowing for the expansion and further creation of an already prolific film industry based in Bombay. Numerous scholars (Dwyer 2001; Kasbekar 2001; Mankekar 1999; Vasudevan 2001) have discussed the extensity of the Hindi film industry's influence in India. Films are the subject of a national obsession and the cult of personality that surrounds some actors and actresses is unlike the adulation given to performers anywhere else in the world (Dickey 1993; Thomas 1995). While this phenomenon long predates structural adjustment, the removal of most restrictions on international media and the concomitant increase in the amount of competition to Hindi films led to a restructuring of the industry that mirrored many of the IMF's broader targets of efficiency, productivity, and "international standards" based upon a European and American template.

One of the most salient changes to the media industry in India was the introduction in 1994 of the international satellite network Star TV, a broadcasting conglomerate that beams American and European programming throughout Asia from its head offices in Hong Kong (Page and Crawley 2001). The implementation of the Prasar Bharathi (Broadcasting Corporation of India) Act in 1997 removed government controls from the formerly state-administered Doordarshan television network (Munshi 1997) and marked a notable change in the media industry. Changes brought about by the introduction of international media were vast and overarching, as were the deregulation of national media and the subsequent proliferation of Indian-run cable television networks.

Individuals began to routinely use the media-centric synecdoche "MTV culture" to describe a philosophy of life whose main tenets included individuality, the right to self-expression, and celebrated conspicuous consumption in a new market economy. Individuals who were possessed of what Mathews calls the "receiving equipment"

(2002:68) to take advantage of this brave new world of "MTV culture" did so with abandon in the newly opened nightclubs and media venues, all the while privileging cultural elements which were European and American in origin. "MTV culture" contained gendered elements as well, particularly in its impact on beauty culture, which underwent a veritable revolution in urban India.

Prior to economic liberalization, women had two brands of lipstick and cold cream to choose from in order to satisfy their beauty needs. In the last five years, however, zaibatsu giant Hindustan Lever Ltd released 250 new beauty products, and international corporations have also subsequently been heavily involved in marketing beauty products in India. French cosmetics giant L'Oreal, for example, has spent over thirty million dollars on local manufacturing since 1994. As a senior executive at Hindustan Lever told me in the course of an interview, "the Indian woman no longer compares herself to other Indians—she uses international concepts of beauty." When I asked the editor of *Femina*, South Asia's most popular women's magazine, what she made of these changes, she was quick to note that images of beauty had "changed amazingly in the last five or six years because of the multinationals coming in. They brought images of beauty with them which were very different from what we had, and therefore we internationalized our images of beauty, and today we see that reflected in the way that young women look."

As Saran's point illustrates, transnational flows of media can move in several directions at once, such as Hong Kong cinema to the United States (Teo 1997) or Hindi cinema to West Africa (Larkin 1997), and these movements both directly and indirectly affect the lives of spectators. Many scholars (Gerke 2000; Kemper 2002; Liechty 2003) have noted that privileged ways of being and thinking are more often than not European or American in origin, and yet to deny the reality that power and agency is exercised at all social levels by all social actors (Foucault 1980) is to oversimplify reality. Operating in tandem within the economic realities of structural adjustment there is also a visual economy of symbols through which individuals negotiate what it means to be Indian that is not without cultural and historical precedent.

Doing Bombay Darshan: "Heritage Buildings" and the Question of History

The Hindi word *darshan* conveys the Hindu religious concept of simultaneously seeing and interacting with the divine in the dialogical process worshippers engage in when they pray to a representation of a god or goddess that embodies its celestial essence. *Darshan* is also used in ordinary Hindi as a verb meaning "to gaze at," although the true connotation is rooted in a religious practice that blurs the distinction between subject and object in ways which are markedly similar to poststructural adjustment patterns of visual consumption. New meanings of what it means to be "Indian" are also constructed through a process of exchange between the viewer and the viewed, so that urban life in Bombay's neoliberal economy is concurrently informed by its colonial past and what is discursively constructed throughout South Asia as its "international" present.

Everyday, visitors from all over India are transported on a sight-seeing tour that extends from the grey-green shores of South Bombay's Marine Drive to the sprawling suburban bungalow that houses legendary Hindi film star Amitabh Bachchan via a curiously named vehicle: The Bombay Darshan Bus.[1] The bus' quasireligious reference is particularly apt given the city's status in South Asia as the source of the celluloid fantasies of the Hindi film industry as well as a place that is believed by many to offer unlimited possibilities to millions of subcontinental migrants. The Bombay Darshan Bus departs every morning from the Gateway of India, which was built at the southernmost tip of the city to commemorate the visit of King George V and Queen Mary in 1911. The Gateway, modelled on the Arc de Triomphe, is engraved in a style that closely resembles the Mughal architecture of North India and was the seaside landmark that visiting imperial dignitaries would see first when they called upon what was then the trade hub of the Jewel in the Imperial Crown.

The bus then briefly passes by a statue of Shivaji, the seventeenth century founder of the Hindu kingdom of Maharashtra, the state of which Bombay is currently the capital. The driver then halts at the sixteenth-century Mughal-style Prince of Wales Museum, so named because its foundation was laid by the Prince of Wales in 1905. This is followed by a stop at the Jehangir Art Gallery, built by the Parsi art patron Sir Jehangir Cowasji in 1952. Passing by Bombay University's nineteenth-century Rajabai Clock Tower, built by a wealthy Indian businessman, the bus slows down near what the British called Flora Fountain, an elaborately carved marble fountain which was renamed Hutatma Chowk (The Square of Sacrifice) in 1994 in honor of the one hundred and five people killed in the independence struggle against the British.

The bus then passes an enormous Gothic train station that was modelled on London's central transportation hub and is used by nearly two million passengers every day. Victoria Terminus is yet another

British-built structure that was renamed (to Chatrapati Shivaji Terminus, after the founder of Maharashtra) in 1996 following the election of a right-wing Hindu political party, although its original name is still used by most individuals. The politics of colonial place names follow a pattern in Bombay so that nearly every structure built prior to 1947 has two names: one Marathi, the indigenous language of the region, and the other English. What this means in practice is that while street signs and place names may be altered by politicians, the vast majority of Bombay residents choose to use the original English names in conversation.

The sidewalks which surround these landmarks are lined with inexpensive imported goods ranging from Chinese radios to bootleg copies of Hollywood films, many of which are displayed under umbrellas to protect them from the afternoon sun, pollution, and salty ocean air. The bus then turns the corner to skirt Marine Drive on the shores of the Arabian Sea, also known as "The Queen's Necklace" because of the electric streetlights that commemorated the arrival of Queen Mary in 1911. Multistoried corporate offices that house former government-controlled companies such as Air India, which have been privatized since the advent of neoliberalism in 1991, line the street opposite Marine Drive. The guide who narrates the tour on The Bombay Darshan Bus invariably announces that while the view of the sea may be beautiful from the bus window, it is unbelievably breathtaking when seen from the vantage point of Malabar Hill, a neighborhood were real estate can cost over five hundred dollars a square foot.

The subtext of The Bombay Darshan Bus Tour is always one that implicitly references both the colonial and corporate histories of the city, including the increasing divisions between rich and poor that have accompanied the implementation of structural adjustment policies. The stark contrasts of city are unmistakable as the bus passes Tarporewala Aquarium, built by one of the wealthiest entrepreneurs in India, to Chowpatty Beach, where homeless migrants and lepers sleep, to the Hanging Gardens, built by the British in 1880 and where the children of the wealthy now play amongst shrubs carefully sculpted to resemble elephants and giraffes.

The bus then passes Kamala Nehru Park, named after the wife of the first prime minister of India and built in 1922, and goes on to Nehru Planetarium, inaugurated by Prime Minister Indira Gandhi in 1976 in honour of her father, former prime minister Jawaharlal Nehru. Following this, the bus stops at the Mahalaxmi Temple, dedicated to the Hindu goddess of wealth and prosperity. As the Hindu passengers file out of the bus to take darshan of the goddess, the tour guide remarks how appropriate such a temple is in Bombay, a city seen throughout India as a place of fabulous wealth.

The passengers are then afforded a view of Haji Ali Dargah, a shrine to a Muslim saint that is situated five hundred yards out to sea. The image of Muslim women walking along the ocean pathway to pray, their black burqas waving poetically in the wind, has been used in countless Hindi films, and many passengers on the bus are rendered speechless at the sight of it. At this point, the tour guide comments on Bombay's heterogeneous ethnic and religious populations, as no other city in South Asia has such a diverse blend of communities living in a single urban area. The bus then spends the next hour in relative silence through the drive to Bombay's northern suburbs where film studios and the homes of many Hindi film stars are located.

The silent drive between the two seemingly distinct worlds of former British colonial power in South Bombay and the more recent film studios in the north of the city speaks to the nuanced and multi-layered realities of life in a vibrant urban center with rich social and cultural histories. An excellent example of the complexities of Bombay's histories can be found in an organization which works to preserve what are known as "heritage buildings," British structures in the southern part of Bombay, housing the families and corporations that have been major features in Bombay's economy since before independence. The Foundation to Preserve Heritage Buildings concerns itself with a relatively small area of the city that can be walked across in about an hour, known as the Kala Ghoda (Black Horse) Crescent, which extends from the southern end of Mahatma Gandhi Road, where the Bombay Gymkhana is located, to Bombay University in the north, with the cricket field of Oval Maidan to the west and the former military barracks of Lion Gate to the east.

As a result of the Foundation's activities, it is forbidden to change the exterior edifice of any structure in Bombay that has been declared a "heritage building." This is of particular note given the amount of money that builders have been willing to pay for space in the southern side of the city in which to construct high-rise apartment buildings for high income families. While neoliberalism resulted in the destruction of mills and other formerly state-owned corporations, its advent also spurred a movement to preserve what are at least superficial reminders of the city's colonial history. This reality complicates at least some of the arguments in Bombay that support neoliberalism as a celebration of a new national self-determinism by presenting very real questions about whose interests are being served and whose socio-economic structures are being privileged.

The Foundation is primarily supported as a hobby by women whose families compose the Indian elite who filled the power vacuum left by the departure of the British colonial administration in 1947. These women meet on a regular basis at the Bombay Gymkhana, a social centre built for colonial administrators to engage in sports and relaxation activities in 1875 and was appropriated by the Indian elite following independence in a not-uncommon practice of assimilation of the built form (King 1990:79). For such women, living in a "heritage building" is not at all about British colonialism, but rather a marker of their families' wealth and prestige in the city, and their efforts at preserving this "heritage" must be construed through a lens which is sensitive to the multiple meanings that such structures take on over time.

Chatterjee (1993) has noted the way in which European and American scholarship serves to "swamp" the history of India, defining the British colonial period as the crucial moment in India's history when much had transpired before and has continued to take place since. This reality notwithstanding, the British East India Company was instrumental in fostering the networks of trade that made Bombay into a city unlike any the subcontinent had ever seen, in which people from different religious and ethnic groups lived side by side (Lawson 1993:58). The Foundation to Preserve Heritage Buildings lies somewhere between these two discrete poles, which posit alternate views of Bombay as an independent entity versus Bombay as a colonial remnant.

I interviewed the President of The Foundation to Preserve Heritage Buildings about whose "heritage" it was that the Foundation sought to protect. When I asked her how she felt about the Bombay Gymkhana's history as a space of imperial domination, she laughed, exclaiming, "That was so long ago!" After a pause to think, however, she became a bit more reflective, using her drink as an example, noting, "It's a bit like my gin fizz, these things. At first glance, it's something of substance, easy to define, a glass of gin and tonic. After a while, though, if one looks at it long enough, it becomes clear that it's all just bubbles, millions of little bubbles." Indeed, like the gin fizz, Bombay's history is also made up of millions of fragmentary pieces.

If the case of Bombay demonstrates anything, it is that power is a process which works in multiple ways, as much enforced from below as imposed from above. Foucault is clear that humans are possessed of agency in the complex schema of power. Not simply targets for the imposition of power, individual social actors "are also the elements of its articulation" (1980:98). The real question, then, is to whom the heritage buildings actually belong. Boyarin suggests that the answer to such questions may lie in envisioning history as a multilinear process in which time is not "a one-dimensional and irreversible phenomenon" (1994:2), but rather a reality that constructs the present as much as it precedes it. Boyarin's argument bears a striking relationship to the metaphor of the gin fizz in his calling for the incorporation of multiple threads of history. Moreover, this approach underscores how hegemonic processes are never quite as simple as they initially appear.

Doing Darshan, Bollywood Style: National Identity and "International Standards"

As the shiny black Lexus stopped in full view of the guests at the opening of a well-known designer's new prêt line, all heads turned to see who would step out of the back seat of such an expensive car, the likes of which had only been available in India for a few months. When Hindi film star and Oscar nominee Aamir Khan emerged onto the street and made his way into the champagne reception being held in his honour, his presence was illuminated by the flashbulbs of press photographers. The shoeless itinerant labourers on the street outside began shouting excitedly to one another that Khan, who had most recently played the lead role of a poor villager who defeats British colonial officials at a game of cricket in the Oscar-nominated Hindi film *Lagaan* (Land Tax), was in their midst. The more minor celebrities inside the party stopped to gaze at Khan as he stylishly lit a cigarette for the benefit of a photographer, an image which featured prominently in the next day's issue of *The Times of India.*

Seeing and being seen are both granted central importance in Hindu canonical traditions, and the notions of darshan and buri nazar (the evil eye) both underscore how the subject of the gaze can sometimes be a source of greater authority than the object of the gaze. Gods and goddesses are often depicted as being possessed of a third eye, which signifies superhuman powers of perception or, in the case of Shiva, the ability to destroy with one unfavorable glance, pointing to a concept of the gaze as the repository of both power and wisdom. Visual representations of the eye are common throughout the subcontinent as talismans against bad luck or ill will, and can be seen in a wide variety of forms, ranging from hand-painted eyes on the backs of beautifully decorated transport trucks to the frequency of eyes in religious art.

Recognizing that ways of seeing are also ways of knowing, anthropologists and art theorists (Goody 1997; Grimshaw 2001; Lee and Munro 2001; Virilio 1994) have acknowledged the ways in which images and representations affect individual understandings of the world. Nandy (1998) refers to Hindi film tales of love plagued by conflict, which is invariably resolved in the end, as "the secret politics of our desires," which posit a happy solution to the inescapable South Asian reality of rigid social structures such as class and ethnicity. These hierarchies have exponentially increased following the advent of neoliberalism and have been compounded by additional competing factors as the Hindi film industry struggles to reconcile its dual reputation: for being the most prolific film industry in the world, and having unoriginal plots and low standards vis-à-vis American and European films.

This struggle came to a head just as Aamir Khan became the subject of incessant adulation and media attention as he prepared to leave for Los Angeles in anticipation of an Oscar for the film *Lagaan*. Khan's Oscar nomination quickly became a symbol that the Hindi film industry had "arrived," and the excitement surrounding it crossed over into the realm of a city-wide obsession just before the Oscar ceremonies. All the Hindi film awards shows I attended held a moment of silence in the midst of the Indian awards, for the audience to pray for *Lagaan* to succeed. One of Bombay's most popular nightclubs held a "*Lagaan* Night," during which guests wrote their wishes for the film's success on a huge roll of paper that was then faxed to Khan's hotel room in Los Angeles.

The excitement quickly died out when *Lagaan* did not receive an Oscar, and press photographers were waiting at the airport to capture Khan's expression as he returned to Bombay from Los Angeles. The *Times of India* featured a photograph of a weeping Aamir Khan that filled half a page the next day with a headline that read almost like an accusation of betrayal: "How Could It Not Win?" This reception made it seem that the hopes of the Hindi film industry had been pinned on *Lagaan*, a fact which did not go unnoticed by many individuals who voiced their contention of this to me privately. As we sat through yet another moment of silence for *Lagaan* at a film awards show, one director whispered, "It's all bullshit, this bowing-down-before-Hollywood stuff. They made the movie for an Indian audience, and they loved it. What more do they want? What can Americans understand about this movie, and why is their award so important? Indians are such suckers. I hate this attitude."

The director's contention that "Indians are such suckers" points to how the obsession over *Lagaan*'s potential to succeed in the United States far exceeded pride over its success in India. Other Hindi film directors and producers were quick to make veiled references to *Lagaan* during the course of interviews I conducted at the height of the enthusiasm surrounding the film. Producer Mahesh Bhatt responded to my question of which audience he had in mind for his most recent film by noting, "I'm not catering to the taste buds of any foreign audience. I'm making basically an Indian movie for the people which are there in my own country." Director Tanuja Chandra, when asked what made a film successful, insisted that, "I think that Indians are still unfortunately colonized in a way. They always feel inferior to the West, which is why everyone is so excited about *Lagaan*." Chandra's linkage of India's colonial history with a film whose plot revolved around the ability of Indian villagers to defeat British colonial administrators at a game of cricket was particularly significant, as it begs the question as to why a nationalist film should require international authentication.

Discussions of national desires and "international standards" were by no means confined to the controversy and excitement surrounding *Lagaan*. During the period of my research at Moksh, South Bombay's most exclusive gym and spa, almost all the individuals with whom I spoke mentioned media as a powerful factor in influencing what they found to be a beautiful body. Elton, a personal trainer at Moksh, cited the reasons for this as follows:

> There's been a certain awakening, actually, due to the international exposure on television. And we're seeing beautiful people most of the time. It's really picked up in the last five or six years. The reason being that most of the models we look up to, most of the actresses we look up to, have started developing a good body. And since most of us put ourselves in their (the actors') shoes when we go to watch a movie, we think, 'Hey, why can't we woo women with the same body?

Elton situates the construction of a "good" body at a confluence between what are usually thought of as two very different medias: international satellite television and Hindi films. When he mentions that actresses "have started developing a good body," he is referring to actresses in the Hindi film industry who, following what are perceived as international trends, have metamorphosized into thinner, more model-like versions of Hindi film actresses. Interestingly, Elton also positions himself as a consumer of films, one who sits in the audience and asks himself why he should not have access to women with the same kind of bodies he sees on the screen.

I spent six months working and conducting participant observation at a major Hindi film production house that was also a publicly traded company, a fairly unusual arrangement in which directors and producers were held accountable to shareholders. During the time I spent with the company, its leadership authored an accounting plan that was poised to revolutionize the way the Hindi film industry conducted business via the incorporation of "international" standards and practices. The opening paragraph read:

> The idea is to create a model accounting policy that will be universally acceptable. It is also the intention to have a model that is acceptable to global investors, fund managers and international bankers so that [the company] is seen to be a company that follows international practices when it comes to accounting policy and valuation. (Accounting Plan 2002)

What this list of goals implicitly aims for is not only the complete privatization of the film industry but also the elimination of the widespread policy of allowing organized criminal groups to launder money by providing financing for films. Noting that, "accounting for cinematic and television content in India is still at its fledgling stage," the company's accounting plan tacitly acknowledges the policy of involving dubious funding sources.

Stories abound about the Hindi film industry's connections to organized criminal networks that primarily operate between Bombay and Dubai. Although individuals who work in the industry never flatly deny that much of the funding for film production comes from such groups, many of them are quick to point out that it is the high-profile nature of the film industry which draws attention to its illegal and semilegal activities, as did director Pankaj Parashar in the course of an interview:

> It's human nature to talk like that. If I say, "Yesterday I went for a walk and saw a beautiful sunset," and then I say, "Yesterday I went for a walk and I saw someone shoot someone," you're going to say "wow" to the second one. But the industry is getting clean now, after Bharat Shah and all, and at the same time it's going corporate to bring in the money.

Parashar employs the example of Bombay diamond merchant and film producer Bharat Shah, who was imprisoned after being accused of using funds from the Chhota Rajan crime syndicate to finance his films. Shah's case was a landmark in that while many directors and producers privately commented that he was being singled out for something that was common industry practice, there were no public rallying cries in support of his innocence.

Producer Subhash Ghai tried unsuccessfully to have films officially considered an "industry" by the Government of India in the early 1990s, a status which would have made it eligible for bank funding and insurance. The company I worked for circumvented this problem entirely by being open to investment, which ensured that it had a ready supply of cash available to make the three or four films per year expected of the average Hindi film production house. The accounting plan sought to standardize film production costs as part of a process of setting standards quite different from preliberalization Indian economic policies. Referencing the Nehruvian model of economic policy on national self-sufficiency, the plan noted, "entertainment, not steel, not autos, not cements, not even telecom, will lead the new economy" (Accounting Plan 2002).

Several interesting analogies were drawn from this new way of thinking about the Hindi film industry as a business, such as the accounting plan's depiction of a film's higher earning potential as opposed to detergent:

> Unlike the detergent, which can be exploited by the producer and enjoyed by the viewer only once, a movie can be exploited by the producer and enjoyed by the viewer over and over again. You can release a movie in a theater, release it on video, cut a soundtrack album, sell satellite rights, show it on Doordarshan, play it on local and overseas cables, merchandise it by selling t-shirts, apparel and related products, novelize it and make it the theme of a string of restaurants, market it on the Internet, and, years later, it can be shown to a nostalgic audience once India has joined the other countries of the world in protecting intellectual property. (Accounting Plan 2002)

This language conveys a dual message that emphasizes the seemingly endless possibilities for lucrative returns under the neoliberal regime, as well as life in a new market economy in which so little is self-evident that detergents and films seem perfect points of comparison. The question of intellectual property, in turn, places India near the bottom of a hierarchy of standards due to the rampant piracy of films and even entire plots.

Implementing "international standards" was not completely without efforts made to incorporate some realities of the Hindi film industry, an attempt that was most salient in the incorporation of words used in Indian English to describe the degree of a film's success or failure. A "blockbuster" film is defined as one that reaps five times the return on investment, a "superhit" has triple the return, a "hit" doubles its return, and an "overflow" makes slightly more than a return on investment, but not enough to be considered a "hit." A "loser" earns .5% less than the initial investment, whereas a "flop" loses more than .5% at the box office (Accounting Plan 2002). This clear delineation of standards for success is particularly interesting because of the way it borrows from the general list of terms that have long been used loosely to gauge a film's success in the industry. Everyone knew, for example, that a film which lost money was a flop, but to objectively evaluate the precise amount of loss that a film requires to be considered a failure is unique to the standardization of practices in the Hindi film industry.

The company I worked for had adopted a set of American accounting standards detailed in the financial accounting standards bulletin (FASB), which it cited as advantageous because of the way it allowed the cost of each film to be reasonably determined and the collection of the full amount of funds agreed upon in contracts reasonably assured. If followed correctly, the FASB standards would mean that there would be no room for money laundering in the industry and all costs and profits would be declared taxable income. This would ideally generate trust and thus encourage foreign investment, which would make the production house's ventures more lucrative and risk-free.

As part of its plan to attract international investors, the company listed the recent trends and advances in the Hindi film industry as follows: the expansion of theater infrastructure in the form of multiplexes and audiovisual effects, curbs on piracy, increased amounts of exports of cinematic content, satellite rights, increased demand for film music rights, increased corporate sponsorship and merchandising, as well as emerging sources of content delivery, such as broadband connections. All of these are examples of a newly privatized company's efforts to move beyond the old stereotypes of the Hindi film industry as rife with corruption, inefficiency, and connections to organized crime. Curiously, these are the very same standards that the IMF sought to implement in the national economy following the implementation of its structural adjustment policies in 1991.

Conclusion

> In earlier days, a big budget film meant you went to Kashmir. Nowadays you go to Switzerland where you get international crews who work more efficiently and locations which are more beautiful, because we have the money to do that now. (Producer Ken Ghosh)

> I film in Switzerland as if it's Kashmir. Switzerland is a beautiful place, but Kashmir is much, much more beautiful, God's paradise on Earth. But because of the insurgency, we can't film in Kashmir anymore, so Switzerland is our only other option. (Producer Mahesh Bhatt)

Both Ghosh and Bhatt cite how what in the past was the common practice of shooting at least part of a film in the alpine scenery of Kashmir has now been substituted with Swiss mountains and valleys, yet each differs on why this is the case. While Ghosh names the increased amount of money available to Hindi film budgets as a reason to film in the almost identical location of Switzerland, Bhatt names the presence of armed insurgents in Kashmir as the prohibitive factor against making a film there. This amounts to much more than a simple difference of opinion, rather speaking to a sea change in ways of thinking about economics, standards, and, indeed, India. Ghosh's assertion that Switzerland offers more efficiency and more attractive scenery is very much in keeping with neoliberal ideology, while Bhatt's statement speaks to the reality of an industry (and, perhaps, a nation) which has no other choice but to change with the times.

That economic policy changes do not take place in a vacuum is evidenced by the Hindi film industry's focus on privatization that closely mirrors that of IMF policy. Structural adjustment policies in Bombay created a surreal world in which mill workers lost their jobs and homes, which were replaced by entertainment complexes in which privileged young people could partake in what they referred to as "MTV culture." While societies and individuals respond to an economy undergoing enormous structural changes by redefining their own sense of identity, the fact remains that the vast majority of citizens in Bombay have been deeply disadvantaged by structural adjustment policies.

Power is embedded in processes through which the gaze molds both self and other, so that over time formerly British colonial "heritage buildings" become much more than symbols of imperial domination. As is the case in the politics of renaming well-known landmarks visited by the Bombay Darshan Bus, multiple meanings surround formerly colonial structures and social systems over time. This directly relates to the visual economy which privileged Hollywood over Bollywood in the case of *Lagaan*, or in the incorporation of "international standards" into the Hindi film industry. As such, this article raises not only the question of who has the right to set standards and who is mandated to follow them, but also of how hierarchies become so entrenched and embedded in socio-cultural processes over time that it is no longer clear where domination stops and agency begins.

Notes

1. Hindi allows for variation in spelling when transliterated into English. I have followed standard Hindi transliteration practices throughout this paper.

References

Appadurai, Arjun. *Modernity at Large*. Chicago: University of Chicago Press, 1996.

Boyarin, Jonathan. "Space, Time, and the Politics of Memory," In *Remapping Memory: The Politics of TimeSpace*, 1994.

Chatterjee, Partha *The Nation and Its Fragments: Colonial and Postcolonial Histories*. Princeton: Princeton University Press, 1993.

Chopra, Ajai, Charles Collins, Richard Hemming, Karen Parker, Woosik Chu, OliverFratzscher. *India: Economic Reforms and Growth. International Monetary Fund Occasional Paper* 134. Washington, DC: International Monetary Fund, 1995.

D'Monte, Darryl. *Ripping the Fabric: The Decline of Mumbai and Its Mills*. Delhi: Oxford University Press, 2002.

Dickey, Sara. *Cinema and the Urban Poor in South India*, 1993

Dwyer, Rachel *All You Want is Money, All You Need is Love: Sex and Romance in Modern India*, 2000.

___. "Bombay Ishtyle" In Bruzzi, Stella and Pamela Church Gibson, eds *Fashion Cultures*. London: Routledge, 2000. 178–190.

Foucault, Michel. *Power/Knowledge*. New York: Pantheon, 1980.

___. *Discipline and Punish*. New York: Vintage, 1975.

Ganti, Tejaswini. *Casting Culture: The Social Life of Hindi Film Production in Contemporary India*. PhD dissertation: NYU, 2000.

Gerke, Solvay "Global Lifestyles under Local Conditions," In Beng-Huat, Chua, ed.

Consumption in Asia: Lifestyles and Identities. London: Routledge, 2000.
Gillespie, Marie. *Television, Ethnicity and Cultural Change*. London: Routledge, 1995.
Goodwin, Andrew. *Dancing in the Distraction Factory: Music Television and Popular Culture*. Minneapolis: University of Minnesota Press, 1992.
Goody, Jack. *Representations and Contradictions: Ambivalence Towards Images, Theater, Fiction, Relics and Sexuality*. Oxford: Blackwell, 1997.
Grimshaw, Anna. *The Ethnographer's Eye: Ways of Seeing in Modern Anthropology*. Cambridge: Cambridge University Press, 2001.
Gupta, Nilanjana. *Switching Channels: Ideologies of TV in India*. Delhi: Oxford. Hindi Film Production Company. Accounting Plan 2002, 1998.
Hutnyk, John. *Critique of Exotica: Music, Politics and the Culture Industry*. London: Pluto Press, 2000.
Kaplan, E Ann. Looking for the Other: Feminism, Film and the Imperial Gaze. New York: Routledge. 1997.
Kasbekar, Asha. "Hidden Pleasures: Negotiating the Myth of the Feminine Ideal in Popular Hindi Cinema" In *Pleasure and the Nation*, 2001. 161–185.
Kemper, Steven. Buying and Believing: Sri Lankan Advertisers and Consumers, 2002.
King, Anthony. *Urbanism, Colonialism and the World Economy: Cultural and Spatial Foundations of the World Urban System*. London: Routledge, 1990.
Kocchar, Kalpana, Khatri, Yougesh, Petya Koeva, Ranil Salgado, Dong He, Jean-Pierre Chauffour. *India: Selected Issues and Statistical Appendix*. Washington, DC: International Monetary Fund, 2002.
Larkin, Brian. "Indian Films and Nigerian Lovers: Media and the Creation of Parallel Modernities" *Africa* 67 (3), 1997. 406–440.
Lawson, Philip. *The East India Company: A History*. London: Longman. 1993.
Lee, Nick and Rolland Munro. *The Consumption of Mass*. Oxford: Blackwell. 2001.
Liechty, Mark. *Suitably Modern: Making Middle Class Culture in a New Consumer Society*. Princeton: Princeton University Press, 2003.
Mankekar, Purnima. *Screening Culture, Viewing Politics*. Durham: Duke. 1999.
Mathews, Gordon. *Global Culture/Individual Identity: Searching for Home in the Cultural Supermarket*. New York: Routledge, 2000.
Mulvey, Laura. *Fetishism and Curiousity*. Bloomington: University of Indiana Press, 1996.
___. *Visual and Other Pleasures: Theories of Representation and Difference*. Bloomington: University of Indiana Press, 1989.
Munshi, Shoma. *Images of the 'Modern Woman' in Asia: Global Media, Local Meanings*. Surrey: Curzon Press, 1997.
Nandy, Ashis. *The Secret Politics of Our Desires: Innocence, Culpability and Indian Popular Cinema*. Delhi: Oxford, 1998.
Nayar, Baldev Raj. *Globalization and Nationalism: The Changing Balance in India's Economic Policy 1950–2000*. Delhi: Sage Publications, 2001.
Page, David and William Crawley. *Satellites Over South Asia*. Delhi: Sage Publications, 2001.
Qadeer, Imrana, Kasturi Sen and KR Nayar, eds. *Public Health and the Poverty of Reforms: The South Asian Predicament*. Delhi: Sage Publications, 2001.
Rangarajan, Chakravati. "India's Balance of Payments: The Emerging Dimensions" Shri Govind Ballabh Memorial Lecture. Delhi: Reserve Bank of India Bulletin, 1994.

Sharma, Satya P. "The Cultural Costs of a Globalized Economy for India" *Dialectical Anthropology* 21, 1996. 299–316.

Silverman, Kaja. *The Threshold of the Visible World.* New York: Routledge. 1996.

Teo, Stephen. *Hong Kong Cinema: The Extra Dimensions.* London: British Film Institute, 1997.

Thomas, Rosie. "Melodrama and the Negotiation of Morality in Mainstream Hindi Film" In Breckenridge, Carol, ed *Consuming Modernity: Public Culture in a South Asian World*, 1995. 157–182.

Vasudevan, Ravi. "Bombay and its Public" In *Pleasure and the Nation*, 2001.

Virdi, Jyotika. *The Cinematic Imagination: Indian Popular Films as Social History.* New York: Routledge, 2003.

Virilio, Paul. *The Vision Machine.* Bloomington: Indiana University Press, 1994.

Globalizing Bombay Cinema
Reproducing the Indian State and Family

MONIKA MEHTA

This article examines the changing relations between Bombay cinema and the Indian state in a global context. In 1998, the Indian state recognized film as an industry. This dramatic shift in state policy occurred during the same period as two other noteworthy developments. First, the Bombay film industry produced and successfully distributed what the Indian state and the audiences approvingly referred to as 'family films.' Second, Indian diasporic communities emerged as valued audiences in Bombay's box-office figures and as desired investors in the Indian state's political, economic, and cultural plans. By examining this historical conjuncture, I seek to show how processes of globalization contribute to the (re)production of Hindi commercial cinema, the Indian state and family.

Opening

On May 11, 1998, news of India's nuclear test exploded onto world headlines. The previous day, another explosive situation was resolved by the Indian government, this one, however, barely generating a murmur in national and international media. On May 10, 1998, after fifty years of independence, the Indian state finally recognized film as an *industry* "proper." In the past, prominent members of the film industry had discussed with various governments the possibility of gaining recognition as an industry; each time, they had been refused. However, on 10 May 1998, when members of the film industry met with the representatives of the government at the national conference on "Challenges Before Indian Cinema" in Mumbai (Bombay), they received an unexpected response.[1] Surprisingly, without any argument or debate whatsoever, the

Union Information and Broadcasting Minister Sushma Swaraj announced that the government had decided to grant industry status to film.[2] This new status meant that the film industry would finally be eligible for the infrastructural and credit support given to other industries.

This noteworthy development was soon followed by a series of other changes instituted by the state. In 1998, Finance Minister Yashwant Sinha granted many long-standing demands of the film industry, including reduction in custom duties on cinematographic film, exemption of recorded audio and video cassettes from excise duties, and tax incentives, to name a few. In 2000, Sinha added further concessions including a complete exemption on export profits, further reduction in import duties on cinematographic equipment, and more tax incentives. In October 2000, under the Industrial Development Bank Act, the film industry became eligible for financial support from "legitimate" institutions. In May 2001, for the very first time, a twenty-five member team led by Sushma Swaraj went to Cannes in order to promote overseas sales of Indian films.

This dramatic shift in state policy towards the commercial film industry occurred during the same period as two other significant developments: First, in the 1990s—the era of economic liberalization—the Bombay film industry began producing what the Indian state and audiences approvingly referred to as "family films" which wove a happy marriage between Indian "traditions" and the global market. Second, during the same period, both the Bombay film industry and the state began pursuing Indian diasporic communities.

How do we make sense of these developments? How are they related to one another? In this article, I seek to examine this historical conjuncture, focusing on how globalization reconfigures the relation between the Indian state and Bombay cinema. Specifically, I will be pursuing the following questions. By which processes and mechanisms does "India as nation state" reproduce itself in the context of globalization? What has been the process of negotiation between the Bombay film industry and the state apparatus? How and why did "family films" become central to the agendas of the film industry and the Indian state?

In the 1990s, despite the successes of *Hum Aapke Hain Kaun/What Is My Relation To You?* and *Dilwale Dulhania Le Jayenge/The Brave-Hearted Will Take Away The Bride*, the Bombay film industry came to the conclusion that chances of producing an "All-India hit" were increasingly low; therefore, it began to pursue diasporic markets to obtain more revenue. This turn to diasporic markets is part of a larger process of market segmentation which is visible in the emergence of a new mode of exhibition in India, namely, the multiplex. Multiplexes provide a menu which, depending upon the region, can consist of various combinations of Hindi, regional, art, crossover, art-commercial hybrid, and Hollywood films (Sharma 2003). Due to an increased number of screens via multiplexes and a larger number of prints which get distributed, a film can become a hit without necessarily filling theatres. The steep cost of tickets at multiplexes and the high currency exchange rate vis-à-vis the rupee, especially from diasporic markets in the US and the UK, further ensure that a film with a smaller audience can be successful. Consequently, producers and distributors no longer need to aim for an "All-India hit"; by earning enough money in profitable segments their films can be financially viable. These changes have both marginalized less profitable segments and have impacted the informal economy, namely, scalping which feeds off high demand for tickets (Joshi 2005).

Unlike the Bombay film industry which sought new markets of its own volition, the advent of liberalization in the 1990s imposed certain economic imperatives on the Indian state, which forced it to open its markets to western products and culture, and to become a player in the global market. This, it could be said, is a part of "globalization." Sassen points out that "Global markets in finance and advanced services partly operate through a "regulatory" umbrella that is not state centered but market centered" (1998: xxvii). These markets, she explains, make "new claims on national states to guarantee the domestic and global rights of capital" and "national states respond through the production of new forms of legality" (1998: xxvii). Understood in this context, in granting film the status of an industry, the Indian state sought to accomplish two tasks: first, to harness the enormous export potential of commercial films, in particular, "Bollywood" films; and second, to tailor the industry to international standards by transforming the mechanisms of film production.

I would argue that by designating film as an industry, and thereby bringing an "unorganized" and "informal" sector of the economy under its purview, the state is actively attempting to (re)inscribe its authority in the context of globalization. By tracing recent events and processes, I suggest that this new legality is productive of a different kind of state, one in which financial institutions assume prominence. One could end the analysis here and say that fiscal reasons compelled the state to grant commercial cinema the status of a legitimate industry. This fiscal rationale does not, however, explain two important developments. (1) The government sought to bring an unregulated sector of the economy under its wing, while it was busy deregulating other sectors. (2) The state began to support big-budget "family films." I would explain the first development by noting that, while the state needed follow the rules laid out by the global market, it also had to show its citizens that it was not powerless to counter one of the most compelling arguments against liberalization, namely, that the state would be controlled by market forces.

Regarding the second development, namely, the state support of "family films," I contend that it is through the process of regulation that the state seeks to produce "good cinema," one which is simultaneously attentive to the global market and to the reproduction of the Indian nation. Thus, state recognition of the film industry can also be seen as a means of controlling content in ways that are more subterranean, more effective, and less public than through the censorship battles of the 1990s to which I refer later in the article. From independence until the mid-1990s, the state had, more or less, viewed the commercial industry as a social vice and subjected it to censorship and taxation.[3] After this period, the repressive apparatus, e.g. censorship and taxation, does not disappear. Rather, a generative apparatus emerges alongside it. This apparatus enables a distinction between "good" commercial films, i.e. family films, such as *Hum Aapke Hain Kaun/What Is My Relation To You?* (1994), *Dilwale Dulhania Le Jayenge/The Brave-Hearted Will Take Away The Bride* (1995), *Pardes/Foreign Land* (1997), *Kuch Kuch Hota Hai/Something Happens* (1998), *Aa Ab Laut Chalein/Let us Return* (1999), *Hum Dil De Chuke Sanam/I have Given my Heart* (1999), *Hum Saath Saath Hain/We Are United* (1999), *Yaadein/Memories* (2001), *Kabhie Khushi Kabhie Gham/A Time for Sadness and a Time for Happiness* (2001), etc. and "bad" commercial films which contain vulgar songs such as "Choli peeche kya hai" (What is Behind the Blouse), from *Khalnayak/The Villain* (1993), "Sexy, Sexy, Sexy, Mujhe Log Bole . . ." (People Say I am Sexy, Sexy, Sexy) from *Khuddar/Self-Respecting Person* (1993), "Meri Pant Bhi Sexy . . ." (My Pant is Sexy) from *Dulaara/The Loved One* (1993); "Sarkayleo Khatiya Jara Lage . . ." (Bring your Cot Closer, I am Feeling Cold) from *Raja Babu/His Lordship* (1993), etc.

In order to elaborate upon these arguments, I will focus on four related issues: first, the state's and the commercial film industry's recent efforts to find legitimate means for financing films; second, the state's claim that clean financing is crucial for producing good cinema; third, the state's role in defining good cinema; and last, Bombay cinema's and the Indian state's persistent efforts in the 1990s and the present to woo diasporic communities. In making these arguments, I seek to intervene in the fields of global studies and film criticism. I contribute to a growing body of work by scholars which interrogates arguments that, regardless of political orientation, presume that globalization is a phenomenon limited exclusively to the expansion of Hollywood (see e.g. Ciecko and Lu 1999; Iwabuchi 2002; Larkin 2003; Lau 2003; Lu 1997; Naficy 2001; Shohat and Stam 1994, 2003; Srinivas 2003; Wong 1999). This scholarship not only intensifies debates on globalization and cinema, but also questions the very theoretical grounds through which we comprehend globalization itself. This scholarship, however, has not attended to the changing relations between the state and media in the era of globalization. I hope to expand this scholarship by examining these issues.

For the most part, in film studies, there has been an insistence upon separating questions about political economy and representations; this separation is manifest in the formation of film studies and mass communications, where the former largely addresses questions of representations and the latter is concerned with political economy. This is, of course, part of a larger divide between the humanities and the social sciences. Studies on Bombay cinema have often reiterated this division by focusing on cinematic representations and overlooking the specific technologies and capital which enable the production, distribution, and exhibition of these representations. Unlike these studies, I seek to locate questions of representation in a wider social field by placing questions of representation alongside political economy.

From Black Market to Legitimate Financing: The Production of a Different State

Film financing in India has generally been a creative endeavor. Given the high risks and lack of state support, banks have tended to refuse to lend money for film productions, "thus forcing filmmakers to turn towards alternative means, which include clear funding of future profit potential or high-cost borrowing from the dubious and the not-so-dubious" (Aiyar and Chopra, 1998). Currently, in the Bombay film industry, prominent producers such as Yash Chopra, Subhash Ghai, Indra Kumar, and the Barjatyas generally do not borrow money. They have, "with repeated success, built reputations strong enough to sell their films the day they are announced" (Aiyar and Chopra 1998). Hence, they are able to acquire funds from distributors.

However, others have been neither as successful nor as lucky:

> Nearly 25 percent of the under-production films are financed by conventional moneylenders, who have traditionally lent money to the film industry at interest rates of 36 to 40 percent per annum. Some are backed by non-conventional but corporate financing while others use the widely-prevalent *hundi*-system (money raised through promissory notes) to fund their projects. Less than 5 percent of the films are funded by the infamous underworld sources[4] and the remaining 70 percent-odd producers get their money from assorted businessmen—builders, jewellers, traders—who, attracted by the glamour, pump in money. (Aiyar and Chopra 1998)

In an interview, Swaraj alluded to this "convoluted state of affairs" and identified film's new status as an industry as a solution to these problems:

> If you are committed to good cinema, you will have to provide good finance. By according the status of industry, we have given pictures the much-needed eligibility to seek funds from legitimate places. Thus, a semblance of order is now possible in what has been a rather confused and convoluted state of affairs. A great step, indeed. (*The Hindu* 1998a)

If we consider that "black" money has funded film productions in India since the 1940s and that the involvement of the mafia in the industry can be traced to the 1970s, we may wonder why the state has chosen to turn its attention to these issues at this juncture.[5] I suggest two reasons for this recent focus on weeding out "mafia-black" money: first, we know that in the international arena Third World nation states have always been characterized as "corrupt."[6] In order to become a worthy contender in the global market and to present India as an attractive and safe site for foreign investment, the Indian state is compelled to erase the blemish of "corruption." Second, the process of constructing and then policing corruption produces another opportunity for the state to "act" and to (re)inscribe its authority. In the era of liberalization, this assumed significance because the state needed to demonstrate to its citizens that it was a potent force and not merely a puppet of market forces.

The relations between the state, Bombay cinema, and "mafia-black" money have always been complex. In state discourses, "black" money, that which the underworld supplies, is part of the larger problem of corruption—a problem which the state is ostensibly hard at work locating and eradicating. While in public discourse the state attempts to distance itself from corruption, a cursory glance at the workings of bureaucracy and politics shows that "illegal" activities supplement the income of officials and politicians, and state coffers. With the pressure of globalization, the state has become more zealous in its efforts to remove corruption. In 2001, the Bombay police arrested film financier Bharat Shah and director/producer Nadeem Rizvi, and seized the prints of a commercial Hindi film *Chori Chori Chukpe Chupke/Secretly, Quietly* on the grounds that the money for its production had come from the underworld. The film was eventually released, but the monies from the sale of the prints to distributors were appropriated by the state. Curiously, one of the distributors for the film happened to be Bharat Shah who was under arrest at the time. This incident not only highlights how "corruption" assists in increasing the economic productivity of the state but also the difficulty of the state in disentangling itself from corruption.

Corporatization, or "Clean" Industry and Clean Films: The Increasing Regulative Authority of State-Supported Financial Institutions

As members of the film industry discussed Swaraj's unexpected announcement, they wondered about a series of issues. What would be legitimate sources of finances? If banks provided funds for films, what would they demand as collateral? Would these new institutions interfere with the process of filmmaking? How would these institutions affect the industry's "work-culture"? Newspapers and magazines generally reported that the film industry was happy with this new state of affairs. In fact, Plus Channel CEO Amit Khanna suggested that these processes would produce a

> . . . Bollywood where films will be insured—banks will not lend without insurance—therefore scripts will be finalised, artists will sign completion bonds and films will be completed in a stipulated period of time. Black money will be totally weeded out and a system of valuation experts will evolve. . . . "There will be a transparent accounting system and underworld rumours, a bad memory." (Aiyar and Chopra 1998)

Some sections of the industry undertook efforts towards materializing this future. For example, in 1999 director/producer Subhash Ghai set a precedent by insuring his film *Taal/Rhythm* (*The Times of India* 2000). In early 2000, the All India Film Producers Council (AIFPC) commissioned the Arthur Andersen Corporation to do a study of the industry and create corporate benchmarks for key players in the future (*Economic Times* 2000). Later in the year, Subhash Ghai went public with his production company Mukta Arts, laying a new road ahead for the country's film industry. Soon after, music giant TIPS Industries and content provider Pritish Nandy Communications followed Ghai's example. These efforts on the part of certain sections of the industry suggest that corporatization of cinema is not simply a vision imposed by the Indian state. Clearly, the industry, "Bollywood" in particular, is eager to become a contender on the stage of world cinema; however, the rules for its entry onto this stage are governed by a global market which demands corporatization.[7] While "Bollywood" seeks many benefits that come from corporatization, such as legitimate financing and larger markets, this process also extends the authority of state-supported financial institutions through a new set of rules imposed on the production and marketing of films.

While the government officials as well as members of the film industry have welcomed these new changes, the financial institutions have been more apprehensive about investing funds in such a risky industry. After more than two years of discussion, the entertainment industry, including film production, was made eligible for financing from banks. According to a notification issued on 16 October 2000 under section 2(C)(xvii) of the Industrial Development Bank of India Act, 1964, the entertainment industry was recognized as an approved entity under "industrial concerns" (*Business Line* 2000a; *India Abroad Daily* 2000).

Approximately six months later, the Industrial Development Bank of India (IDBI) issued a set of "norms" for financing films:

> The IDBI has said that to be eligible for its film-financing scheme, the movie should have a capital of Rs. 5 crore [50 million] to Rs. 25 crore [250 million] for Hindi films and Rs. 30 lakh [300,000] to Rs. 10 lakh [100,000] for regional films. The scheme says no two films should be the same and the investment would vary depending on the "treatment" of the story or concept and scale of production. Materials and technicians cost should constitute about 55% of the capital outlay. Said IDBI executive director RS Agarwal, "'The film should be comprehensively insured and a guarantee for the timely

> completion within the estimated cost of film should be provided by the applicant. The borrower should be a corporate entity, backed by established directors/producers having a satisfactory record. The quantum of assistance will be normally not less than Rs. 5 crore[8] and not exceeding 50 percent of the film's cost. The promoter's contribution should be normally not less than 30 percent of the cost of the film. The period of loan should not be more than two years. The security towards the loan will be a lab letter, assignment of Intellectual Property Right of the proposed films as also existing rights on old films, hypothecation of movable assets, personal guarantee and receivables IPRs to be routed through TRA." (*Financial Express* 2001)

The IDBI policy is no simple program for providing finance to the film industry. Rather, through a host of rules mandated and enforced by state-supported financial institutions, the policy seeks to transform the nature of the film industry. The objective of these rules is to produce a disciplined Indian film industry by increasing professionalization and in the process weeding out "non-professional" filmmakers and "amateur"/ "lower-grade" films. While earlier rules limited the assistance to films with a budget of at least 10 crores, the recent guidelines have reduced this amount to 4 crores, but even the reduced amount excludes low-budget filmmakers. For example, the successful, progressive film, *My Brother Nikhil* (2005), which was made on a budget of 2.25 crores, would not have been eligible for assistance from IDBI (Jha 2005). Government officials, bankers, and members of the industry hope that in this professional environment, film production will decrease, but the quality of films as well as film marketing will increase. In their view, these transformations would create a truly productive film industry (see e.g. Aiyar and Chopra 1998; *Financial Express* 1998; IndiaInfo.com 2000; Rediff on The Net 1999; Responservice 2000). In recognizing film as property, the state which is formally in charge of protecting and safeguarding the rights to property is able to control the kind of films produced. In making a distinction between Hindi and regional films and prescribing a larger amount of initial capital for the former and a lesser one for the latter, this policy seeks to (re)inscribe the dominance of Hindi and Bombay cinema both nationally and internationally.

Making Good Cinema: The Role of the State in Producing the Nation

In the following section, I seek to explore why the state's investment in family films occurs at the same moment as financial regulation of the industry. I ask how it is that family films become the cultural articulation of liberalization, and analyze the conjuncture of such films with the development of the diaspora market. In the 1990s, the state sought to regulate film production not only through film financing, but also through official and unofficial measures aimed at defining good cinema. Government officials endorsed and gave awards to big-budget, family films; this new genre emerged in the 1990s and has been very successful in India and abroad (*The Hindu* 1998b). Discussions about genre have focused on three primary issues: (1) the semantic elements through which one can identify a genre, (2) genre as a site of negotiation between the film industry and audience, and (3) genre as reflective of ideology or a particular historical period.[9] I would like to suggest that through mechanisms of censorship as well as national awards the state plays a crucial role in producing genres. Furthermore, genres, in this case, the family films, in turn contribute to fostering new relations between the Bombay film industry, the Indian state, and the Indian diasporic communities.

In the era of globalization, family films have played a significant role in reimagining the nation, audiences, and markets. These films affirm India's moral foundations by representing its "traditions" and announce India's triumphant entry into the global market by managing to persistently include a wide array of multinational brand names in its narratives. In these films, women become pivotal for the production of the patriarchal Indian family and men are charged with spreading seeds of liberalization within and beyond the borders of the Indian nation state. In the era of globalization, Indian diasporic communities have emerged as valued audiences in Bombay box-office figures and as desired investors in the state's political, economic, and cultural plans. The family has been an important site for the construction of diasporic communities. The gendered division of labor operative within the territorial boundaries of the nation state has been intensified in the diaspora, which assiduously seeks to (re)create Indian traditions. The narratives of Bombay cinema have become increasingly significant in accomplishing this task. The desires of the diaspora appear to have been inscribed within the texts of "Bollywood" films, which often contain characters who live in the UK or the US and continue to maintain Indian traditions. These films invite the diaspora to make libidinal and material investments by supporting Indian traditions and commercial film production. In making these investments, the diaspora is being both imaginatively and materially drawn into the nation.[10] Scholars have noted the importance diasporic markets for the Bombay film industry (Dwyer and Patel 2002; Ganti 2004; Mankekar 1999; Mishra 2002; Pendakur and Subramanyam 1996). Ganti points out that Hindi film distribution has been divided into five major territories in India; a "sixth territory, known as the "overseas territory," previously used to be undifferentiated from the point of view of distributors in India, but is now subdivided into North America, United Kingdom, Gulf States, South Africa etc" (Ganti 2004:57–8). According to box-office collection figures, the earnings of "family films" from the overseas market range from approximately 15 to 45 percent of the film's total collections. Interestingly, most websites and trade analysts that provide box-office figures for overseas territories focus on the earnings from the US and UK markets.

A Family Love Story

To elaborate and extend these points, I would like to examine *Dilwale Dulhania Le Jayenge*, the 1995 blockbuster which has become the longest running film in the history of Indian cinema. *Dilwale Dulhania Le Jayenge* followed on the heels of the immensely successful film, *Hum Aapke Hain Kaun* which began the trend for big-budget family films.[11] Both films are credited with bringing audiences who had been lured away by other technologies, namely, videocassettes and cable television, back to the theaters. It is important to situate these films as well as the genre that they heralded in the context of economic liberalization. The plans for economic liberalization were crafted by Dr Manmohan Singh (the Prime Minister of India at the time of writing) and implemented under Congress rule in the early 1990s. It is important to note that debates about the liberalization process in India centered not just around economic disadvantages of opening up the markets, but also about the impact of the "West" on "Indian culture." Both supporters and opponents of the process framed their arguments in terms of the need to protect "Indian culture" from the West and of the strength of "Indian civilization."

In this era, the state and the film industry encountered a powerful adversary in the form of satellite television. Since satellite television was not subject to state censorship, it provided viewers easy access to films and programs that were prohibited by the state. As satellite television easily breached state authority, state censorship appeared to be a superfluous activity.[12] The film industry added to the troubles of the state by pressing for more liberal censorship guidelines with respect to sex and violence so that it could compete with satellite television. The vociferous censorship battles in the 1990s reflected the anxieties of the state, the film industry, and the citizenry with regard to these changes. How would the state reestablish its authority? How would the film industry compete with new forms of entertainment? How would the social fabric change due to both the quantity and quality of entertainment available? How could India protect its *culture and traditions* from the onslaught of western culture and values represented in films, sitcoms, and soap operas shown via satellite television?

In order to address these concerns and to bolster its own authority, the Congress government, in 1991 and 1994, asserted that various complaints regarding objectionable scenes and songs compelled it to revise and reissue the censorship guidelines. The Ministry of Information and Broadcasting issued the following list of objectionable visuals and asked the Central Board of Film Certification to ensure that:

> . . . human sensibilities are not offended by vulgarity, obscenity or depravity; such dual meaning words which obviously cater to baser instincts are not allowed; scenes degrading or denigrating women in any manner are not presented; scenes involving sexual violence against women like attempt to rape, rape or any form of molestation, or scenes of a similar nature are avoided, and if any such incident is germane to the theme, they shall be reduced to the minimum and no details are shown . . . (1992a:8–9)

In addition, the guidelines urged the Certification Board to ensure that a film which is granted a "U" certificate is "suitable for family viewing, that is to say, the film should be such that all members of the family including children can view it together" (Ministry of Information 1992b). Through these guidelines, the state sought to regulate representations of sexuality which were the sites for debates on Indian traditions and culture.

It appeared that in films such as *Hum Aapke Hain Kaun*, *Dilwale Dulhania Le Jayenge* and their subsequent reincarnations, the state had found allies for combating the "vulgarity, obscenity, depravity" which presumably plagued Indian screens. These family films assisted the

Bombay industry in securing its domestic market and in reaching the diasporic market, while educating Indian nationals, both at home and abroad, in "Indian traditions" and the pleasures of consumerism. Released in theaters in India, England, and the US, Aditya Chopra's *Dilwale Dulhania Le Jayenge*, affectionately known as *DDLJ*, became a mega box-office hit; *DDLJ*'s success helped establish the overseas territory as a major market for Bombay filmmakers. The film bagged all the important Filmfare awards—the Oscars of India. Aditya Chopra was effusively praised for his first effort at direction and screen-play writing. He was commended for the script, cinematography, the picturization of songs in scenic European locales—and most importantly—for creating a good family film, one devoid of vulgarity and violence. The Indian government expressed its approval for the film and assisted in its marketing by giving it the award for the "BEST POPULAR FILM PROVIDING WHOLESOME ENTERTAINMENT." As a national award winner, *DDLJ* was also granted the privilege of being *tax-free*.[13] Relieved of the extra charge ranging from 25 to 70 percent depending upon the state, *DDLJ* could be enjoyed for a reasonable price.[14]

Earlier, *DDLJ* had sailed smoothly through the Central Board of Film Certification (CBFC) in Bombay which granted it a clear "U" certificate. According to censorship guidelines which were introduced by colonial administrators and subsequently maintained by the postcolonial state, the letter "U" stands for unrestricted exhibition, allowing all audiences to see the film. As stated earlier, the 1991 censorship guidelines reasserted that only those films which were appropriate for "family viewing" be granted a "U" certificate. Cognizant of these guidelines, the CBFC's examining committee's report on *DDLJ* states that, "Subsequent to the screening of the film and initial reactions, members felt the film is made for the family audience and there is nothing objectionable in the film hence the film may be recommended a clear "U" certificate" (Central Board 1995). Since the state certificate assists in classifying films and identifying proper audiences for films, one could argue that the state contributes to the production of genres. Moreover, the letter rating serves as a marketing device. It appears in advertisements about the films, indicating to habitual audiences the content of the film as well as the state-designated audience. In light of this, one could claim that the mechanisms of censorship not only assist in producing genres, but also that the letter rating itself represents a genre.

While the process of certification deemed *DDLJ* as a film suitable for the "entire family," one wonders what kind of film is considered suitable for the family, specifically the Indian family? To answer this, I'd like to quote the summary of the film provided by the examining committee:

> The film is a family love story. Raj and Simran fall in love when they meet each other in Europe. Baljit father of Simran believes in arranged marriage and wants Simran to marry Kuljeet son of his friend. Simran is heart broken but Raj travels all the way to Punjab from London. As the marriage preparations for Simran and Kuljeet's wedding begin, Raj enters the family as a stranger's friend and wins the confidence of all the family members with his friendly behaviour. Finally Baljeet becomes very angry knowing the intention of Raj. However, he agrees at the end to give away his daughter to Raj when he knows that his daughter is really in love with Raj and not Kuljeet. (Central Board 1995)

The examining committee members are the first to identify this genre precisely, calling it a "family love story." The appellation is ironic considering that the love story in popular Hindi films generally, *DDLJ* among them, takes place against the wishes of the family. In what way then would this film be a "family love story"? If one thinks of *DDLJ* in the context of film production in India in the late 1980s and 1990s, I think the answer becomes clearer. While the love story has always been prominent in Hindi films, there was a palpable shift at this time. The romantic pair moved to the forefront in a way which diminished the role of other characters and other relationships, specifically familial ones.

Unlike most of its contemporaries, *DDLJ* re-establishes the importance of familial relations even as it appears to imagine their transgression. Most obviously, within the story, the family is accorded significance and value. For example, within the narrative, Raj, the hero of the film, refuses to elope with Simran, his lover, despite her many pleadings. He repeatedly tells her that their union needs to be blessed by her family, in particular her father. The family's prominent position is reinforced by the amount of screen time given to characters who play aunts, uncles, parents, siblings, and grandparents. Finally, the references within *DDLJ* to previous commercial films—in other words, inter-texuality—weave a relation between Bombay cinema present and past, constructing *DDLJ*'s genealogy and in the process producing the cinema as familial. The title of the film is taken from a song in *Chor Machaye Shor/A Thief Creates a Commotion* (1974), and within the diegesis, the family members play *antakshari* (a collective singing game) which refers to older film songs.

The most moving reference to Bombay cinema's past occurs during the pre-wedding festivities when Baljeet sings a song to his wife from *Waqt/Time* (1965)—an evocative film about a family which is separated and then reunited. The reference is perhaps made more poignant by the knowledge that the actress who plays Baljeet's mother in *DDLJ* was the heroine in *Waqt* to whom the song was sung. *DDLJ* is read as a film which is attentive to both the family and the love story. Hence, the appellation family love story.

So far, I have primarily discussed the role the state plays in identifying and producing a genre. I would like to now discuss the ways in which this genre assists in reformulating the relations between the Indian state, Bombay cinema, and the Indian diasporic communities. In order to do so, I'd like to discuss two scenes from *DDLJ*. The first scene that I would like to examine takes place early in the narrative as a postman arrives bearing a letter from India concerning Simran's engagement. After accepting the letter from the postman, Baljit enthusiastically runs into the kitchen announcing that a letter from his friend in Punjab has arrived. Strains of "Ghar Aaaja Pardesi" (Come home, foreigner) play in the background as Baljit twirls Lajhoo around, telling her to smell the fragrance of Punjab which is enveloped in the letter.[15] The dialogue, the music, and Baljit's excitement indicate that, even though he has lived in London for 20 years, he is still quite attached to "India." For him, "India" is a series of cultural values and traditions largely associated with Punjab.

Baljit, Lajhoo, and Chutki (Simran's younger sister) gather around Simran in what appears to be a picture-perfect family portrait as she begins to read the letter. Simran's crisp and clear pronunciation in Hindi establishes that, despite being raised in London, she is literate in India's national language.[16] Her smooth reading falters when she arrives at the section of the letter where Baljit is asked to honor a promise made between the two friends, namely, the marriage of their respective son and daughter, the reproduction of tradition. She ceases to speak Hindi at the moment when the totality of which it is a part—Indian tradition—threatens to envelop her or more precisely, her desire. It is a traumatic moment. Simran's voice fades and the camera pans to the left, briefly holding Lajhoo and Simran in a frame. Simran shoots a troubled glance at her mother and hands her the crumpled letter before quickly exiting the living room. Baljit misses this glance because he is positioned to the right of his daughter in such a way that her reaction does not fall within his field of view. The framing suggests that a relation, one of mother and daughter, enables *insight*; we as privileged spectators are shown this insight and are invited to sympathize with Simran's predicament.

Blind to his daughter's state of mind, Baljit is thrilled by the proposal and interprets his daughter's unwillingness to meet his eyes and her exit not only as consent to the marriage, but also as a sign of modesty. He misreads her refusal to embody the promise, and by extension, tradition, as its very opposite: the extension of tradition, its reproduction. In his view, she exhibits a "proper" reaction, namely embarrassment, when the topic of marriage is raised in the company of her father. He proudly declares to Lajhoo that, even though Simran has been raised in London, her embarrassed reaction demonstrates that he has been successful in raising a good Indian daughter. Simran's identity as a "good Indian daughter" is crucial for constituting Baljit as a "good Indian father"—and for reproducing the Indian family.

While one consequence of Baljit's promise to his friend is Simran's imminent engagement, another is a trip to Europe on which Simran will meet Raj, her dream lover. Simran requests her father to send her on a Eurorail trip with her friends so that she can enjoy their company before departing to India to marry a stranger. On this trip, she encounters Raj who continually harasses and annoys her. We, as privileged spectators, know from a previous song sequence that Raj is her dream lover. We are invited to read Raj's pranks not as signs of sexual harassment, but as rituals of courtship. One such event takes place when Simran and Raj accidentally miss the train and spend a night in Switzerland. After Simran drinks too much cognac, Raj brings her to a bed and breakfast.[17]

When Simran wakes up, she notices that she is wearing a man's shirt—and the camera slowly moves about the room to show us her strewn clothes. Simran's confusion is heightened when Raj enters the room with a tea-tray and a rose. In a series of tight close-ups, the camera makes Simran's distress visible as she begs Raj to relate the previous night's events. He insinuates that they slept together and when she does not believe him, he provides the lipstick marks on his chest as evidence.[18]

Whereas the camera shows us Raj's suppressed laughter, Simran is not granted this view. Our privileged glimpse not only enables us to read the scenario as yet another prank, but also to see that Simran has retained her "honor," namely, her virginity. Meanwhile, Simran believes that she made those marks and as such, is "marked," i.e. she is no longer a "virgin surface" and is cut off from tradition. When Simran begins to cry, Raj realizes the joke has reached its limit and quickly tells her that he stole the lipstick from her purse and painted his chest and that nothing happened between them the previous night. Through Raj's confession, tradition is reaffirmed: Simran is still a virgin, which is to say she is still within the scope of tradition. When Simran continues to wail, he pulls her head back and asserts:

> Listen to me, Simran—Listen to me. I know what you think about me. You think I'm a no-good, low-down creep, but I'm not a creep. I'm an *Indian*. I know what an Indian[19] girl's honor means to her. I would never even imagine doing such a thing to you. I'm telling you the truth—nothing happened last night. It was a joke. (*Dilwale Dulhania Le Jayenge* 2001; my translation)

In this gendered version of *Indian* cultural values, a woman's honor is lodged in her body; it is sexual purity that constitutes her as an *Indian* woman. And an *Indian* man is one who recognizes the importance of sexual purity. Raj's explanation reinforces an old patriarchal association between sexuality, honor, and the female body. This association is fueled by both Simran's initial distress and her subsequent relief upon hearing Raj's explanation. Embracing Raj, she tells him, "Don't ever joke like that—you don't know what I would have done" (*Dilwale Dulhania Le Jayenge* 2001). Later in the film, Raj gains access to Simran's family and her future in-laws by posing as a non-resident Indian (NRI) who wishes to open a Stroh's beer factory in Punjab. As Mankekar notes, *DDLJ* re-establishes the male hero as an agent by constructing him as a NRI investor as well as the guardian of an Indian woman's sexual purity and by extension, the virtue of the nation (Mankekar 1999:750–1).

The construction of the NRI as a potential investor, the assertion of Indian national identity, the identification of particular cultural values as Indian, the expression of a commitment to those values as shown in films like *DDLJ* overlap with the Indian state's political, cultural, and economic agendas, which seeks to attract the investments of non-resident Indians and to constitute new national subjects. In the Union Budget speech given a month after film received industry status, Finance Minister Yashwant Sinha stated:

> I believe NRIs constitute a huge, untapped potential for India's development. I propose the following steps to encourage NRIs to participate in the development of their country of origin: (purchase shares, easier procedures, buy bonds, bank in India—)—I have one more significant announcement to make for the NRIs. The Government has decided to draw up a scheme for issuance of a

> Persons of Indian Origin (PIO) Card for those living abroad and having foreign passports. The PIO Card, 'would be extended to persons of Indian Origin settled in countries to be specified by government would besides introducing a visa-free regime, also confer some special economic, educational, financial, and cultural benefits. The details are being worked out.[20]

I would argue that that cinema is central to forging this new relationship with non-resident Indians. It is through cinema that the state (re)imagines the nation, one which is not bound by territory—a nation which includes the Indian diasporic communities.

I believe that this new relationship between Bombay cinema and the Indian state is illuminated by a quip made by Sinha after granting the film industry a series of concessions: "I hope these concessions combined with what I have already done on the indirect tax side will reassure the entertainment industry that *Hum Saath Saath Hain* [We Are United] . . ." (*Business Line* 2000b). Sinha's use of the title of a big-budget Bombay "family" film to characterize the relationship between Bombay cinema and Indian state was by no means insignificant. It not only highlighted the twin goals of the Bhartiya Janata Party (the Hindu Nationalist Party in power at the time), namely, to globalize but in the Indian way, but also pointed to the patriarchal alliance between the state and Bombay cinema. While the Congress-led government, which came to power in 2004, has installed its own representatives at key cultural institutions, it has not changed the BJP's policies towards the film industry, e.g. it has not rescinded industry status for film. Furthermore, it has recently announced that it will soon offer dual citizenship to non-resident Indians; in doing so, it is continuing an initiative formulated by the BJP. Let me end by recalling the nuclear explosion that I referred to at the beginning of this piece. I suggest that the explosion and the recognition of film as an industry are part of the same process, the production of a different kind of state in the era of globalization.

Notes

I have drawn upon sections of my dissertation (Mehta, 2001) in writing this article. I would like to thank Rajesh Bhaskaran, Anupama Prabhala-Kapse, Latha Varadarajan, and Kamala Visweswaran for their comments.

1. The event, "Challenges Before Indian Cinema," was co-organized by the

Federation of Indian Chambers of Commerce and Industry (FICCI) and the Film Federation of India.

2. After independence, the film industry hoped to participate in the task of nation-building by developing film as an industry. To achieve this goal, it asked the government to recognize it as a legitimate industry and, as such, to grant it the infrastructural and credit support that the economic policy promised for other industries. The "developmentalist" Indian state had no time for such frivolous pleas. It reserved its economic aid for *useful* projects such as agriculture and heavy industry. It viewed commercial cinema as excess—at best, an entertaining luxury that needed to be heavily taxed and, at worst, a corrupter of morals which needed to be regulated via censorship. For further information on the Bombay film industry and the postcolonial Indian state, see Mehta (2001). For articles on the granting of industry status, see *Indian Express* (1998a, 1998b, 1998d).

3. See n. 2.

4. Although the statistics indicate that the amount of money supplied by the underworld is quite small, the state, in its efforts to curb illegitimate financing, has focused on the underworld. Various accounts in the media show that the state has cast the "underworld" as the "villain" so that it can play the "hero."

5. Black money and white money are terms used to describe illegitimately and legitimately acquired wealth. This distinction is of course open to debate. It is also important to consider how the terms black and white as ways to distinguish illegitimate and legitimate money (re)produce racist discourses in the context of India.

6. Approximately a month before the BJP government announced its decision to grant industry status to film, the Minister of State for Information and Broadcasting Mukhtar Abbas Naqvi declared that the government was considering proposals which would "enable filmmakers to tap institutional sources for finance," thereby decreasing filmmakers' dependence on "mafia-black" money. He appealed to "the talented and nationalistic sections of the film industry to support the government in its bid to rid the industry from the clutches of the 'mafia.'" See *Indian Express*, 1998c.

7. The emergence of the term "Bollywood" in the 1990s indicates a desire to be like Hollywood, as a large-scale, if a much less socially and financially legitimate, form, but with similar drives. The goal is to establish a form which is both national and international and which can move into non-national territories with considerable success. For further discussion regarding this term, see Rajadhyaksha, 2003; Prasad, 2003.

8. The more recent guidelines on the IDBI website state that the IDBI will not grant assistance of less than 2 crores (IDBI, 2005).

9. For a discussion on film genres, see the select references: Altman, 1984; Buscombe, 1970; Neale, 1990; Schatz, 1977; Sobchack, 1975; Tudor, 1973; Williams, 1991; Wood, 1977.

10. For further discussion on gender, diaspora and Hindi films, see Mankekar, 1999; Mishra, 2002: 235–69; Uberoi, 1998; Virdi, 2003: 192–204.

11. Patricia Uberoi (2001) provides an engaging analysis of *Hum Aapke Hain Kaun*. In her article, she interviews a set of middle/upper-middle class viewers in Delhi to analyze the appeal of this film.

12. The state did institute the Cable Television Networks Rules in 1994, and the Cable Television Networks (Regulation) Act, 1995, in an effort to regulate the influence

of cable and satellite programming (Ministry of Information, 1994, 1995).

13. According to an agreement among all the states, films which are national award winners are tax-free.

14. Instead of spending 40 rupees ($1) or more per ticket, one can buy tickets for Rs 9 (25 cents) for stalls, Rs 11 (26 cents) for family circle seats and Rs 13 (27 cents) for balcony seats. At this rate, the film is affordable entertainment for many. (These figures are based upon the exchange rate in 1996.)

15. Punjab is a state in India. Punjabi immigrants were and continue to be important contributors to the Bombay film industry.

16. The question of language is interesting here as Hindi is the official language of India—not of the Punjab, although many Hindu Punjabis after the Partition of India claimed Hindi rather than Punjabi to be their mother tongue. In doing so, they not only distinguished themselves from the Muslim Punjabis but also the Sikh Punjabis. Language in this case was linked to religion: Urdu for Muslims, Hindi for Hindus, and Punjabi for Sikhs.

17. In this scene, Simran at first refuses to drink alcohol and scolds Raj for drinking in front of a woman. Presumably, Indian women are supposed to refrain from consuming alcohol. In commercial films, this is a device for distinguishing the "vamp," the "western" or "westernized" woman, from the "Indian" woman.

18. In a television show about the making of *DDLJ*, the stars of the film, Shah Rukh Khan and Kajol, revealed that this shot had been completed after 20 takes, largely because one or the other would begin laughing when "Raj" pulls down his shirt zipper to show the lipstick marks.

19. *Hindustani* is commonly translated as "Indian." More specifically, the word refers to a person who lives in Hindustan, namely, the place of Hindus.

20. Sinha, 1998: Purnima Mankekar (1999: 743–8) also notes this overlap.

References

Aiyar, V Shankar and Anupama Chopra. "Waiting for Action," *India Today* (25 May), http://www.india-today.com/itoday/25051998/biz-html 1998.

Altman, Rick. "A Semantic/Syntactic Approach to Film Genre," *Cinema Journal* 23(3), 1984. 6–18.

Buscombe, Edward. "The Idea of Genre in American Cinema," *Screen* 11(2), 1970. 33–45.

Business Line. "Film Accorded Industry Status" (19 Oct.), http://www.indiaserver.com/businessline/2000/10/19/stories/141918re.htm, 2000a.

Business Line. "Sops Set Film Industry on a Roll" (2 March), http://www.indiaserver.com/businessline/2000/03/02/stories/030244s2.htm, 2000b.

Central Board of Film Certification. *Certification Board Report for* Dilwale Dulhania Lejayenge. Bombay: Central Board of Film Certification, 1995.

Ciecko, Anne and Sheldon Lu. "The Heroic Trio: Anita Mui, Maggie Cheung, Michelle Yeoh—Self-Reflexivity and the Globalization of the Hong Kong Action Heroine," *Post Script: Essays in Film and the Humanities* 19(1), 1999. 70–86.

Dilwale Dulhania Le Jayenge. Directed by Aditya Chopra. DVD, Yash Raj Productions,

2001.

Dwyer, Rachel and Divia Patel. *Cinema India*. New Delhi: Oxford University Press, 2002.

Economic Times. "Entertainment Industry Wants Parity with Infotech Sector, and More Tax Benefits" (23 Feb.), http://www.economictimes.com/230200/23indu0.htm, 2000

Financial Express. "Money for Movies" (18 May), http://www.expressindia.com/fe/daily/19980518/13855654.html 1998.

Financial Express. "IDBI Outlines Norms for Film-Financing" (31 March), http://www.financialexpress.com/fe/daily/20010331/fco31005.html. 2001.

Ganti, Tejaswini. *Bollywood: A Guidebook to Popular Hindi Cinema*. New York: Routledge, 2004.

India Abroad Daily. "Film Industry Becomes Eligible for Bank Finance" (18 Oct.), http://www.indiaabroaddaily.com/2000/10/18/18filmfin.html, 2000.

IndiaInfo.com. "Underworld Nexus with Filmdom Worries FICCI" (23 March), http://www.news.indiainfo.com/2001/03/23/23under.html (accessed 20 April 2001), 2000.

Indian Express. "Bollywood's Woes to Get a Hearing Finally" (9 May), http://www.expressindia.com/ie/daily/19980509/12950624.html, 1998a.

Indian Express. "Finally an Industry" (12 May), http://www.expressindia.com/ie/daily/19980512/13250064.html, 1998b.

Indian Express. "Govt Script to Rid Film Industry of Mafia" (20 April), 1998c.

Indian Express. "Industry Status for Film World" (11 May), http://www.expressindia.com/daily/19980511/13150654.html, 1998d.

Industrial Development Bank of India. "Film Financing," http://www.idbi.com/film_fin.html (accessed 24 June 2005), 2005.

Iwabuchi, Koichi. *Globalization: Popular Culture and Japanese Transnationalism*. Durham, NC: Duke University Press, 2002.

Jha, Subhash K. "*My Brother Nikhil* Releases at a Time When Unconventional Cinema is Getting Surprisingly Successful," *Desi Talk* (22 April), http://desitalk.newsindia-times.com/2005/04/22/cinema25-my.html (accessed 23 June 2005), 2005.

Joshi, Namrata. "Housefull! (But . . . Kitne Aadmi Thhe?)," *Outlook India.com* (27 June),http://www.outlookindia.com/full.asp?fodname=20050627&fname=Cinema+%28F%29&sid=1&pn=1, 2005.

Larkin, Brian. "Itineraries of Indian Cinema: African Videos, Bollywood, and Global Media," in Ella Shohat and Robert Stam (eds) *Multiculturalism, Postcoloniality, and Transnational Media*, New Brunswick, NJ: Rutgers University Press, 2003. 170–92.

Lau, Jenny Kwok Wah, ed. *Multiple Modernities: Cinemas and Popular Media in Transcultural East Asia*. Philadelphia, PA: Temple University Press, 2003.

Lu, Sheldon, ed. *Transnational Chinese Cinemas: Identity, Nationhood, Gender*. Honolulu: University of Hawaii Press, 1997.

Mankekar, Purnima. "Brides who Travel: Gender, Transnationalism, and Nationalism in Hindi Film," *Positions* 7(3), 1999. 731–61.

Mehta, Monika. "Selections: Cutting, Classifying and Certifying in Bombay Cinema," PhD, University of Minnesota, 2001.

Ministry of Information and Broadcasting, Government of India. *Film Censorship:*

What Everyone Should Know. Delhi: Bengal Printing Press, 1992a.

Ministry of Information and Broadcasting, Government of India. *The Cinematograph Act, 1952 (37 of 1952) and Censorship Guidelines*. New Delhi: Rakesh Press, 1992b.

Ministry of Information and Broadcasting, Government of India. "Cable Television Networks Rules," http://mib.nic.in/informationb/media/actsrules/frames.htm (accessed 23 April 2001), 1994.

Ministry of Information and Broadcasting, Government of India. "Cable Television Networks (Regulation) Act," http://mib.nic.in/infor-mationb/media/actsrules/frames.htm 1995.

Mishra, Vijay. *Bollywood Cinema: Temples of Desire*. New York: Routledge, 2002.

Naficy, Hamid. *Accented Cinema: Exilic and Diasporic Filmmaking*. Princeton, NJ: Princeton University Press, 2001.

Neale, Steve. "Questions of Genre," *Screen* 31(1), 1990. 45–66.

Pendakar, Manjunath and Radha Subramanyam. "Indian Cinema Beyond National Boundaries," in John Sinclair, Elizabeth Jacka and Stuart Cunningham (eds) *New Patterns in Global Television*. New York: Oxford University Press, 1996. 67–82

Prasad, Madhava. "This Thing Called Bollywood," *Seminar* 525, 2003. 17–20.

Rajadhyaksha, Ashish. "The "Bollywoodisation" of the Indian Cinema: Cultural Nationalism in a Global Arena," *Inter-Asia Cultural Studies* 4(1), 2003. 25–39.

Rediff on The Net. "Industry Status Remains a Mirage for Dream Merchants" (3 July), http://www.rediff.com/business/1999/jul/03film.htm (accessed 20 April 2001), 1999.

Responservice. "Bollywood Biggies Take a "Capital" Step to Get Organised" (Oct.), http://www.responservicearchives/oct2000_issue2/media/cinema.htm (accessed 20 April 2001), 2000.

Sassen, Saskia. *Globalization and its Discontents*. New York: New Press. 1998.

Schatz, Thomas. "The Structural Influence: New Directions in Film Genre Study," *Quarterly Review of Film Studies* 2(3), 1977. 302–12.

Sharma, Aparna. "India's Experience with the Multiplex," *Seminar* 25, 2003.42–6.

Shohat, Ella and Robert Stam, eds. *Unthinking Eurocentrism: Multiculturalism and the Media*. New York: Routledge, 1994.

Shohat, Ella and Robert Stam, eds. *Multiculturalism, Postcoloniality, and Transnational Media*. New Brunswick, NJ : Rutgers University Press, 2003.

Sinha, Yashwant. "Union Budget Speech 1998–1999," Ministry of Finance, Government of India, 1 June, http://indiabudget.nic.in/ub1998–99/bs/speech.htm (accessed 25 April 2001), 1998.

Sobchack, Thomas. "Genre Films: A Classical Experience," *Literature/Film Quarterly* 3(3), 1975. 196–204.

Srinivas, SV. "Hong Kong Action Film in the Indian B Circuit," *Inter-Asia Cultural Studies* 4(1), 2003.40–62.

The Hindu. "Focus, Please (Indian Movies)" (23 Sept.), http://www.webpage.com/hindu/daily/980923/05/05232512.htm, 1998a.

The Hindu. "It is Darkest before Dawn" (6 Sept.), http://www.webpage.com/hindu/daily/980906/09/09060227.htm, 1998b.

The Times of India. "Mukta Arts Float First Film Production IPO" (7 July), http://timesofindia.com/070700/07boll1.htm, 2000.

Tudor, Andrew. "Genre," in *Theories of Film*. New York: Viking Press, 1973. 131–50.

Uberoi, Patricia. "The Diaspora Comes Home: Disciplining Desire in DDLJ," *Contributions to Indian Sociology*, new series 32(3), 1998. 305–36.

Uberoi, Patricia. "Imagining the Family: An Ethnography of Viewing *Hum Aapke Hain Kaun . . .!*," in Rachel Dwyer and Christopher Pinney (eds) *Pleasure and the Nation*. New Delhi: Oxford University Press, 2001. 309–51

Virdi, Jyotika. *The Cinematic Imagination: Indian Popular Films as Social History*. New Brunswick, NJ: Rutgers University Press, 2003.

Williams, Linda. "Film Bodies: Gender, Genre, and Excess," *Film Quarterly* 44(4), 1991. 2–13.

Wong, Cindy Hing-yuk. "Cities, Cultures and Cassettes: Hong Kong Cinema and Transnational Audiences," *Post Script: Essays in Film and the Humanities* 19(1), 1999. 87–106.

Wood, Robin. "Ideology, Genre, Auteur," *Film Comment* 13(1), 1977. 46–51.

Imagi Nation: The Reconfiguration of National Identity in Bombay Cinema in the 1990s

RADHIKA DESAI

Nations imagine themselves eternal and immutable just as fervently as they must reinvent themselves continuously. If they are, as Tom Nairn puts it, "a modern form of community," they embody the contradiction between the noun and the adjective. They can be, at best, precarious balancing acts between modernity's capitalism and commodification, which corrode community, and the compulsion to create minimal meanings and solidarities. As modern capitalist societies, nations are not serial sums of their members. National communities are hierarchically structured by the inequalities that capitalism creates among the groups that constitute them, and national cultures and ideologies of nationalism must somehow manage to articulate community out of, and despite, the inequalities. Changes in the orders of inequality which nations really are must be articulated in the national discourse by changes in its characteristic themes, idioms, and figures, by new inclusions, exclusions, and re-orderings. This paper is about an instance of such changes.

As socio-economic and political change accelerated in India over the 1990s, as neoliberalism created deeper inequalities, and Hindu nationalism or Hindutva sought to give them new political and cultural expressions, the boundaries of the Indian nation, as delineated in its national culture, began to be redrawn. Certain national groups came to be constructed as outsiders, and even enemies, while certain others, formally outside the nation, were not only included in it, but were placed at its core. In this process the nation renegotiated its relationship with the territories and populations that are India, and with the national culture that hitherto articulated them. It did not thereby dissolve into some *global* community, as per the talk of globalization, however. The Indian nation remained anchored securely to the state that is the Republic of

India with all its various cultural, bureaucratic and military apparatuses. At the same time, new boundaries were drawn and others dissolved in a complex process.

Among the many sectors of culture where this process could be observed, none manifested it more clearly than the nationally, and increasingly globally, popular Bombay cinema. Indeed, its fate was intricately intertwined with this process. In the 1980s, as this restructuring of the Indian nation got going, Bombay cinema lost its feel for the national pulse. When, after a decade of groping, it found that pulse again, it poured everything it had into amplifying it, adopting new themes and tropes and even creating new genres. This re-imagination of the Indian nation on the big screen was one of the central cultural events of our time. And it testified to the continuing centrality of Bombay cinema to Indian culture.

I propose to examine two recent films, exemplars of two new genres in which the cultural work of exclusion and inclusion in the reconfiguration of India's national culture was performed. The "nation in danger" genre and the "NRI" genre were both popular in recent decades in India and in the international market for Indian films, mainly among South Asian émigrés. The first gave voice to anxieties about threats, mainly from "terrorists" from Pakistan, to the nation. It was instrumental in expressing, and at the same time gentrifying and popularizing, the more extreme and unreasonable anti-Pakistan and anti-Muslim sentiments which had hitherto been the idiolect of the more extreme elements of the Hindu right. The second was a new genre focussed on the large and influential community of émigré Indians in metropolitan countries and serves not only to depict them in glamourous lifestyles which most in India adulate and aspire to emulate, but inflected them towards upper-caste Hindu lifestyles, prejudices, and values in a manner that made the sectarian discourse of Hindutva more widely acceptable. *Sarfarosh* and *Dilwale Dulhania Le Jayenge,* represent each of these two genres. The one revolved around the character of a young career police officer, an Assistant Commissioner of Police, engaged in the task of stopping the smuggling of arms for terrorist and subversive forces from across the India-Pakistan border. He was up against the smugglers, against elements of the corrupt Indian state who were complicit in this gravely antinational activity, and against his own trusting nature and love for the culture which India and Pakistan share. The other was a love story which, as so often in Bombay cinema, involves two young people of Indian origin who are residents of a Western country, in this case Britain. It was, however, difficult to tell whether the hero loved the heroine or the high caste and patriarchal values and culture of her family more. This was certainly the partial result of the increasingly vapid treatment of female characters in Indian cinema: she was beautiful, no more, and as such only the trailer for the much bigger love to follow. The hero spent more time wooing her family, in particular her father, than her. Perhaps a latent homosexuality is a feature of all patriarchies. The film climaxed in the bonding not of the hero and the heroine, which is only the climax of its first and rather frivolous chapter, but in that of the hero and his prospective father-in-law.

The reconfiguration of the nation of which these films were at once the instrument and the expression, pointed to the centrality of the nation, and the nation-state, to politics today. All the rhetoric of globalization notwithstanding, the nation remained central to any politics as a terrain of struggle, as I discuss in the following section. However, the reconfiguration of the nation also made clear that the nation as a terrain of struggle and resistance was redefined in important ways. The third section briefly discusses Bombay cinema's place in India's national culture and traces some of the changes it has undergone over recent decades, so that a fuller understanding of the work which the two films and their genres do in the reconfiguration of the Indian nation can follow in the final section.

Global and National Terrains of Resistance

By the turn of the twentieth century the activist or intellectual who was not aware that the ground of politics had shifted beneath her feet was rare. The idea of "globalization" captured imaginations across the political spectrum. Whereas neoliberal boosters of globalization argued that globalization was desirable, the swelling army of those who constituted a veritable global flying picket against globalization and its principal institutions—demonstrating against meetings of the WTO or the IMF or the World Economic Forum wherever they took place around the world—thought it must be stopped in its tracks. For the latter, resistance required a specifically *global* strategy which transcended national borders and concerns. Both sides agreed that the terrain of politics—of both domination and resistance—was no longer national, it had become global.

This conviction was, however, ill-founded. Many scholars forcefully argued that globalization implied no "decline of the nation-state." Rather than being the victims of globalization, nation-states had been its architects. Over the last decades of the twentieth century nation-states constructed globalization's complex international economic and political architecture and they did this to register and reinforce a massive shift in the balance of power to the right, in favour of capitalist and propertied elites within them (Panitch 1998 and 2000; Weiss 1998; Hirst and Thompson 1999). Globalization was therefore not the unstoppable and inevitable process its boosters claimed it was, but the result of the deliberate actions of nation-states taken to serve the interests that stood behind them. The portrayal of globalization as inevitable was only a fall-back position of its boosters when its critics questioned their claim that globalization was desirable and pointed to the poverty, inequality, environmental destruction, social breakdown and, for good measure, slow-down in economic growth, which it brought in its train.

Critics of globalization also noted that it was not about knitting the world into a closer community, based on closer economic relations. Rather, it gave freedom of movement to capital above all. While global flows of people and trade in commodities increased during the 1990s, these increases nowhere matched the unprecedented increase in global financial flows. Moreover, this predominantly financial globalization was biased towards speculative flows of money seeking to profit from small changes in the value of currencies, financial instruments, and certain highly traded commodities, rather than flows of productive capital, of direct foreign investment of multinational corporations. Finally, globalization was not an enterprise in which all nations, and not even all the rich nations of the world, participated equally. Rather it was a particular strategy of US hegemony, and the actions of the United States government were preponderant in its making, both in extent and effect. Arguably, as such a strategy, globalization had ended at the turn of the century. Let me explain.

The United States' majority share of world production, which had formed the basis of its hegemony at the middle of the twentieth century, was eroded in the course of the long boom in the world capitalist economy as Western Europe and Japan recovered from the war and enhanced their productive capacities. By the late 1960s they had emerged as major economic competitors of the United States, eating into its share of the world economy. From the late 1960s onwards, the United States attempted to work to advance its interests in a context where its hegemony was rendered unstable by this development. The strategies it adopted seemed to pit US interests against those of the rest of the capitalist world, including the next most powerful economies. Financial globalization seemed for a short time to be a reliable means for securing the US's economic dominance. During the 1990s the new world financial structure created and dominated by American financial institutions and their allies in the United Kingdom under the sponsorship of the two governments and the international financial institutions such as the IMF which they dominated, acted to suck up capital from all over the world to create an investment boom in the US. American firms and corporations also gained control over greater portions of world productive capacity through the mechanisms of financial control. The US economy grew at a fast clip while its most important competitors, the Japanese and the Europeans, stagnated.

This strategy began to overreach itself by the late 1990s and its symptoms were a series of financial crises, particularly the Asian, the ensuing bursting of the dotcom bubble, and the collapse of certain US corporate giants which had engaged most thoroughly and innovatively in the new financial economy. Together, these events spelled the end of the financial globalization strategy of preserving a leading position for the United States in the world order. However, the lineaments of the US's next strategy did not emerge clearly until after the War on Terrorism was launched. Once it was, it seemed as though the US was engaged in a drive not for financial but more direct—political and military—forms of control over the world's productive capacity and resources. Kyoto, the Asian steel wars, the military and political drive for the control of oil, and the return of competitive devaluations are all instances of this new strategy. In contrast to the relatively peaceful operation of purely financial control (though the Clinton years, which were almost exactly contemporaneous with financial globalization, did see much military activity also, in Afghanistan, Sudan, Iraq, and the Balkans), this new strategy required the direct or indirect control of territories and productive capacities, and greater violence naturally went with it. It was not without significance that in the new century the term "globalization" fell out of use while the term "imperialism" was favoured, not just by critics of American power but also by those who concluded that American imperialism was the best way forward for the world and urged the United States to avow its imperial function and role. If globalization had not implied any decline of the nation-state, the War on Terrorism did so even less. The powers of nation-states, and their differential powers in the larger world order, remained central determinants of world and domestic politics, no matter the degree of international activity registered in various economic indices.

In its universalism, the idea of global resistance has an undeniable charm, just as in the past that of internationalism had constituted the lodestar of working-class movements. However, as the Italian Communist Antonio Gramsci long ago argued, the struggle against national ruling classes, their hegemonies, and their nationally organized domination was the first step in any global emancipation from capitalist domination. While capitalism was international, and the working-class struggle had to be the same, each national working class also had to settle its scores with its national ruling class. "To be sure the line of development is towards internationalism, but the point of departure is national and it is from this point of departure that one must begin" (Gramsci 1971:240). Gramsci had no time for empty or abstract universalisms which ignored the reality—economic, political and moral-cultural—of the nation. Through the central concept of the "national-popular" he sought to place the idea of the nation centrally in any Communist understanding of the terrain of struggle. In particular, he sought to make Communism's internationalism more concrete (Gramsci 1971a:236–241). In doing so, he also criticised the role of the "cosmopolitanism . . . of the Catholic Middle Ages, centred on Italy" which had contributed to the "absence of any Italian 'political and national history'" which he so brilliantly analysed and lamented (Gramsci 1971a:274; Gramsci 1971b; Gramsci 1983:28–51).

As he understood it, the national-popular was the modern terrain of politics. It came into existence as a result of the popular energies aroused by successful bourgeois revolution and the task of socialists within the capitalist order thus constituted was to radicalize these national-popular energies further towards socialism. In Italy, this task was difficult precisely because of an only partially successful bourgeois revolution, which had failed to lay the basis of a truly national culture (Gramsci 1971:131–133). National cultures provided the popular medium through which socialist parties and their intellectuals could lay the basis of a deep communicative, cultural, and political bond with the "people-nation"(Gramsci 1971:418) for the purposes of revolution. Gramsci was critical of intellectuals who, with a breezy internationalism, neglected the task of bonding with the people through the national culture. Without this bond, socialism was impossible.

> The popular element "feels" but does not always know or understand; the intellectual element "knows" but does not always understand, and in particular does not always feel. The two extremes are

> therefore pedantry and philistinism on the one hand and blind passion and sectarianism on the other . . . The intellectual's error consists in believing that one can know without understanding and even more without feeling and being impassioned . . . : in other words, that the intellectual can be an intellectual . . . if distinct and separate from the people-nation, that is, without feeling the elementary passions of the people, understanding them and therefore explaining and justifying them in the particular historical situation and connecting them dialectically to the laws of history and to a superior conception of the world, scientifically and coherently elaborated—i.e. knowledge. One cannot make politics-history without this passion, without this sentimental connection between intellectuals and people-nation. In the absence of such a nexus the relations between the intellectual and the people-nation are, or are reduced to, relationships of a purely bureaucratic and formal order; the intellectuals become a caste, or a priesthood . . . (Gramsci 1971:418)

If the character of the national culture, the nature of the popular imaginings, and conceptions of the nation are important terrains of struggle, they can also become both targets and instruments of resistance. It is in this context that the reconfiguration of the Indian nation through one of its most popular cultural media, Bombay cinema, becomes significant.

Many critical accounts of Hindutva noted the transition from Indian nationalism to Hindu nationalism. This change had counterparts in other countries and, in an attempt to theorize it, I envisaged, more generally, a transition from *developmental nationalisms* which sought to create out of colonized or deeply unequal and hierarchical societies, more equal and productive ones, and took internationalist and anti-imperialist positions on the international stage to *cultural nationalisms* which, more and less brazenly, seek to reinforce the structures of hierarchy and inequality at home by entrenching their expression in the national culture. They also projected aggressive and (and this is only apparently a paradox) pro-imperialist identities internationally (Desai 2004a, 2004b, and 2008). In this conception, the category of cultural nationalism includes all nation alisms that are focused on identities, whether religious, national, or ethnic. They also include various forms of "multicultural" nationalisms, for they too privilege a dominant "national" identity against those of various "minorities." Indeed, the two are not necessarily mutually exclusive: Hindutva in India, for example, insists that the dominant Hindu culture is inherently secular, tolerant, and multicultural, while, to take a very different example, conservative discourses of German national culture today make a concession to "multiculturalism" while also demanding that the minorities accept that Germany has a *lietkultur*, a leading culture. In multiculturalism, cultural differences are only hypocritically valorized while underlying socio-economic inequalities reinforce cultural hierarchies.

The cultural dynamics of nationalisms cannot be investigated in isolation from the changing political economies of nations. Nationalisms and capitalisms have emerged in tandem with one another. Etienne Balibar and Immanuel Wallerstein (1990) have attempted to theorize the relationship between the cultural dynamics and the political economies of nations more intricately. Mechanisms of inclusion and othering, and associated mechanisms of structuring the nation hierarchically within, both in ways which are intertwined with the inequalities which capitalisms create, maintain, and modify as they develop are central to their account.

The mechanisms of exclusion and othering order groups within the nation in a hierarchy of belonging in which some are more national than others. In the Indian case, whereas its early, developmental nationalism seemed to be inclusive (albeit more in aspiration than in reality), contemporary Hindu nationalism reinforces the hierarchies which compose the nation ever more brazenly while seeking to include within it a small number of new entrants into the elite, to *give them a place* within a restructured nation. Meanwhile, violence and intimidation directed at hapless minorities are designed to *show them their place* in the emerging India.

As long as the structured community of the nation resided largely within its territorial borders, in particular as long as the peak of this hierarchically structured national community remained both objectively and subjectively within its territories, the idea of nation and territory remained consonant. Today, however, they are out of joint. It is the fate of many nations in the third world, in particular, to sport a propertied elite whose business, leisure, and kinship networks are flung across the globe. In many ways these elites are more transnational than the elites of the first world.

One of the chief ways in which Hindutva's project is being reinforced in the wider culture is through the projection of new national stereotypes. What is truly "Indian" is being redefined in new and politically reactionary ways. Older themes of a new secular and diverse nation emerging under the benevolent tutelage of the state, with socialistic policies of development, to take its place in an international community of the nonaligned nations with their anti-imperialist unity, are being replaced by new ones of an assertive Hindu nation, with its roots in a traditional—rural—Hindu milieu, adroitly managing to assert itself economically and militarily within an imperialist international order. Themes and tropes of the new agrarianism are freely deployed: "Bharat" versus "India," the countryside as the repository of national identity, of its unsullied soul. All the contradictions and oppressions involved in the development of capitalist relations of production in agriculture and the consequent sharpening of class conflict in the countryside are airbrushed away. These themes obviously address the numerically most important segment of the Indian bourgeoisie: the provincial propertied class (Balagopal). This class emerged from the agrarian bourgeoisie as it began to acquire interests and investments in India's urban and industrial sectors in its small towns and industries. Today India's capitalist classes span vast distances—geographically, culturally, and socially—from the dominant classes of the villages through small-town bourgeoisies to national and international networks of business, family, and social links. Hindutva can now deploy rustic rhetoric as a myth of agrarian "traditional" origins for this class. This trope views the "traditional" village, much like mainstream Bombay cinema, as a harmonious organic whole without exploiters or exploited. It can serve as the chief myth of the authoritarian nation, delegitimizing cleavages within it, while remaining within the framework of the capitalism into which its constituencies are deeply implicated.

In the new cultural definition of "Indianness," membership of the nation is no longer a matter of citizenship. It has, according to Hindutva, an identitarian logic with important global and émigré dimensions. While Non-Resident Indians (NRIs) who retain their Indian identity can now be considered more or less Indian, certain sections of the nation—Muslim, first and foremost but also liberals, socialists or feminists, that is to say "unindian" and "Westernized"—can be othered as "resident non-Indians."

Bombay Cinema

The century-old Indian film industry has been the subject of investigation and analysis by scholars of film studies, cultural studies, semiotics, and sociology. However, the analysis of the *political* aspect of films, their content, style, form, their makers and actors, and the configuration of the film industry itself have rarely come under systematic investigation. Bombay cinema's complex and reflexive relationship with India's political evolution should be of interest to more than just Indian audiences or scholars of film studies. Not only is Bombay cinema a major centre for the production and reproduction of India's culture, the new century has seen it make a bid, quite successful in its initial stages, to be counted among the producers of culture globally. The politics embedded in the products of this industry should then interest a global scholarly and popular audience.

Films are not usually watched for their political message, nor do their makers usually claim to have one. This is what makes the politics implicit in every film so effective. The mass audiences which films generally attract make their political messages far more effective and potent than those carried by print or even electronic media. Bombay cinema has not only reflected the politics of India, it is also often in the forefront of their making. In the 1950s, Bombay cinema had a broadly developmentalist, protosocialist egalitarian character. In the 1960s, it represented the disappointment of the hopes of the nationalist movement. In the 1970s, Bombay films focused on social themes—caste, gender, and class—and included a very substantial number of films combining high quality, box office success and social criticism. After a "lost decade" of the 1980s, when the video revolution and its very specific class patterning in India changed the demographics of movie audiences drastically, and Bombay cinema seemed to descend into a morass of underfunding, bad quality, sex, and violence, the 1990s and the new century have seen a major new revival.

It is this revival within which we must place the new politics of cultural nationalism. Economically, India has seen two decades of market liberalization, and this can be seen today in the unabashed valorization of free market and corporate values and characters, not to mention the simple, uncritical celebration of wealth, in Bombay cinema. Socially, with rising inequality and the emergence of a bigger and more powerful capitalist class, India has seen the sharpening of class, gender, certain ethnic and religious divides, and their new politics are now manifest on screens: no longer the critique of caste or patriarchy, for instance, but rather the uncritical acceptance of caste, gender, and religious structures of privilege. Such acceptance takes place on a changed cultural terrain given India's opening to global cultural trends, its increasing distance from the rural world, and the emergence of a new youth culture. A good part of the cultural labour being performed by Bombay cinema is to re-stabilize caste, gender, and religious hierarchies on this new terrain.

Finally, politically, the rise of Hindu nationalism in Indian politics has been the dominant political phenomenon of the last few decades. Except for some of its more extreme organizations, such as the Bombay-based Shiv Sena, few of the organizations or activities of Hindu nationalism have come in for critique in Bombay cinema: on the contrary, many of Bombay's new themes are closely associated with the characteristic themes of Hindutva politics: a new emphasis on piety; the "modern" but not "Western" woman; the importance of diasporic Indians as models and as a core part of the nation (not to mention their centrality to the market for these films); the venality and corruption of India's old-style (read Congress and other non-BJP) politicians; and finally, the centrality of the theme of Kashmir, terrorism, and Pakistan.

At the same time the industry itself has been undergoing many important changes: the eclipse of the studio system; the vast, international distribution networks; the international market; the high value market for videos and DVDs and related promotional materials; the new centrality of the predominantly Hindu upper and middle caste and class audience; the financing of films through more respectable and open means through a favourable taxation and credit regime, and so on.

The Re-Imagination of India and Indians

Among the foremost films in the "nation in danger" genre were *Roja*, *Sarfarosh*, and *Mission Kashmir*. Each of them was ostensibly about the Kashmir problem and the threat it represented for the Indian nation. Each began with title sequences which impressed upon the audience the seriousness and the tragedy of the situation. The audience was assured that the film was entirely cognizant of these and intended to tell a story within their parameters. *Mission Kashmir* was directed by Vidhu Vinod Chopra, a Kashmiri Hindu and the most recognized talent in the Bombay cinema of the 1990s. *Sarfarosh* was the debut of John Mathew Mathan. *Roja* was made by Mani Ratnam. What was interesting about the last, which set the trend for making films about Kashmir and the problem of terrorism generally, was that it was made by a South Indian director. South Indians had hitherto been, and were seen to have been, relatively detached from the issues of Kashmir and Partition, a detachment which had its counterpart in the south's lower susceptibility to anti-Muslim attitudes and violence. Ratnam's *Roja* represented a claim on behalf of the south to full membership in the new Indian nation, where the membership fee was, in part at least, an expression of concern, involvement, and commitment with regard to Kashmir. Its political counterpart was the gradual penetration of Hindutva into the south, and quite possibly, a break from the region's historic traditions of communal harmony. On the other hand, it was the beginning of a trend where, as in Pakistan, commitment to the issue of Kashmir was accepted as being the most authentic testimonial of national loyalty.

The most obvious of the three films' common themes was that of national unity and safety. These needed to be secured against a number of enemies: Pakistan, which, either by malignant design or because it was a failed state or some combination of the two, harboured terrorists; the terrorists themselves; and disloyal Indians who, in the simple iconography for which Bombay cinema was always distinguished, were usually portrayed as seedy and malignant, completely unlike the idealized Indian men, women, children, families, and communities who were urbane and benevolent. These categories of enemies resembled the stereotypes of all othered groups: Muslims, Christians, tribals, lower-caste and -class people, and corrupt Indian politicians. These last most often resembled the middle- and lower-class politicians who came to be so resented in India for increasing their numbers in parliament and "lowering the standards" in politics.

Apart from the new villains, there were some characters whose virtues were cast as crucial weaknesses: the message was that some virtues had to be forsaken in a larger national cause. There was the laidback political leadership, which remained unaware of the true extent of the dangers. There was the trusting Indian, who must be more suspicious. The Indian state was typically portrayed as lackadaisical, the underlying message being that it needed to become more tough, harsh, and businesslike to deal with terrorism and other dangers facing the nation. Finally, of course, there were the heroes and heroines (these latter had ceased to have any quality other than appearance and are called here "heroines" because that is the convention) who all come from "good" families (for which read upper-caste or those who dutifully emulate them and show reverence for the upper-caste norms of Indian life). Typically at some point in the film, an idyllic family life was interrupted by an outbreak of terror.

In none of these films did the issue of the indigenous movement for Kashmiri independence get much coverage. One was left with the impression that the cause of Kashmiri independence was that of terrorists alone. Where, in *Mission Kashmir*, a native-born Kashmiri, Altaaf, became a terrorist, this was entirely due to the trauma of watching his entire family perish in a bloody orgy of police brutality. Even then the hero became a terrorist only because this trauma was exploited by a foreign terrorist. The film was lauded for being exceptionally candid about the brutality of the Indian armed forces in Kashmir. However, this viewpoint ignored the fact that the film also depicted this brutality as inevitable. The violence sponsored by foreign terrorists made this brutality necessary, however tragic its consequences for individual Kashmiris. It had to be accepted above all by Kashmiris who wished to be considered "good Muslims," and its sometimes dangerous and tragic consequences had to be managed, if necessary, with more brutality.

Muslim characters appeared in the three films to different degrees and in different ways. The portrayals ranged from simple, uncomplicated othering as in *Roja*, where they were only terrorists, to a more complex discourse in which they were on the point of being othered and would be readmitted into the nation provided they accepted certain terms, i.e. a conditional inclusion. In *Sarfarosh* there were two important Muslim characters. One was a police officer under the command of the hero, Assistant Commissioner of Police, Ajay Singh Rathod. The other was the mastermind behind the gun-running operation, who appeared in public as a singer beloved in India and Pakistan and whose celebrity was a cloak for his activities. The former was resentful of the discrimination he faced and was told off by his boss, the ACP, who chastised him for thinking only of himself and reminded him of his duty to his country. It was a scene noteworthy for breaking one of the most important conventions of the portrayal of good behaviour, respect for age. Indeed, it was this which gave the scene its power: an older Muslim was chastised for his infantile concern for himself by a younger, truly national Hindu hero. The character of the Muslim singer and gun-runner contained two very important features: the danger of duplicitous Muslims to trusting Indians, and the shared culture of India and Pakistan which could be exploited by the latter. In *Mission Kashmir* both the leading male characters, the Inspector General of Police and his errant adopted son, Altaaf, are Kashmiri Muslims. Good Muslims were loyal to India. Other Muslims who did not constantly protest their loyalty to India and did not seek to demonstrate it in ways which would never be required of Hindus were not. Moreover, they also exemplifed the notion that good Muslims, so defined, were better off in India than in Pakistan.

From the mechanisms of exclusion and conditional inclusion in the "nation in danger" genre, we can now move on to the NRI genre's mechanisms of inclusion and privileged inclusion. In *Dilwale Dulhania Le Jayange* (DDLJ,) the London-based hero, the only son of a widowed and indulgent father, pursued the heroine, also living in London, to Punjab, where she was to have an arranged marriage with the son of a childhood friend of her father's. The story revolved not around the hero winning the love of the heroine, all of which happened within a few song sequences set in picture-postcard-perfect European locations at the beginning of the film. Rather, it revolved around the hero wooing the heroine's farther for his consent. Indeed, the drama of the film was provided by the hero's refusal to marry against the wishes of the heroine's father. He even refused her mother's advice to elope with her daughter in the face of the bitter opposition of the father. In *Pardes*, the chief protagonist was, once again, an Indian émigré who became fabulously wealthy in the United States, living in Los Angeles, and seeking the hand of an old friend's daughter for his son. The beautiful young daughter, Ganga, was brought up in the Indian countryside. She was unspoiled, Indian, traditional, and simply beautiful: she was India. Her much-indulged fiancé, however, was, unbeknownst to his father who was merely blinded by his love for his son, completely undeserving of the young Ganga. The film unfolded as a story about how Ganga, pure and unspoiled as her namesake, the river Ganges, gradually came to the conclusion that the person she loved was not her fiancé, but his adopted brother who remained more Indian despite living abroad. Here, too, parental consent trumped love and the young Ganga only made the final choice once she was permitted to do so by her prospective father-in-law.

The NRI genre revived a declining Bombay film industry practically single-handed. During the 1980s the industry was assaulted by the video revolution and had been sinking into a mire of lost markets and lack of legitimate funding (and thus involvement with the underworld), resorting ultimately to depictions of sex and violence. Such films were thought to meet the tastes of the largely male and middle and lower class and caste movie-going public, which remained once the respectable middle classes withdrew to their drawing rooms furnished with video players. In this new genre, the émigrés, mainly upper-caste Hindus, made their debut among the chief protagonists in Bombay cinema.

This appearance was not simply an innocent reflection of the changes taking place in the life of Indians—i.e. the ubiquity of relatives and friends abroad. Rather it was a specific process in which a certain type of émigré Hindu—a nearly impossible combination of high-caste origin, economic success, and cultural competence within the Western world, and a carefully preserved traditional Hindu identity—was written into the script of the Indian nation as one of the chief mechanisms through which its transformation into a Hindu nation would be accomplished. Among other things, this involved a deterritorialization of the nation and its conversion into a community defined exclusively in terms of participation in an elite culture.

One might add in passing, and it is not at all irrelevant to the de-territorialization of the nation under discussion here, that in the late 1990s Bombay cinema sought to rise as a subordinate, if not exactly a rival, centre for the production of films and culture for a global audience. Indian actors and technicians sought work abroad. This trend was accompanied by the elevation of Indian popular culture to the status of flavour-of-the-month in the institutions of Western high culture—with major exhibits on Indian cinema at the V&A in London, for example, and the attempt to elevate Indian calendar art from its former consignment as kitsch to something worthy of great interest for its creativity and artistic merit.

In one sense, whether or not they involved émigré Indian protagonists, the most successful Bombay films were transformed by their social, ideological, and cultural presence. All portrayals of the good life now involved a reimagination of Indian middle-class life in a way which closely corresponded to popular ideas about the life of émigré Indians abroad. That is to say the "abroad"—still referred to quaintly as "vilayet," (Urdu for mother-country), "foreign" (which has come to mean "abroad" in popular usage in several Indian languages), or simply a privileged "there" in contrast to the more problematic 'here'—appears in Indian cinema in a way which reflects the continuation of a colonial awe in a consumerist reverence. It has already arrived and settled down comfortably in India's metropolises. Whether it was the home (*Hum Apke Hain Kaun*) or a boarding school (*Mohabbatein*) or a police station (*Sarfarosh*) or a television studio (*Mission Kashmir*), all locations in India now had a certain airbrushed foreign quality. This was part of the claim that Bombay cinema made to become a centre of cultural production for the world as a whole. In making this claim successfully it had to rival Hollywood in terms of technical proficiency and accept the norms which the latter set in visualization. (*Mission Kashmir* and *Lagaan* are good examples of this trend. So is *Devdas*, which was screened at Cannes, but in an entirely different manner. The latter's central stylistic gesture—indeed its principal gesture given the dominance of style over all other elements in the film—was to grab the Western viewer by the collar with its unapologetic, even excessive, "Bollywood" cinematic style and idiom in order to stun him into forgetting his condension towards it once and for all.) However, this translocation of the "there" into the "here" also reflects the extent to which a life abroad, more particularly a life in the West, or the recreation of that life in India, represented the pinnacle of the aspirations of the Indian propertied classes. The fact that many middle-class Indians had achieved either or both merely fuelled the aspirations of those who had yet to do so. In that sense this revisualization of India had an objective reality: living in the aspirations of Indian propertied elites it moulded their dreams and desires, their projects and plans.

Indian life, as it came to be portrayed in the NRI genre, whether it was located in India or abroad, was the life of the upper-caste and upper-class Indians. This was the principal reason why films in this genre seemed little more than the portrayal of an endless series of rituals. These conveniently combined the chief leisure activity of the propertied elites, conspicuous consumption, with claims to ritual privilege. Among the invariably opulently performed Hindu rituals that crowded the big screen, marriages were the most prominent (and one may be forgiven for suspecting that these films were sponsored by the federation of marriage-catering businesses). But any number of other rituals, all upper-caste and patriarchal, also figured prominently in the stories. There was no hint that these may not be the rituals performed by all Indians, or even all Hindu Indians. The portrayals constituted a sort of unacknowledged benchmark which all Indians, particularly all Hindu Indians, were expected to seek to emulate. Given that Hindutva operates to unite the Hindus largely on the basis of the dynamics of this sort of emulation—Sanskritization, as MN Srinivas had called it—and to other those who cannot or will not so emulate, these films constituted a major mechanism for the diffusion of these benchmarks into the wider society. The intertwining of upper-caste rituals with the secularly attractive lifestyles of the upper-caste elites in India and abroad merely served to legitimize these rituals and the values they represented. Indeed very often a central theme of these films was that the leading characters' material successes were based on conformity to tradition.

A significant discrepancy existed between the political economy of Indian emigration and the ideological representation of it in Bombay cinema. By the 1990s émigré Indians became central to India's political economy through the remittances which they sent back and which helped balance India's international payments. What was not widely appreciated was that the vast bulk of these remittances came from those émigrés who were working temporarily in much less privileged parts of the world than the Western countries, and in much less privileged positions. For instance, a very large and substantial proportion of Indians who lived and worked abroad were in the countries of the Persian Gulf. They did not choose to emigrate permanently. And the émigrés who worked in these countries usually left their families, or parts of them, behind and their remittances back to them constituted the chief mode of support. Indians who emigrated to the West usually left lock, stock, and barrel, and had hardly any reason or opportunity to send much money back. Nevertheless, the latter types of émigrés became ideologically valorized. They were indeed disproportionately upper-caste, not the least reason for the valorization: they were the kin of India's upper-caste elite. They also resided in parts of the world to which the no-longer anti-imperialist bourgeoisie would happily subordinate itself.

A third theme which emerged in the new Bombay cinema increasingly portrayed the purported cultural authenticity of these groups as the privileged form of nationalism. Émigré Indians were often portrayed as more truly nationalist, preserving their Indian cultural identity, and genuinely caring more about India's future, than their hapless kin who remained in India. These latter only sought to go abroad, disliked having to live in India, cared only about their own geographical and economic mobility and nothing of the nation's future. This new centrality of émigré Indians clearly rearticulated the very idea of a nation in such a way as to detach it from territory more or less completely.

Another related theme was the increasing centrality of the family to the film plots, such as they were. In contrast to the lives of their relatives in India, who may have access to, and feel a close connection with a large number of social institutions, whether political parties, clubs, unions, universities, or business groups, the structures of racism within which the lives of the émigrés were embedded ensured that the family was the only social institution to which they had privileged access. The increasing centrality of the family was clearly connected in important respects to this reality. It was also connected to another reality in India. The assertion of upper-caste privilege was deeply tied up with the performance of certain family-based rituals. This too ensured that the family would be the privileged social institution in the ideological universe of India's middle classes today.

Finally, it is widely appreciated that women as the repository of tradition constitute a feature common to all nationalisms. Whereas this feature was not absent in early Bombay cinema's conception of national identity, it coexisted with a progressive notion of woman's place in the nation, a more progressive idea which looked forward to greater equality, agency, and valorization, and was critical, if often insufficiently so, of the restrictions of tradition and patriarchy. Indeed Bombay cinema of the 1970s, in particular, produced some of the finest feminist films anywhere, more important than many a more esoteric feminist text for reaching a wide audience. But, the 1990s witnessed a resurgence of the idea of woman as the repository not only of tradition but of upper-caste upper-class tradition.

References

Anderson, B. "The New World Disorder." *New Left Review*, Vol. 193, May/June, 1992.

Balagopal, K. "An Ideology for the Provincial Propertied Class," *Economic and Political Weekly*, Vol. XXII, Nos. 36 and 37, September 5–12, 1987. 1546-7.

Desai, R. *Slouching Towards Ayodhya*, Three Essays Press, New Dehli, 2004a.

___. "From National Bourgeoisies to Rogues, Failures and Bullies: The Contradictions of 21st century imperialism and the unravelling of the Third World." *Third World Quarterly*, Vol. 25, no. 1, 2004, 25th Anniversary Issue, Special Issue on 'After the Third World,' Guest Editor, Mark T Berger, dedicated to the Memory of Edward Said (1935–2003), 2004b. 169–185.

___. "Nation Against Democracy: The Rise of Cultural Nationalism in Asia," in Fahimul Quadir and Jayant Lele (eds.), *Democracy and Civil Society in Asia*, Vol. I (London: Palgrave and Macmillan, 2004. 81–110, 2004c.

___. *The Nationalisms of Asia: From Developmental Nationalism to Cultural Nationalism*, Special Issue of *Third World Quarterly* Guest Editor, Radhika Desai, assigned date of publication Vol. 29, No. 5, 2008.

Desai, R et al. *From Developmental to Cultural Nationalisms in Asia*, a SSHRC funded research Development Initiative, Available from: <http://web.uvic.ca/~anp/>.

Gramsci, A. *Selections from the Prison Notebooks*, ed. and trans. Q Hoare & GN Smith, Lawrence and Wishart, London, 1971a.

___. "Notes on Italian History" in *ibid*, 1971b.

___. *The Modern Prince and Other Writings*, International Publishers, New York, 1983.

Hirst, P and G Thompson. *Globalization in Question: The International Economy and the Possibilities of Governance*, Polity Press, Cambridge, 1999.

Nairn, Tom. Faces of Nationalism, Verso, London,1997.

Panitch, Leo. "The State in a Changing World," *Monthly Review* Vol. 50, October 5, 1998.

___. "The New Imperial State," *New Left Review* Vol. 2, March–April, 2000.

Weiss, Linda. *The Myth of the Powerless State*, Cornell University Press, Ithaca, 1998.

From Artist-as-Hero to the Creative Young Man: Bollywood and the Aestheticization of Indian Masculinity

NITIN DECKHA

In her essay, "Globalisation, Sexuality and the Visual Field," Mary E John seeks to connect the globalization and liberalization of the Indian economy with the explosion of visual representations of sexuality in urban Indian consumer culture. At the heart of this explosion is the sexualization of the "new middle-class woman" as a desiring, consuming subject (2000:382). John echoes other feminist scholars, such as Chaudhuri (2001), who point to the transformation of female agency and its sexualization in commodity culture as the simultaneous consequences of globalization and liberalization.

In this essay, I suggest that the urban, consuming-class Indian male can be understood in terms of the "liberalization" of urban Indian masculinity. That is, if liberalization—with its attendant processes of deregulation, privatization, the opening up of new markets and so forth—jeopardizes the efforts of the state to plan and control its economy, the liberalization of masculinity brings to crisis the "traditional" confines of Indian patriarchy and the sites and representations of masculine identity. Moreover, while this liberalization occurs at a time when the urban young Indian male risks being stereotyped as a faceless technology worker, Bollywood is creating heroes whose inclinations and ambitions seem decidedly antitechnological.

Using examples from the films *Dil Chahta Hai* (2001), *Salaam Namaste* (2005), and *Parineeta* (2005), I argue that a new model of masculinity is being articulated and idealized for the burgeoning South Asian consuming classes; that of the Creative Young Man. As I trace the shift from the artist-as-hero of newly independent India as depicted in *Parineeta* to the self-realized Creative Young Man in *Salaam Namaste*, I further suggest that, following the aestheticization of everyday life

(Featherstone 1991), the aestheticization of masculinity enacts a cultural politics of a late, globalized, hybrid Indian modernity. Such kinds of cultural politics, which I have discussed elsewhere in the UK context (Deckha 2004), create anxieties about national identity and belonging. Indeed, as Chaudhuri notes in her study of urban Indian newspaper ads in the late 1990s, the cultural politics of aestheticized masculinity (and femininity) are exclusionary, marginalizing the nonconsuming classes—the urban and rural poor, the Dalits and Adivasis—from their claims to normative citizenship (Chaudhuri 2001).

As a model of masculinity, the Creative Young Man displaces earlier forms of Indian masculinity that intertwine the concerns of the Indian middle class and its struggle to determine its identity and its modernity vis-à-vis the West. These forms have included the Bengali babu described by Sinha (1995), the emasculated upper-caste recipient of English education and work in the colonial administration; the "Five Year Plan" hero of the Bollywood cinema of the 1950s and 60s, the "engineer, doctor, scientist, and bureaucrat" committed to Nehruvian technocratic nation-building (Srivastava 1996 in Srivastava 2004; see also Chaudhuri 2001:379–80); and the "Angry Young Man" of the 1970s, typified by a youthful Amitabh Bachchan (Mishra 1985).

In addition, this model finds resonance with Favero's ethnography, *India Dreams* (2005). Focused on the lives of twenty- and thirty-something single men in Delhi working particularly in tourism, Favero captures the parallel liberalization of the Indian economy and the related expansion of consumerism with his respondents' perceptions of the shifting terrain of love, sex, women, "India," and the "West." Unlike Srivastava's (2004) work on the "footpath modernity" of poor urban men who visit "sex and vitality clinics" at railway stations or consume vernacular-language pornography sold on the street, Favero's young men are the male counterparts of John's sexualized new middle-class Indian women. They are active participants in the globalized, hybridized consumer culture to whom the Bollywood portraits of the Creative Young Man as hero are likely to be most resonant. Nonetheless, common to both categories of urban men are negotiations with modernity. With the urban poor, such negotiations take place within the confines of the Indian vernaculars and tradition. For the liberalized young urban Indian male, they occur in the sites and practices of aestheticized consumption, an indication that even the hype of the "metrosexual" has gone global. To trace the evolution of the Creative Young Man as Hero, I now turn to a discussion of the films.

In *Parineeta*, Saif Ali Khan's character, Shekhar Roy, elaborates a modernist masculinity in India in opposition to that of his father, Navin Roy. While the latter is the stereotype of the cunning, wealthy industrialist loyal to nothing but money, Shekhar presents an aesthetic masculinity centred on his vocation and passion as a musician, composing music for playback singers, listening to jazz and Elvis. His musical passion overlaps with his love, even obsession, with Lolita, played by Vidya Balan. Lolita, orphaned as a young girl and taken in by her *mama* and *mami*, is a neighbour who grows up as Shekhar's playmate and friend.

While always generous with his father's money, Shekhar retains the upper hand in an unequal relationship, his birthright of wealth and privilege a stark contrast to that of Lolita's. She is dependent on others who themselves are dependent. Her guileless mama has accepted money from Navin to pay his mortgage, without realizing that Navin knows that he will never be able to pay it off and has plans to seize his house. Moreover, to contribute to her family's income, Lolita works for Navin. Indeed, it is only when Shekhar's father introduces his son to the socialite daughter of a fellow titan, and Girish, the self-made businessmen played by Sanjay Dutt, enters Lolita's circle of cousins, that the love between Shekhar and Lolita is tested.

In *Parineeta*, the love of Art and the love of Woman are intertwined in the formation of a resistant, alternative aesthetic masculinity that extends Shekhar's stylization of himself as an artist, a way of life as an artist that is at odds with the mercenary world of his father. Until the entrance of Girish, Shekhar takes Lolita's love for granted. Only when Shekhar becomes jealous of a potential suitor does he transform his rebellion through aestheticism—his appropriations of the Western modernist musical forms of jazz, rock, and the blues—into a flagrant and aggressive defiance of his father's wishes. This is symbolized graphically by the destruction of the brick wall that Navin Roy had built between him and his neighbour, when his plans to seize Lolita's *mama*'s house backfires. With the destruction of the wall, and the recognition that Girish has married not Lolita but her cousin, Shekhar and Lolita are free to love, marry, and start a life together with the blessing of everyone around them, except his father.

Throughout the film, Lolita's own subjectivity is constantly circumscribed by the "self-extensions" of men (cf Chopra, Osella, Osella, eds. 2004:14). Her genuine love for Shekhar, her subservience at work, her devotion to her *mama*, her reliance on Girish's money to repay her *mama*'s loan, are responses to these self-extensions that culminate in the antagonism and struggle between Father and Son, the Capitalist and the Artist.

In *Dil Chahta Hai*, we have the (refreshing) absence of the struggle with the father, because the Creative Young Man of the film, Siddharth Sinha, played by Akshaye Khanna, is presented as living with his (presumably widowed) mother. Here the driving force is not the father-son conflict but the stresses of the friendship among three young post-college men. Against the backdrop of the 1990s, the first decade of globalization and liberalization, we see signs of the expanding, hybridizing landscape of India's consumer classes: night clubs, restaurants, vacations in Goa, opera in Sydney. It is also within this landscape that we get a shift in the representation of the Creative Young Man from merely being antagonistic to capitalist, as in the case of *Parineeta*. In *Dil Chahta Hai*, Siddharth—or Sid, as everyone calls him—straddles both worlds: one that of a hybridized consumerism, in what Kazi Ashraf (2005) has called the "masala" landscapes of new urban India, and the other that of a introspection, emotion, and aestheticism of a painter. Once again, the Creative Young Man is presented as being in love with a socially illegitimate woman—Tara, played by Dimple Kapadia—a relationship pivotal to the elaboration of an artistic masculine identity.

Sid meets Tara, an interior designer, when she moves down the road from his own house, as she struggles with carrying luggage to her company-owned flat. Sid quickly realizes that she is a kindred spirit in whom he may confide his true self. When Tara asks him what he does for a living, Sid admits that he usually makes something up depending on what floats into his head. However, when he sees some paintings in the crates amongst her luggage, he reveals to her his true vocation: painting. When Tara responds with excitement and expresses a desire to see his work, a relationship begins.

Tara arrives the next day, just as Sid is planning to be dropped off by his mother. Tara's sensual presence throughout the film—loose hair, subtle prints, open-necked kurta and jeans, shawls strewn over her shoulders, a white sari—is repeatedly juxtaposed with the colourful, heavy saries of Sid's and his friends' mothers. Moreover, as Sid's first female viewer of his work, Tara strikes a deep chord within him. Sid nervously shows her his paintings, laid on the floor of the attic, and quickly Tara comments on the recurring themes: tightly-bound boxes, doors that don't open, shut eyelids—not-so-subtle allusions to an interior world to which even his friends lack access. On another occasion, while Sid watches Tara work, he announces that he would like to paint her. Again, as in *Parineeta*, we get a clear indication of the intertwining of artistic and romantic desire. When she agrees, Sid sprints home to bring his materials, only to return to see her leaving for an emergency meeting at a building site.

This twinned desire continues to prosper. Sid invites Tara to his solo show at an art gallery. While his friends lurk in the background, outsiders to Sid's artistic world, the editor of *Art India* showers praise on Sid's talent to his mother and suggests he apply for a residency at Kasauli. Yet Sid is most pleased when Tara shows up. Afterwards we get a song-and-dream sequence of Tara modelling for Sid, resplendent in a white sari, Sid dreaming and painting Tara's portrait, romance now completely overlapping with art.

Lolita was a penniless orphan; Tara is older, divorced, and, as Sid discovers, an alcoholic. When he announces to his friends that he loves Tara, they laugh and are incredulous. When Sid persists, admitting that "she won't marry me or be mine," Akash explains away his desire as that of a young man for an "experienced" woman. When Sid responds by striking Akash, telling him that "in every friendship there is a line and Akash had crossed that line," the trio of friends—Akash, Sameer, and Sid—breaks up.

As in *Parineeta*, male desire melds with the pursuit of creativity in an alternative way of life. The breakup between Akash and Sid triggers Akash's concession to his parent's demands that he manage the family business in Sydney. Meanwhile Sid gets the artist's residency in Kasauli. Yet Sid proves to be prescient when he said Tara can't be his. Towards the end of the film, Tara dies from cirrhosis, her social illegitimacy and Sid's contamination at once extinguished. This allows the friendship to be rebuilt and leaves Sid available to fall in love again, this time (hinted at in the film's conclusion) with a more socially acceptable woman.

The landscape of the consumer classes that anchors *Dil Chahta Hai* is more fully centred in the film *Salaam Namaste*. If in *Parineeta* and *Dil Chahta Hai* the Creative Young Man constructs an alternative masculinity based on pursuing art as a way of life, in *Salaam Namaste* the hero's masculinity is fully aestheticized, and creativity itself is presented as aestheticized lifestyle. "Saif" as Nikhil Arora—or Nick as he prefers—is an architect-turned-chef who has left India to "live for himself" and "make himself happy" by being a chef-entrepreneur in Melbourne. Like the heroine of the film, Ambar Malhotra, played by "Preity," Nick's affirmation of creativity is part of a self-stylized and self-realized identity that is severed from the family—there are no parents or relatives in *Salaam Namaste*—and is emblematic of the imagined optimism and opportunity encountered by the younger generations of post-liberalized, globalized India, like those whom we met in Delhi in Favero (2005), whose imagined selves extend globally (Appadurai 1996). Moreover, Nick's stylization of self dovetails with the ongoing aestheticization of masculinity, well-captured by the term "metrosexuality."

First coined by Mark Simpson in 1994, and popularized by marketers, metrosexuality reveals the increasingly marked nature of masculinity and the sexualization of the male body that parallels that of the middle-class Indian woman discussed by John (2000) and Chaudhuri (2001). Indeed, Nick's body seems even more on display than Ambar's, reversing a traditional Bollywood aesthetic code. Sporting hairless, tanned, and muscled arms, legs, and, especially, chest, Nick's body is a symbol of the new globalized Indian. In Nick's case, this aestheticization marks not only his participation in a sexualized, hybridized consumer society, but also his status as a "creative" worker in the global service economy. As a chef with an eponymous restaurant and catering company, Nick is a creator and manipulator of signs and ideas, representative of the reflexive, postmodern worker (Lash and Urry 1994). Telling is Nick's own logic of how he presents himself to others, as revealed on the radio when interviewed by Ambar, the RJ (radio jockey) who is putting herself through medical school. "If the person asking is educated, like a doctor or lawyer, I say I'm an architect"; "if it's a creative type, like a writer or a RJ, I say chef."

It is this opposition between educated—read reason—and creative—read passion—that also underwrites the ethic of "living for oneself." In this sense the idealized self-stylized, self-made global Indian is the Creative Young Man. He is finding his way, carving his niche, and creating his own style. Yet, in this process, lifestyle trumps love. Unlike in *Parineeta* and *Dil Chahta Hai*, the Creative Young Man does not need to be in love with a woman to extend and express his artistic self and define his aesthetic masculinity against more dominant forms. Rather, Nick compartmentalizes love, keeps it outside of his egoist endeavours. Only after he convinces Ambar to live with him and she becomes pregnant do notions of responsibility, fatherhood, marriage, and living for something or someone beyond oneself enter the picture. Importantly, when Nick and Ambar decide to reconcile, it's as "equals," a huge departure from the relationships between Lolita and Shekhar, Sid and Tara. Indeed, in the liberalized, globalized Indian imaginary of the consuming classes, male-female relationships are severed from the legacies of cultural, caste, religious, and national forms of gender inequality, and replaced by the chimera of gender equality in the romantic couple.

As a negotiation with modernity, the Creative Young Man epitomizes what I've called the ongoing liberalization of masculinity within the globalized framework of Indian/Bollywood culture as well as elsewhere. Central to this idea is the aestheticization of masculinity and of everyday life. Featherstone (1991) discusses three senses of the aestheticization of everyday life that, uncannily, mirrors the transformation of the Artist-Hero to the Creative Young Man that I've charted here.

The first sense seeks to "efface the boundary between art and everyday life" and finds examples in early twentieth century Dada and Surrealism (1991:66). The second sense seeks to turn life into a work of art—a project that has long fascinated intellectuals and artists in their own critiques of modernity, such as the Bloomsbury group in Britain and the "the bohème and avant-gardes in mid-to-late nineteenth century Paris." Indeed, this critique of modernity is nascent in the oppositional stance of Shekhar as a musician vis-à-vis his father's capitalism and in Sid's efforts to retreat into an emotional, interior world in his paintings. Featherstone's third sense refers to the flow of images and signs and their saturation and commodification of everyday life, and thus describes the contemporary aestheticization of masculinity and the practices of the urban, consuming, Indian male, typified by Nick and his peers in Favero (2005).

While this aestheticization is often easily written off as marketing ploy, it is also a symptom of the changing forces in defining, representing and imagining masculinity in imagined worlds where "traditional" dominant modes of masculinity are obsolete or undesirable. Indeed, representations of, and appetite for, aggressive and violent masculinity in popular culture persist, as Katz (1999) and Derné (2002) have shown in the contexts of American media and Hindi filmgoers in Fiji, respectively. As both note, the appeal of aggressive and violent masculinities reflects the crisis of patriarchy and male identity in the age of globalization, at a time when more and more work is being feminized; stable, blue collar work is beleaguered; and access to contraception and reproductive technologies transforms the meaning of families and the status of women. As male spectators and consumers seek grounds to assert their manhood and masculinity, society (including Bollywood) tells them to turn to their bodies: the desire for muscular bodies is not merely a reflection of aestheticization, but aestheticization as a partial response to the real and imagined loss of male power. Indeed, this attention to the body and male sexuality is not lost to the urban poor who frequent the clinics that offer "traditional" remedies to improve their clients' sexual drives and energy levels (Srivastava 2004). In fact, both the aesthetic masculinity of the Creative Young Man and the frequenting of sex and vitality clinics of the marginalized urban poor are bodily tactics that must be situated in the context of the liberalization of urban masculinities in India. The anxieties they reflect suggest the intensified significance of the male body across the socio-economic divide and in the everyday articulations of gender, class, nationality, and "masala modernity" in contemporary India.

References

Appadurai, Arjun. *Modernity at Large: Cultural Dimensions of Globalization.* Minneapolis: University of Minnesota, 1996.

Ashraf, Kazi K. "Masala City: Urban Stories From South Asia." *Architectural Design*, 75(5), 2005. 62–9.

Chaudhuri, Maitrayee. "Gender and Advertisements: The Rhetoric of Globalisation." *Women's Studies International Forum*, 24 (3/4), 2001. 373–85.

Chopra, Radhika, Caroline Osella, and Filippo Osella, eds. "Introduction: Toward a More Nuanced Approach to Masculinity, Towards a Richer Understanding of South Asian Men." *South Asian Masculinities: Context of Change, Sites of Continuity*. New Delhi: Women Unlimited, 2004.

Deckha, Nityanand. "Beyond the Country House: Historic Conservation as Aesthetic Politics." *European Journal of Cultural Studies*, 7(4), 2004. 403–423.

Dil Chahta Hai. Farhan Akhtar, dir. Excel Entertainment. Mumbai, 2001.

Derné, Steve. "Globalization and the Reconstitution of Local Gender Arrangements." *Men and Masculinities*, 5(2), 2002. 144–164.

Favero, Paolo. *India Dreams: Cultural Identity Among Young Middle Class Men in New Delhi*. Stockholm: Stockholm University, 2005.

Featherstone, John. *Consumer Culture and Postmodernism*. London: Sage. 1991.

John, Mary E. "Globalisation, Sexuality and the Visual Field: Issues and Non-Issues for Cultural Critique." In Mary E John and Janaki Nair, eds., *A Question of Silence?: The Sexual Economies of Modern India*. London and New York: Zed Books, 2000.

Katz, Jackson (presenter) and Sut Jhally (director). *Tough Guise: Violence, Media & the Crisis in Masculinity*. Northampton, Mass: Media Education Foundation, 1999.

Lash, Scott and John Urry. *Economies of Signs and Space*. London: Sage. 1994.

Mishra, Vijay. "Towards a Theoretical Critique of Bombay Cinema." *Screen* 26(3/4), 1985.

Parineeta. Pradeep Sarkar, dir. Vinod Chopra Films. Mumbai, 2005.
Salaam Namaste. Siddharth Anand, dir. Yash Raj Films Pvt. Ltd. Mumbai. 2005.
Sinha, Mrinalini. *Colonial Masculinity: The 'Manly' Englishman' and the 'Effeminate Bengali' in the Late Nineteenth Century*. Manchester: Manchester University Press, 1995.
Srivastava, Sanjay. "The Garden of Rational Delights: The Nation as Experiment, Science as Masculinity" *Social Analysis*, 39, 1996. 119–148.
Srivastava, Sanjay. "Non-Gandhian Sexuality, Commodity Cultures and a 'Happy Married Life': Masculine and Sexual Cultures in the Metropolis." In Sanjay Srivastava, ed. *Sexual Sites, Seminal Attitudes: Sexualities, Masculinities and Culture in South Asia*. New Delhi: Sage, 2004. 342–390.

Gender, Nation, and Globalization in *Monsoon Wedding* and *Dilwale Dulhania Le Jayenge*

JENNY SHARPE

The crossover success of Mira Nair's *Monsoon Wedding* (2001), whose characters speak English, Hindi, and Punjabi, lies in the skill with which the film acquaints a Western audience with the sights and sounds of the new global India. Set in a burgeoning New Delhi suburb, the film uses a lavish Punjabi wedding as an occasion for staging the reunion of family members who are scattered across the globe. But the idea of a global India does not simply refer to the large numbers of Indians (known as Non-Resident Indians or NRIs) living in the diaspora.[1] The term also signifies the social and cultural transformation India has undergone since 1991, when a new economic policy eliminated the bureaucratic red tape restricting imports and foreign investment. For the first time, the marketplace became flooded with consumer goods that had previously been available only on the black market, and designer labels became commonplace. Indian television went from the two channels of the state TV to the more than sixty channels available on cable and satellite in some urban areas. Whereas the state-controlled television programming promoted, for example, agricultural shows aimed at farmers, the new satellite TV channels broadcast sexually explicit music videos and Hollywood soap operas such as *Santa Barbara* and *Baywatch* that engendered Indian imitations. Sexual topics that were previously unmentionable were now openly discussed, and television brought these discussions into the inner sanctum of the home.

Monsoon Wedding presents the contradictions of everyday life that an opening of India to globalization has introduced. The film destroys any lingering image of a nation mired in some premodern space as a traditional land with ancient customs and beliefs. Rather, it reveals a postmodern world in which cell phones and e-mail coexist with age-old rituals and occupations.[2] The audience witnesses Delhi street scenes of pushcarts and bicycle rickshaws weaving in and out of cars driving by a monolithic statue of Shiva.[3] Golfers ride in golf carts across an immaculately landscaped golf course, while a row of women carrying sand in baskets on their heads (presumably for the sand pits) passes behind them. The camera often zooms in on television screens and monitors to emphasize the power of the new media, and it presents a TV talk show on film censorship, where guests debate the erosion of Indian morality and Hindu tradition. The heroine, Aditi (Vasundhara Das), represents a new generation of Indian women who live double lives in order to reconcile their desires with the wishes of their parents. Aditi secretly meets the man she loves the night before she is to marry the Houston NRI her parents have arranged for her to marry.

In foregrounding the clash of modernity and tradition, Nair makes explicit the anxieties about a national identity underlying the commercially successful films of Indian cinema, commonly known as Bollywood in reference to Bombay as the Hollywood of the Indian film industry.[4] A hybrid form from its inception, Bombay cinema reworked the melodrama, musical, slapstick comedy, and gangster genres of the classic Hollywood era, by infusing them with Indian epic plots, Orientalist exoticism, and the visual and aural overload of Indian culture to create a new aesthetic style. Once derided for its melodrama and derivative plots, Bollywood has more recently begun to infiltrate a Euro-American consciousness through what can be identified as a new transnational cultural literacy. Indian films have always enjoyed an international audience, being popular among Arabs, Africans, Mexicans, and Southeast Asians. Indian film stars such as Raj Kapoor had an enormous following in third world countries as well as the former Soviet Union, where loyal fans equally consumed the visual spectacle of his movies as his depiction of the angst of the common man. What is different today is that a Bollywood audience has expanded to include Western populations, while its cinematic style has been mainstreamed into British and American theater, film, and television.[5] Bollywood's crossover success can be attributed to the increased availability of Indian films on DVD, cable TV, and in theaters catering to South Asians living in the diaspora. But it is also an indication of how Indian films are becoming more global in appearance.

Glossy, high budget films shot on location in Europe and the United States and influenced by the slick cinematography of commercials are far removed from the feudal village drama of the 1950s and 1960s belonging to the golden age of Indian cinema. The story of the strength and courage of a peasant woman to overcome debt bondage in the classic postindependence film, Mehboob's *Mother India* (1957), served as an allegory for the heroic effort of the Indian nation to achieve self-sufficiency through modernization. The 1970s and 1980s witnessed a shift to action films featuring the angry young man who embodied the triumph of India's underclasses over social injustice and political corruption.[6] The commercially successful films made since the mid-1990s, in contrast, emphasize wealth, fast cars, youth culture, and cosmopolitan lifestyles. Moreover, the folk-inspired song-and-dance sequences that were standard Bollywood fare have been replaced with a hip-hop style, Michael Jackson–inspired choreography, accompanied by the rapid editing and unconventional camera angles of MTV music videos—all appropriately "Indianized." The rural exists in the post-1990s films not as a geographical location so much as a signifier for a simpler way of life prior to globalization. As a member of the new generation of directors declares: "The village has been pushed to the farthest periphery of our imagination. Any reference to a rural background today is only a synthetic nod to the roots. The insistence is on gloss" (cited in Chopra 1997). Instead of the folkloric scenes belonging to earlier generations of films, the rural is emptied of the culture of everyday life.

The most successful genre to deploy the new cinematic style is the family melodrama, which was the most popular genre of the 1990s.[7] Instead of featuring India's underclasses as did earlier generations of films, the 1990s melodrama centers on wealthy Indian families with traditional values. These big-budget films, often shot on location in Europe and the United States, present "endless rounds of parties, beach dances, wedding celebrations, festive occasions, and an all-round feeling of well-being" (Kripalani 2001, 45). Films such as *Hum Aapke Hain Kaun . . . !* (What am I to you! 1994); *Dilwale Dulhania Le Jayenge* (The brave-hearted will take the bride, 1995); *Pardes* (Foreign land, 1997); and *Kuch Kuch Hota Hai* (Something is happening, 1998) allow their audiences to share in the extravagant lifestyles of the elite classes and cross the threshold of their luxurious homes, whether Western-style mansions or traditional *havelis*. Instead of the class conflict that dominated the angry young man films of the prior two decades, the conflict staged in these films is between modernity and tradition.[8] The 1990s family melodrama endorses traditional values through its staging of elaborate northern Indian marriage ceremonies and by making the joint family into the locus of the nation at a moment in time when the nuclear family was replacing the extended family among India's middle class (Uberoi 2001). The indebtedness of *Monsoon Wedding* to this genre of Bollywood film is unmistakable in its integration of song-and-dance sequences into the storyline, its indulgence in the rich culture of Punjabi weddings, and its tribute to the extended family.[9] In addition, through the shared knowledge its characters have of songs from popular Hindi films, Nair's film dramatizes how a commercialized, hybridized, and low cultural form such as Bombay cinema operates as the site of a collective Indian identity throughout the diaspora.[10]

But even as Nair integrates a Bollywood aesthetic into her film, she is critical of the rosy picture presented in its family dramas. Made under the aegis of her New York–based company, Mirabai Films, *Monsoon Wedding* moves fluidly from happy family reunion scenes to sexually intimate ones, and it weaves into its wedding motif the disturbing topic of sexual molestation—a subject too controversial for popular Indian cinema. Inasmuch as Nair eschews the glossy patina of blockbuster Bollywood films in favour of a documentary cinematic style by shooting with a handheld Super 16 camera, she merges the realism of American independent filmmaking with Bollywood's narrative style. Still, *Monsoon Wedding* was not only successful in Britain and the United States but in India as well, at least among its urban middle class. Its celebration of the Indian family aligns it more closely with the 1990s Bollywood blockbusters than its maverick approach to questions of female sexuality might lead one to suspect.

Nair reinvents even as she reproduces the lavish Punjabi wedding film that Yash Chopra popularized and that experienced a comeback with the success of *Hum Aapke Hain Kaun . . . !* and Yash Chopra and Aditya Chopra's *Dilwale Dulhania Le Jayenge* (commonly referred to as *DDLJ*). Although *Monsoon Wedding* is generally located within a Hollywood tradition of wedding films ranging from Robert Altman's *A Wedding* (1978) to Ang Lee's *The Wedding Banquet* (1993), I want to consider it alongside a Bollywood wedding film such as *DDLJ*, which also uses the marriage between an Indian and an NRI as an occasion for exploring the contradictions of the new global India. The first Bollywood film to fuse elements of Eastern and Western cultures into what one director calls "believable fantasies" (cited in Anupama Chopra's seminal study of the film 2002, 54–58), *DDLJ* perfected the cinematic style of "Western gloss-*desi* soul" that became endlessly repeated in subsequent films hoping to reproduce its success.[11]

Although the hybridities of global cultures are generally explained as postnational phenomena, I want to examine how they constitute a new nationalism in India.[12] The vanishing rural in Bombay cinema undoubtedly reflects a turn in Indian films towards catering to urban and overseas markets, where the profit margin is greater than that of rural areas.[13] But it is also a sign of what Leela Fernandes (2001) identifies as a shift in the Indian national imaginary from an elimination of rural poverty through development to social mobility through consumerism. She argues that, rather than denoting a deterritorialization of the nation, "the global" is produced through nationalist narratives that shuttle between cultural hybridities and purities. "The lure of hybridity in this context," she explains, "holds within it the dangers of impurity. The potential disruption is managed through a remapping of the nation's boundaries through a politics of gender which centers around conflicts over the preservation of the purity of women's sexuality, a process which once again conflates the preservation of nationness with the protection of women" (2001:157). Fernandes is alluding to how the purity of the Indian nation has historically been identified with the purity of the Hindu woman through the value attributed to Sita, the pure and devoted wife of Rama.[14]

Bollywood heroines commonly serve an iconic function in representing family values that Western decadence and materialism have undermined. In *Pardes* (which invites comparison with *DDLJ* because it not only has the same leading male actors—Shah Rukh Khan and Amrish Puri—but also tells the story of an arranged marriage between an Indian and an NRI), the heroine is explicitly identified with traditional Indian values. A deeply religious woman who responds to the world with childlike innocence, she is appropriately named Ganga, meaning "pure," since the Hindu goddess Ganga is synonymous with the pure and chaste woman. The association between Ganga and the nation is reinforced throughout the film through patently allegorical statements expressing disapproval of an NRI father's attempt to reconnect with India through the marriage of his American born son to Ganga. *Pardes* explicitly rejects the hybrid Indian identity of *DDLJ* in favour of cultural purity. The NRI is informed that he is "trying to bring India's pure Ganges to these concrete jungles of America" and accused of "wish[ing] to nestle an Indian girl, India itself, in America" (*Pardes* 1997).

The potential violation of Indian values is presented through a trip Ganga takes to the entertainment capital of the world, Los Angeles, and the sin city of Las Vegas. Her introduction to amusement parks, nightclubs, and casinos in the two cities creates desire in the audience for "fascinating America" (Uberoi 1998, 330–31). But, even as the film offers the viewing pleasure of urban cool, foreign locales, and extravagant lifestyles, it also exhibits an anxiety about the loss of traditional Indian values. Although Ganga is seduced by the glamour and glitter of an American lifestyle, she refuses to engage in premarital sex with her fiancé. The positing of tradition as a pure origin at the moment of its perceived loss is enacted through her sexual purity and incorruptible nature.

As scholars of colonial and postcolonial cultures remind us, modernity is less the negation of tradition than the grounds for its formation (Makdisi 1995:111; Sharpe 1997; Mani 1998; Grewal and Kaplan 2001:669–70). With this in mind, I want to consider the commodity culture of the new global India as a driving force behind the desire to see traditional family values in Bollywood cinema. The ascendance of the Bharatiya Janata Party (BJP), with its strong Hindu nationalist or Hindutva identity, has paralleled India's economic liberalization policy.[15] Its constituency includes an urban Hindu middle class and wealthy NRIs desiring to reconnect with their birthplace through the idea of a glorious Hindu past (Mishra 2004, 30–31). The strong assertion of a Hindustani identity in the 1990s family melodrama can be considered a response to the crisis in national identity produced by an embracing of values that were previously rejected for being synonymous with a Western lifestyle. With the introduction of the new commodity culture, individual desires began to be placed before social ones, and credit card purchases gained credence over the idea of financial conservatism.[16]

Historically the moral universe of commercial Indian cinema is a world in which social duties, love of nation, and kinship bonds outweigh individualism and personal desires (Thomas 1995:164–66). The 1990s family melodrama broke with this convention by giving value to the acquisition of new wealth and the pursuit of personal desires. Its moral universe is maintained, however, through the symbolic functioning of the heroine as that which defines the boundaries of "Indianness." We have already seen this functioning in a film such as *Pardes*, whose heroine is a traditional Indian woman. What interests me about *DDLJ* is how the materialism of consumer culture is reconciled with traditional Indian values through its presentation of an Indian woman who is sexually chaste but who also has desires of her own. If, as Stuart Hall suggests, cinema is not "a second-order mirror held up to reflect what already exists, but . . . that form of representation which is able to constitute us as new kinds of subjects" (1996:221), what kinds of female subjectivity does this film attempt to constitute? I want to argue that the cinematic staging of Indian tradition through transnational cultural hybridities relies on a female subject who is simultaneously modern and traditional, Westernized and Indian. I am interested in seeing how, on the one hand, a Bollywood film such as *DDLJ* appropriates feminist values in the service of tradition and, on the other, a diasporic film such as *Monsoon Wedding* expands the heteronormative female sexual desire introduced into the family melodrama formula in order to explode it.[17] At the same time, Nair's splitting of Indian femininity along class lines leads one to question the gender politics of her feminist intervention.

The plot of DDLJ is simple enough to be captured by its promotional invitation to "come . . . fall in love." The heroine, Simran (Kajol), is the British-born daughter of a modestly middle-class Punjabi shopkeeper, Chaudhury Baldev Singh (Amrish Puri), while the hero, Raj (Shah Rukh Kahn), is also British-born, except that he is an idle millionaire's son who wears a Harley-Davidson jacket, drives a Lamborghini, and jet-sets across the globe. While Simran's family represents a prior era of migration when Indians had to struggle in small businesses to succeed, Raj's family history belongs more to a more recent past in which enterprising NRIs have made their fortunes in computer and Internet-related businesses. The film presents the problem of the NRI's national identity through Baldev's desire to reconnect with his homeland by arranging a marriage between his daughter and the son of his best friend in Punjab. Although DDLJ ends in the idyllic Punjabi countryside, it does not tell the story of rural poverty. Rather, the rural exists as the nostalgic image of an uncontaminated homeland that resides in the expatriate's imagination. While feeding pigeons at London's Trafalgar Square, Baldev is magically transported to the golden mustard fields of Punjab, where women in colourful salwar kameez, the traditional Punjabi garb, are dancing.[18] The truth value of this image is reconfirmed when he moves his family back home after twenty years of living abroad and sees from the train the same scene that he imagined.

DDLJ is considered a watershed film in Bombay cinema's depiction of NRIs inasmuch as its leading characters are British-born Indians. The NRI had always been a marginal character in Bollywood films, being stereotyped as a decadent debauchee and confused individual who smoked, drank, and gambled. *DDLJ* plays with and overturns this image or, to quote Anupama Chopra, it "turned Bollywood's NRI stereotype on its head" (2002:11–12). The film begins by leading the audience to believe that Raj is yet another decadent NRI who has been corrupted by living in the West. As a youth who relies on family fortune rather than his own intelligence for making his way in life, he is the first student in the history of a prestigious English university to have failed his exams. An early scene shows him tricking Baldev into selling him beer after he has closed his Southall shop for the night. The director wanted the disputed item to be a condom but decided that it would have been too transgressive for the audience to accept (Chopra 2002, 63). As a result, Raj's sexual dalliances are alluded to but not confirmed. By the end of the film, however, the audience realizes that the lazy, inept, beer-drinking, motorcycle-riding playboy does, after all, have traditional Indian values. The message of *DDLJ* is that, although the hero and heroine wear Western clothing and embrace youth culture, they have maintained their Indian values, particularly around questions of sexual morality. Raj will not challenge the authority of Simran's father by eloping with her, while Simran is hot spirited and independent, but also chaste and morally upright.

Even though Simran is not a traditional Indian woman, she is not exactly the second generation NRI that she is supposed to be. The intergenerational strife that is the subject of British-made Indian films such as *My Beautiful Laundrette* (1985), *Bhaji on the Beach* (1993), and *Bend it Like Bekham* (2002) is muted in *DDLJ*. Whereas the British-Indian films show immigrant parents who do not recognize their British-born daughters because their tastes, language, and customs are Westernized, the closest Simran comes to displaying such second-generation traits is to dance surreptitiously to pop music and to wear Western-style clothing. As Vijay Mishra observes in *Bollywood Cinema*, both Baldev's daughters "speak Hindi without an accent and, more important, have a body language that is totally Indian" (2002:251). Despite its overturning of the NRI stereotype, then, the film is not about the overseas Indians coming home so much as the India that never left them. *DDLJ* does not attempt to reproduce the reality of the British Indian experience so much as to transplant a typically Indian family to a foreign locale.

The transformation of the NRI stereotype in Bollywood cinema is less an indication of the increased respectability of the NRI than the emergence of a new urban class in India. *DDLJ* lends credibility to the cosmopolitan lifestyles of India's urban middle class, which overlaps with but is not the same as Indians living in the diaspora. The "Indianness" of an Indian national identity can be established through the hybridized NRI precisely because the new consumer culture threw into crisis the home/world opposition underpinning the nationalist claim to an authentic, spiritual self that the British were unable to colonize.[19] *DDLJ* invokes the perceived independence of NRI daughters to establish Simran's desires for a love match that conflicts with her father's wishes. At the same time, even though she is not happy at the idea of an arranged marriage, she accepts his decision by tearing up the love poems she has written to the unknown man of her dreams.

Once she is in India, Simran abandons her Western clothing in favour of the Punjabi *salwar kameez*, which follows the Bollywood formula of the heroines (more so than heroes) wearing Indian clothes as a sign of their national identity. And, in preparation for her marriage, she decides to keep *karva chauth*, which is a northern Indian ritual in which women engage in a daylong fast for the prosperity of their husbands. The feminist twist on this gender-biased tradition is that Simran is secretly fasting for Raj as the man she wants to marry rather than her husband-to-be, and Raj, out of love and sympathy for her, also refrains from eating or drinking. Yet he does not take the ritual as seriously as she does, as he attempts to sneak her some sweets when she complains of hunger. Since it is women who define the boundaries of "Indianness," Raj can be depicted as playing with traditional practices while Simran has to observe them. The film nonetheless establishes her as a strong, independent woman, and a sexual being with desires of her own.

The song-and-dance sequence, which generally serves as a fantasy space in Bollywood films, provides an occasion for staging female desire, even if in the last instance this desire is contained. The audience is first introduced to Simran as she stands at the window with a dreamy look on her face, the wind blowing in her hair. Her mother, Lajjo (Farida Jalal), has found her daughter's diary and enters reading aloud the love poem she has committed to its pages. After Simran recites the poem to her mother, the film cuts to a song, "Mere Khwabon Mein" (The one who comes in my dreams), which is about the man she hopes to meet. There is considerable ambivalence to the film's staging of Simran's desires. Although the lyrics position the unknown man as the object of her desire, the sequence of images that presents Raj as the embodiment of this man establishes him as agent. He is shown scoring in soccer and bowling, picking up an attractive female hitchhiker on his motorcycle, driving a racing car, and even attempting to outrun an aeroplane.

Unlike Raj who is out in the rough and competitive world of sports, Simran is in the inner sanctuary of her bedroom—one that, with its stuffed animals and lace décor, belongs to a girl who is not quite a woman. Yet, at the same time, her dreams are constitutive of him as an ideal type, since the real Raj is much more bumbling and ineffectual than the almost superhuman man of her dreams. In this regard, the film gives value to Simran's dreams as the expression of female desire. When she moves outside the home to help her mother bring in clothes from the rain, her dance and clothing become more sensual. The domestic chore of removing clothes from the clothesline is an occasion for offering voyeuristic pleasure to the audience. Since the rain song has conventionally been used as a metaphor for sex in order to circumvent the restrictions of the Censor Board, the song plays with this convention in order to hint at Simran as a sexual—but not necessarily a sexually active—being (Chopra 2002, 60). The film entertains (even if it does not go so far as to declare) the possibility for female sexual agency.

In a subsequent song, "Zara Sa Jhoom Loon Main" (What madness love is), Simran does act on her desires, even if, because she is drunk on cognac, she is not quite herself. She steals a red mini-skirted dress (surely the sign of a sexually promiscuous woman) from a store window and wears it while chasing Raj through the Swiss Alps out of a desire to embrace him. The song ends when she wakes up in his bed wearing his shirt and has no memory of how she got there. Raj leads her to believe that they have spent a passionate night together but, on seeing how much his words upset her, exclaims: "I know what you think of me. You think I'm a wastrel. I'm not scum, Simran. I'm Hindustani. And I know what honour means for a Hindustani woman" (*DDLJ,* 1995). This moment constitutes a turning point in the film, one in which both Raj's and Simran's true Indian identities are established. Both of them observe traditional Indian rules of moral conduct prior to marriage, and it is only after exercising restraint that they realize they have fallen in love. The assertion of a hybrid (rather than a pure) Indian identity is thus contingent on the containment (rather than negation) of female sexuality.

There exists a gender difference in each leading character's fulfilment of his or her desire inasmuch as Simran, aided and abetted by her mother, is willing to elope, while Raj is not. Although rebellion is built into the Bollywood formula for romance, it is generally the hero, rather than the heroine, who goes against the parents' wishes (Chopra 2002, 75). This is not the case in *DDLJ*, which endorses a woman's right to choose. As a film genre, Indian women's melodrama has characteristically raised the issue of women's choice and desires within an overarching frame of patriarchal discourse (Prasad 1998, 86). Although *DDLJ* establishes Simran's right to choose her marriage partner, it displaces agency away from the youthful female protagonist by having patriarchal authority questioned by a prior generation of women, who had greater restrictions placed on them.

The most moving scene in the film occurs when Lajjo confesses to Simran that, although she vowed her daughter would not have to make the same sacrifices she did, she wants her to give up Raj in order to make her father happy. As Patricia Uberoi remarks about this scene, "the condemnation of the injustice of 'tradition' (*parampara*) is paradoxically the *very* ground on which the mother asks Simran to *give up* her own aspirations and 'sacrifice' her personal happiness" (1998, 324, original emphasis). Yet the film does not leave this paradox unresolved. Lajjo later reverses her position, saying—"I was wrong, Simran! My daughter won't sacrifice her happiness. She isn't going to sacrifice her love"—and encourages her to elope with Raj (*DDLJ*, 1995).[20] Lajjo's words reconfirm her earlier belief that daughters should not be expected to sacrifice their personal happiness. Simran's mother exhibits an independence and bravery in her willingness to side with her daughter against her husband. Baldev, however, does not possess the patriarchal virtues of wisdom and selfsacrifice that the fathers in Bollywood films have conventionally held.[21] The value he ascribes to his personal desires over the welfare of his family compromises his role as patriarch. The arranged marriage is revealed to be not in his daughter's best interest as the man he has chosen for her is an uncouth lout, who plans to commit adultery after marriage. Since *DDLJ* shows that Baldev has made the wrong choice for his daughter by placing his desires for reconnecting with his homeland above the well-being of his family, it questions a patriarchal authority based on personal desires. At the same time, the male authority that Lajjo challenges in her husband is reconstituted in the man that Simran wishes to marry.

Although Simran rejects the husband her father has chosen for her in favour of eloping with Raj, Raj refuses to marry her unless he has her father's approval. He follows her to India, thereby undermining Baldev's efforts to separate the lovers. But he also dashes Simran's hopes that he has come to take her away. "No, Simran," he informs her, "I haven't come here to steal you. I might have been born in England, but I am Hindustani. I've come here to take you as my bride. I'll take you only when your Babaji gives me your hand" (*DDLJ*, 1995). Raj's refusal to undermine Baldev's parental authority is identified with the Indian values he possesses despite being British-born. Hence, when Lajjo brings the couple her jewellery so that they might elope, she is forced to concur with Raj when he says: "I want to be given Simran. I don't want to steal her" (1995). His repeated phrasing of elopement as a "theft" reaffirms Baldev's propriety over his daughter.

In the film's final scene, when Simran begs her father to let her go to Raj, the camera focuses on the two men looking at each other followed by a literal handing over of daughter from father to future son-in-law. The audience is presented with a close-up shot of Baldev releasing Simran's hand as she struggles to run after Raj, who is leaving on a train. There is a second close-up of Raj grasping her hand to pull her on board the train and, as he clasps her, he exchanges a thumbs-up with Baldev. This closing scene reassures the audience that any choice Simran might have exercised conforms to the rules of patriarchal authority. The traditional values of arranged marriages are affirmed in the love match through the handing over of the daughter from father to husband. The triumph of romantic love over an arranged marriage thus occurs through what Uberoi identifies as an "arranged love marriage" (1998, 306), which is a love match that receives parental approval and consequently is treated as if it were an arranged marriage.[22] The assertion of tradition is contingent on demonstrating that women can exercise their choice, but it is a choice that should not undermine patriarchal authority, even if the father's decision is proven to be wrong.

I have been establishing the cinematic conventions of the family melodrama as well as the uniqueness of *DDLJ* in order to situate *Monsoon Wedding* as a metanarrative commentary on the 1990s genre. Calling her film "a Bollywood movie, made on my own terms" (cited in Hoffman 2002:28), Nair exposes the myth of nation at work in Bollywood films about the NRI. Rather than transporting the Indian experience of globalization to Britain or the United States, Nair stages the identity crisis it is creating within India. The wealthy father is not the tenth-standard drop-out turned London millionaire or immigrant shopkeeper of *DDLJ*. He is the homespun Punjabi Lalit Verma (Naseeruddin Shah), who has made his fortune as a garment exporter for American clothing stores.[23] The setting is not the golden mustard fields of rural Punjab with its pastoral harmony of joint family life but the suburban sprawl of New Delhi with its high-rises and carefully manicured golf course. Sexual frankness is not simply a Western import, for a Hindi film dubbist is shown simulating the sounds of sexual pleasure on a talk show called Delhi.com. The question that one of the show's panelists raises makes explicit the anxieties underpinning Bollywood's endorsement of traditional values. "Just because India has gone global," he queries, "should we embrace everything? What about our ancient culture, our traditions, our values?" (*Monsoon Wedding* 2001).

Countering the tendency in Bollywood cinema to make the Indian woman into a receptacle of traditional Indian values, Nair centres her film on an upper-middle-class Hindu woman's desires and subjectivity. Unlike the heroine of *Pardes*, Aditi is not an innocent Punjabi girl whose honour is potentially under attack; rather, she is a savvy Delhi woman who reads *Cosmopolitan* magazine and is having an affair with a married man. She is the ideal type of a Punjabi beauty—fair-skinned with big doe eyes (although the actress who plays her is from Bangalore)—but she is also a modern Indian woman with cropped, hennaed hair. The audience is first introduced to Aditi when she visits a TV station to meet her lover, Vikram Mehta, the host of Delhi.com. We are immediately confronted with an extreme close-up, over-the-shoulder shot of her face as her lover kisses her in a scene that self-consciously thumbs its nose at the Indian prohibition of on-screen kissing.[24]

Nair melds the sexual frankness of Hollywood with the visual and affective extravagance of Bollywood in order to establish her heroine as a desiring subject. Much of the film's dramatic action focuses on Aditi attempting to arrange a liason with Vikram and agonizing over the difficult choices she has to make. She has agreed to an arranged marriage with a Houston computer engineer, Hemant (Parvin Dabas), but only because she is tired of waiting for Vikram to divorce his wife. Aditi nonetheless is still in love with Vikram and sneaks out to meet him on the night before her wedding. The police catch (and humiliate) the lovers, however, when they are in a state of half-undress in Vikram's car, which is parked in a remote spot in the middle of a torrential rainstorm. Aditi decides to reveal the affair to her future husband so that she can enter the marriage with a clean slate. Hemant is initially upset but then admits to having been in love himself and decides to make a go of it anyway, saying: "What marriage isn't a risk? Whether our parents introduce us or we meet in a club, what difference does it make?" (*Monsoon Wedding* 2001). These words are directed at a Western audience that regards arranged marriages to be a holdover from India's feudal past. For an Indian audience, though, they endorse the idea of an arranged love marriage that has been incorporated into the Bollywood family film formula.

Monsoon Wedding reveals that at the heart of the battle between tradition and modernity is not the question of a woman's sexual abstinence prior to marriage but her right to choose that is withheld through the double standards upheld for men and women. The monsoon that is regarded in India as a cathartic release from the oppressive summer heat serves as a metaphor for Indian women's liberation from the patriarchal strictures imposed on them. One such instance occurs when Uncle Tej (Rajat Kapoor), the man who has served as the family benefactor after Lalit's older brother died, is exposed as having sexually abused his niece, Ria (Shefali Shetty), when she was a child. Noticing the attention that Tej is giving her younger cousin, Aliya, Ria publicly denounces him. Lalit is able to prevent his family from unravelling, not by deferring to Tej's authority as elder male relative and family benefactor but by respecting his niece's right not to have to face her molester anymore.

Tej's ejection from the wedding involves a symbolic removal of the traditional Punjabi turban he is wearing for the wedding. While posing for the formal wedding photo, Ria is made to sit at the feet of her Uncle Tej, who is seated in a chair next to the bride in deference to his status as the extended family's patriarch. In the scene in which Lalit asks Tej to leave the wedding, the camera pans across the female family members to emphasize that the father is making his choice out of respect for them over his obligations to an elder male relative. The film's dramatization of Tej removing his turban before leaving the Verma home makes explicit the superficiality of locating traditional values in appearances. Lalit's decision demonstrates that the strength of the Indian family lies in a male head of household who respects all of its members' needs over his own desire to save face in public. The torrential rain represents not only the freeing of women's sexual desire through a disengagement of male honour from women's virginity but also a refusal to sacrifice women in the name of family honour. Rather than reaffirming traditional patriarchal values through the ruse of modernity as does *DDLJ*, *Monsoon Wedding* reworks these values for the modern Indian family.

But even as Nair infuses the Punjabi wedding film with the grittiness of art house cinema and a feminist sensibility, she adheres to the conventions of Bollywood filmmaking in the parallel love story between the wedding planner, PK Dubey (Vijay Raaz), and the Verma family servant, Alice (Tilotama Shome). Dubey's upward mobility is evident through his frequent conversations with his mother over stock options and his claim to be running a YK2 dotcom operation he calls "event management," which is essentially the age-old task of wedding decorating gone high-tech. He is shown continuously talking on his cell phone or using one or another consumer gadget such as a wristwatch calculator or pager. Dubey represents the much larger group of India's lower middle class that aspires to participate in the new wealth being generated by economic liberalization.

When he gives Alice his business card, he tries to explain to her the electronic transmission of letters to which she responds with a single, knowing word—"e-mail." The exchange suggests that the new information technology extends far beyond the upwardly mobile classes to the servant classes. At the same time, the lowly servant girl serves as a visual image of a nation that has been untouched by the commodity culture of globalization.

Although *Monsoon Wedding* abandons the traditional Bollywood heroine in Aditi, she is reconstituted in Alice, who appears as a pure and virginal object of desire. While decorating the outside of the house, Dubey spies Alice through the window and watches as she surreptitiously tries on Aditi's jewellery. The image of Alice posing in the mirror all adorned in jewels is shot from the voyeuristic angle of a camera that embodies the male gaze. The audience views her reflection in the mirror from Dubey's perspective outside the room looking through the window. Alice is unaware that she is being watched because she is too engrossed in admiring herself in the mirror. As a feminist filmmaker, Nair is careful to show the pleasure a member of the servant class derives from adorning herself in fineries she can never hope to own.

Yet the woman as surveyor is displaced in favour of what John Berger in *Ways of Seeing* calls "the surveyed female," which is a woman who does not act but rather appears as an "object of vision" (1972, 47). The camera lingers on Alice putting on Aditi's necklace, earrings, bindi, and ankle bracelets. As she lets down her hair and strikes the pose of a Bollywood heroine's seductive coyness by wrapping the end of her sari around her head and face, she is transformed into the virginal woman of Bombay cinema. Alice, however, does not embody the perfect vision of upper-caste Hindu femininity that Bollywood has created, as Nair avoids using the soft lens designed to make the heroine emit an aura of beauty. Rather, she operates as a figure of working-class authenticity. When Dubey leaves the soap-opera drama of Lalit's unravelling family to return to his home in the ancient city of Old Delhi, he recalls the vision of Alice's adorned reflection. The juxtaposition of her image with Delhi street scenes shot in the cinema vérité style of documentary filmmaking identifies her with the less materialistic and hence "more authentic" world of India's working classes.

Alice's singularity makes her iconic status in the film all the more apparent. She is the only servant present in the Verma home, which would be unusual for a country in which even a modestly middle-class family can afford several servants. She is also the only Christian—identified by the cross around her neck and a larger one hanging on the kitchen wall—among Hindus and only villager in an urban setting, since she claims to be from the largely rural state of Bihar. Having a Christian occupy the position of the pure Indian woman undermines the Hindutva identification of the nation with the chaste, upper-caste Hindu woman and a Bollywood stereotyping of Indian Christians as mini-skirted, sexually loose women. Yet a reliance on Indian cinematic conventions for filming the parallel love story begs the question as to the narrative function of Alice's character.

I would go so far as to argue that Nair's feminist endorsement of arranged marriages—which are as much determined by class, money, and family alliances as they are by a couple's compatibility—is structurally contingent on the relationship between Dubey and Alice. The latter relationship is not for material gain (that is, a dowry) since Dubey is marrying beneath his class and outside his caste. Dubey and Alice share a propensity for eating marigolds, which are used to decorate the Verma home for the wedding. Dubey declares his love by presenting Alice with a heart of marigolds, which she accepts with a nod of assent. The chasteness of their mutual declaration of affection places the exchange firmly within a trope of romantic love. Dubey says he is looking for a "decent, simple girl" (*Monsoon Wedding* 2001), and there is no indication that Alice is looking for the sexual passion that Aditi desires in a man. The camera cuts from Hemant and Aditi passionately kissing to Alice accepting Dubey's chaste declaration of love, thereby reinforcing the audience's belief that Aditi will find love in her arranged marriage. If the marriage between a woman from Delhi's wealthy cosmopolitan class and the son of a Houston NRI is complicated by prior relationships and family obligations, the relationship between Dubey and Alice is extraordinarily uncomplicated.[25] The latter belongs to the film's utopian desires for an egalitarian nation.

Through its parallel story of a pure and innocent love, *Monsoon Wedding* expresses an anxiety about a widening of the gap between rich and poor in the new global India. In the director's commentary on the DVD release of *Monsoon Wedding*, Nair remarks that she did not know how to end her film and then knew that it had to be with a shot of Lalit happy with where his family had taken him. The film's final shot, however, shows Lalit reaching out for Alice's hand as he invites her to join the wedding guests dancing exuberantly to a Bally Sangoo fusion of bhangra and disco music. Are we to understand this closing scene as a gesture towards a classless society? If so, the utopian vision needs to be located within the frame of the new global nation for which the film creates desire in the audience.

The film's locating of the love between Dubey and Alice outside of the global network that structures the post-1990s family melodramas is evident in Nair's citation of films from the golden age of Bombay cinema for staging their romance. In contrast to the extravagant wedding taking place on the same premises, Dubey and Alice exchange simple vows under a marigold umbrella that alludes to a scene between Raj Kapoor and Nargis in *Awaara* (The vagabond, 1951). The scene in which Dubey declares his love for Alice by presenting her with a heart made of marigolds invokes the ending of Guru Dutt's *Pyaasa* (Thirst, 1957), where Gulabo, who is a prostitute, decides to leave with the idealistic poet Vijay, played by Dutt. It is not inconsequential to Nair's film that Dutt's film denounces the corrupt and materialistic world in which the hero finds himself. However, despite her efforts to remain faithful to his shooting of the scene from the perspective of a mobile camera that heightens Gulabo's (and by extension, Alice's) agency, she cannot escape the Bollywood cliché that Dutt's signature shot has become for representing Indian women as objects of desire. In other words, there is no possibility for a simple return to an earlier (and perhaps purer) moment of Bombay cinema.

Just as *DDLJ* gives value to the hybridized Indian through the traditional values of the NRI, *Monsoon Wedding* requires the innocence of the parallel love story for its endorsement of the materialism of India's wealthy cosmopolitan class. The film suggests that the marginal groups to which Alice belongs—a Christian minority in the face of an increasingly Hindu-identified nation, a servant class that journeys from impoverished rural areas to urban centres seeking employment—can participate in the social mobility that economic liberalization has introduced. Since Bihar is India's most underdeveloped state with the lowest per capita income in the nation, what does it mean for Alice to share in a knowledge of e-mail? *Monsoon Wedding* does not allow the audience to entertain this question. Its vision of a dotcom nation follows a cartography in which the "global" consists of a series of urban centres connecting India's cosmopolitan classes to Indians in the diaspora. It is not inconsequential to its storyline that guests travel from the four corners of the South Asian diaspora—the United States, Britain, the Gulf States, and Australia—for the wedding.

The idea of a global India is endorsed through the visibility of those classes that have the financial ability to participate in the transnational cultures of globalization. However, despite the media's fascination with the success stories of India's growing middle class, its economic liberalization policy has been much more uneven in its effects. The government's incentives for foreign investments were accompanied by cuts in agricultural spending and subsidies during the 1990s. Moreover, agribusiness and biotechnology have not brought wealth to small farmers as have the new technologies in urban areas. Rather, transnational agricultural giants such as DuPont and Cargill engage in practices that activists call biopiracy—namely, the patenting of seeds and indigenous knowledge that prevents farmers from saving seed to replant the following year (Mehta 1994; Shiva 2000). As a result, farmers are forced to plant patented hybrid seed, which requires more water and fertilizers. An increased reliance on purchased seeds, fertilizers, and irrigation systems has placed small farmers even deeper in debt. In Bihar, Monsanto's introduction of hybrid corn resulted in a four billion rupee loss for small farmers. The late 1990s witnessed the emergence of farmer suicides, which has reached the proportion of a national crisis. Approximately twenty-five thousand farmers have committed suicide during the past five years over their increased indebtedness to lenders charging exorbitant rates (Shiva 2004; Huggler 2004).

The diminished iconic value of the village in Bombay cinema does not mean that the problems of rural development have been resolved. 97 percent of rural Indians still do not have basic facilities, and debt bondage remains as much of a problem as ever. The rural vote that helped Sonia Gandhi and the Congress Party defeat the BJP in the 2004 Indian elections has forced the media to address the disastrous cost of economic liberalization on the rural poor. The BJP had hoped to win a second term in office by running a glossy "India Shining" advertising campaign that capitalized on its economic achievements. However, the 1990s enthusiasm for economic liberalization has been replaced with a more sober attitude. "'Shining' India Fails to Lighten Gloom in Villages" declared a *London Times* headline just prior to the April elections (Philp 2004). The difficulty I have with *Monsoon Wedding* is not that it centres on a wealthy Delhi family so much as it suggests, through its "upstairs, downstairs" narrative, that their world is the entire story. Although Nair makes visible the anxieties about globalization that Bollywood family melodramas gloss over, her film renders invisible the widening gap between rich and poor, and urban and rural areas under India's economic liberalization policy. The vanishing rural in Bollywood cinema is mirrored in an independent film such as *Monsoon Wedding* through a universalizing of the class experience that lends credibility to the image of a Shining India.

Notes

This essay was written while in residence at the Center for Ideas and Society at the University of California at Riverside with the generous support of a Rockefeller Foundation Fellowship. It has benefited immensely from the helpful suggestions and critical commentary of seminar participants Leo Chavez, Frances Hasso, Dylan Rodriguez, Parama Roy, and Carole-Anne Tyler. I am also grateful to Joseph Nagy, an avid Bollywood fan, for renewing my interest in Indian cinema.

1. The term "Non-Resident Indian" generally refers to the post-1960s migrants from India to Australia, Britain, Canada, and the United States. The profile of the NRI has changed since the 1990s, when a US immigration reform act tripled the quotas for skilled immigrants, thereby producing a surge in migration from India to the United States. Unlike previous generations of Indians, particularly those who went to Britain in the 1960s and 1970s, this new group constitutes a transnational class that has the financial ability to live between their country of origin and place of residence. It is not unusual for this new class of NRIs to maintain strong ties with India not only through their participation in cultural clubs and religious centres but also by sending their children to India so that they might maintain the cultural identity they would otherwise risk losing.

2. It is estimated that there are now approximately ten million cellphone users in India.

3. The Shiva statue, a modern replica, is on the Delhi-Jaipur road.

4. Approximately two hundred of the eight hundred films made in India each year are made in Bombay, which was renamed Mumbai in 1995.

5. The 2001 nomination of *Lagaan* for an Academy Award in the best foreign film category is one of the many indications of the increased respectability of commercial Indian cinema in the United States. Other indications are the numerous British and American productions of films, television shows, and musicals that Bollywood has influenced. Baz Luhrmann's film *Moulin Rouge* (2001) and Andrew Lloyd Webber's West End and Broadway theatrical productions of *Bombay Dreams* (2002) pay homage to Bollywood's "filmi" style, while Daisy von Scherler Mayer's parody of Bollywood's musical interludes in her disappointing film *The Guru* (2002) presumes the audience's prior knowledge of Hindi film conventions. Nair is currently working on a television series for ABC about a diasporic Indian family in New Jersey, while Gurinder Chadha, whose British-made soccer comedy *Bend it Like Beckham* (2002) did surprisingly well with an American audience, has also made *Bride and Prejudice* (2004), a Bollywood rendition of Jane Austen's novel.

6. The film most representative of this genre is *Sholay* (Embers, 1975), which was released the same year that Indira Gandhi declared a state of emergency in India.

Sholay, which reworked the spaghetti western for an Indian audience, starred Amitabh Bachchan, India's greatest actor of all time, in his characteristic angry young rebel role.

7. Although Bollywood directors have more recently experimented with less traditional genres such as the thriller, science fiction, and gangster film, these are considered niche films and do not have the popular appeal of the family melodrama.

8. *Sholay* was the longest running film in Indian cinema until *Dilwale Dulhania Le Jayenge* broke its record in 2001 (Chopra 2002, 8–9).

9. Interestingly enough, the Indian press treats *Monsoon Wedding* as a Bollywood film, even though it was not made in Mumbai. Bollywood has more recently witnessed the phenomenon of the "Hinglish" film, which are made in both Hindi and English. Both of these events are an indication of the increasingly symbiotic relationship between the Bollywood film industry and the NRIs, who have also emerged as financial backers for Indian films.

10. For discussions of Bollywood as one of the primary cultural sites for constructing an imaginary of the modern Indian nation, see Chakravarty (1993), Prasad (1998), Mishra (2002:235–69), and Rajadhyaksha (2003).

11. Aditya Chopra, who was only twenty-three years old when he made *DDLJ*, belongs to a group identified as Bollywood's Generation Next: "Raised on Hollywood but firmly grounded in Bollywood, the new kids on the block—directors, writers, musicians, choreographers, art directors, editors, stylists, distributors, publicists—are serving up a clever cocktail of *desi* values draped in Yankee slickness" (Chopra and Chowdhury 1999).

12. For explanations of globalization as a process of cultural hybridization rather than homogenization, see Appadurai (1990) and Pieterse (2003).

13. The ticket price in a multiplex theater in Indian cities is fifty rupees compared to the five rupees charged in rural areas. The profit margin for tickets sold in Western nations is even larger, if one considers the exchange rate of forty-five rupees per US dollar.

14. For a reading of the gender politics of national articulations of the *Ramayana* between 1920 and 1990, see Zacharias (2001).

15. The BJP's efforts to remove the mosque built on top of Rama's birthplace in the northern city of Ayodhya culminated in the December 1992 communal violence during which thousands of Muslims were killed.

16. During the mid-1990s, middle-class savings gave way to debt accumulation as the use of credit cards grew by 100 percent (Varma 1998:177).

17. For discussions of how *Monsoon Wedding* asserts the heteronormativity of female sexual desire through a containment of queerness in the effeminate male character of Aditi's brother, Varun, see Desai 2004:223–28 and Gopinath 2005, chap. 4.

18. Vijay Mishra attributes the replacement of a northern Indian ethos in Hindi films with a Punjabi one to the predominance of Punjabis in the diaspora and an identification of the Punjab with a pastoral way of life (2002:260).

19. For a discussion of the home/world opposition in Indian nationalist discourse, see Chatterjee (1993:119–21).

20. A similar moment occurs in *Pardes* when Ganga's grandmother helps her escape from the barn in which her father has locked her for refusing to go through with the arranged marriage. The family matriarch informs the two fathers who have

arranged the marriage that "for centuries we women have been taking poison only" and instructs Ganga not to swallow the poison anymore (1997).

21. I am grateful to Parama Roy for pointing this out to me.

22. The term "arranged love marriage" was first used by the hero of *Hum Aapke Hain Kaun . . . !* in response to the question of whether he preferred an arranged or love marriage.

23. *Monsoon Wedding* alludes to the stereotyping of the NRI as one who returns after having made his fortune abroad when Lalit exclaims—"I'm not a Non-Resident Indian!"—to a price quote of two lakhs for a waterproof wedding canopy (2001).

24. The censorship of kissing is a holdover from strict British censorship codes that were established when India was still a colony. Although the prohibition of kissing has been lifted, filmmakers are reluctant to depict it since public displays of intimacy are considered to be un-Indian. The increasing availability of cell phone cameras has begun to undermine this particular form of Bollywood myth making. The video clip of an actor and his costar passionately kissing in a Mumbai restaurant, which was surreptitiously filmed with the assistance of a cell phone camera, caused an uproar when shown on national TV.

25. One wonders what Dubey's stock-obsessed mother would think of his marriage to a servant girl.

References

Appadurai, Arjun. *Modernity at Large: Cultural Dimensions of Globalization.* Minneapolis: University of Minnesota Press, 1990.

Berger, John. *Ways of Seeing.* London: Penguin, 1972.

Chakravarty, Sumita S. *National Identity in Indian Popular Cinema, 1947–1987.* Austin: University of Texas Press, 1993.

Chatterjee, Partha. *The Nation and Its Fragments.* Princeton: Princeton University Press, 1993.

Chopra, Anupama. "Bollywood: Bye-Bye Bharat." *India Today.* 1 December, 1997.

___. *Dilwale Dulhania Le Jayenge* (The brave-hearted will take the bride). London: British Film Institute, 2002.

Chopra, Anupama, and Nanda Chowdhury. "New Blood: The New Bollywood Brigade." *India Today,* 28 June, 1999. 66+.

Desai, Jignai. *Beyond Bollywood: The Cultural Politics of South Asian Diasporic Film.* New York: Routledge, 2004.

Dilwale Dulhania Le Jayenge. Directed by Aditya Chopra. Mumbai, India: Yash Raj Studios, 1995.

Fernandes, Leela. "Rethinking Globalization: Gender and the Nation in India." In *Feminist Locations: Global and Local, Theory and Practice.* Marianne DeKoven, ed. Piscataway, NJ: Rutgers University Press, 2001. 147–67.

Gopinath, Gayatri. *Impossible Desires: Queer Diasporas and South Asian Public Cultures.* Durham, NC: Duke University Press, 2005.

Grewal, Inderpal, and Caren Kaplan. "Global Identities: Theorizing Transnational Studies of Sexuality." *GLQ* 7, no. 4, 2001. 663–79.

Hall, Stuart. "Cultural Identity and Cinematic Representation." In *Black British Cultural Studies*. Houston A Baker Jr., Manthia Diawara, and Ruth H Lindeborg, ed. Chicago: University of Chicago Press, 1996. 210–22.

Hoffman, Adina. "The Big Bash Theory: Mira Nair's Latest Movie Revels and Reels." *The American Prospect, 25* March, 2002. 28–29.

Huggler, Justin. "India Acts over Suicide Crisis on Farms." *The Independent* (London), 2 July, 2004. 31.

Kripalani, Coonoor. "Coming of Age: Bollywood Productions of the Nineties." *Asian Cinema* 12, Spring–Summer, 2001. 29–48.

Makdisi, Saree. "'Postcolonial' Literature in a Neocolonial World: Modern Arabic Culture and the End of Modernity." *boundary 2* 22, no. 1, Spring, 1995. 85–115.

Mani, Lata. *Contentious Traditions: The Debate on Sati in Colonial India*. Berkeley: University of California Press, 1998.

Mehta, Chirag. "The Seed *Satyagraha*: Indian Farmers and Global Capital Face Off." *Dollars & Sense* 125, September–October, 1994. 25–27.

Mishra, Pankaj. "India: The Neglected Majority Wins!" *The New York Review of Books*, 12 August, 2004. 30–32, 37.

Mishra, Vijay. *Bollywood Cinema: Temples of Desire*. London: Routledge, 2002.

Monsoon Wedding. Directed by Mira Nair. New York: Mirabai Films, 2001.

Pardes. Directed and produced by Subhash Ghai. Mumbai, India: Mukta Arts, 1997.

Philp, Catherine. "'Shining' India Fails to Lighten Gloom in Villages." *The London Times*, 6 April, 2004. 16.

Pieterse, Jan Nederveen. *Globalization and Culture*. Lanham, Md.: Rowman & Littlefield, 2003.

Prasad, M Madhava. *Ideology of the Hindi Film: A Historical Construction*. New Delhi: Oxford University Press, 1998.

Rajadhyaksha, Ashish. "The 'Bollywoodization' of the Indian Cinema: Cultural Nationalism in a Global Arena." *Inter-Asia Cultural Studies* 4, no. 1, 2003. 25–39.

Sharpe, Jenny. "'The Limits of What Is Possible': Reimagining *sharam* in Salman Rushdie's *Shame*." *jouvert* 1 (Fall): 18 paragraphs. 1997.

Shiva, Vandana. "War against Nature and the People of the South." In *Views from the South: The Effects of Globalization and the WTO on Third World Countries*. Sarah Anderson, ed. Oakland, Calif.: Food First Books and International Forum on Globalization, 2000. 91–125.

___. "The Suicide Economy of Corporate Globalisation." *Znet*. http://www.countercurrents.org/glo-shiva050404.html. Accessed 5 April, 2004.

Thomas, Rosie. "Melodrama and the Negotiation of Morality in Mainstream Hindi Film." In *Consuming Modernity: Public Culture in a South Asian World*. Carol A Breckenridge, ed. Minneapolis: University of Minnesota Press, 1995. 157–82

Uberoi, Patricia. "The Diaspora Comes Home: Disciplining Desire in *DDLJ*." *Contributions to Indian Sociology* 32, no. 2, 1998. 305–36.

___. "Imagining the Family: An Ethnography of Viewing *Hum Aapke Hain Kaun . . . !*" In *Pleasure and the Nation: The History, Politics and Consumption of Public Culture in India*. Rachel Dwyer and Christopher Pinney, ed. Oxford: Oxford University Press, 2001. 309–51.

Varma, Pavan K. *The Great Indian Middle Class*. New Delhi: Viking. 1998.

Zacharias, Usha. "Trial by Fire: Gender, Power, and Citizenship in Narratives of the Nation." *Social Text* 19, Winter, 2001. 29–51.

Viewing the West Through Bollywood: A Celluloid Occident in the Making

RAVINDER KAUR

Since the 1990s, the popular film industry in India has successfully renewed its popularity among the South Asian diaspora and the globalised Indian middle class. Its recent films have undergone a thematic shift where the characters encounter the West in a variety of situations reached through travel and migration. The films sport a fantasy-like, rich look, trendy locations, and designer clothes worn by young men and women. The present article locates the Hindi films in the realm of a fast-changing contemporary India with its new market-friendly economy, a globalized and upwardly mobile middle class, a vast dispora that constantly searches for authentic Indian values, and a huge, exportable, techno-savvy workforce that thrives on growing Western pop-dominated cultural forms such as Bhangra/Indi pop music and Hinglish theatre. The search for authentic Indian values, however unintentionally, reveals the long-held images of the West and the eventual making of a celluloid Occident.

Place: Europe.

Characters: A rebellious, young out-of-teens Indian girl out to experience the world and a young man, who has set out to win her as his wife as per his father's wishes.

Scene: A busy nightclub somewhere in Switzerland.

Rebellious girl: Will you buy me a beer?
Man: No, I have no money to spare for alcohol.

At this, another man comes forward to buy her the drink and asks her for a dance. They began dancing and are joined by a couple of more men. As the dance and general merrymaking proceeds, the men start making sexual advances on her. She resists, but is overpowered. She cries to her companion for help. He does respond, but by slapping her hard, thereby shocking everyone around, including the potential molesters. The girl, visibly shocked and embarrassed, walks away.

Man (*confronting her*): Are you French?
Rebellious girl: No
Man: Are you German?
Rebellious girl: No
Man: Are you British or Russian?
Rebellious girl: No, I am Indian.
Man: Then, do Indian girls act shamelessly like this?
Rebellious girl: What do Indian men do while an innocent girl is being molested, just stand as onlookers?
Man: If a woman encourages men, then they are exactly going to respond like this. What do you expect, that I should go and beat them up?
Rebellious girl: If you are an Indian, then yes.
(*After thrashing the offenders, the man has the final word.*)
Man: Nevertheless, it was your mistake.

(A scene from *Dulhan Hum Le Jayenge* 2000)

It was while sitting in a smoke-filled, makeshift cinema hall in Copenhagen that I got engaged in East–West cultural confrontation. The audience reaction to the aforementioned scene almost divided them into two groups; the ones who applauded when the girl is slapped and reminded of her un-Indian behaviour, and the ones who sighed in shocked disbelief. The most vocal in the former category were young men of Indian and Pakistani origin who clapped wildly each time the theme song *Munda Kamaul Hai* (Oh! What a wonderful man) was played to the catchy Punjabi rhythm.

The European background of the scene above—typical of many Hindi films increasingly shot in locations like the Swiss Alps, or the Scottish highlands—was in sharp contrast to traditional Indian values. Throughout the movie, although the main characters dressed in trendy Western labels, they protected each other from succumbing to Western influences. Even when they declared their love for each other, the man refused to make any sexual contact with the girl, reminding her that in

India it is always *shaadi ke baad*, after the marriage. They must not forget their traditions and values in a foreign land.

The Indian film industry produces between 850 and 1000 films a year that are viewed by millions across Asia, Africa, and the Middle East, and by Non-Resident Indians (NRIs) of the West. The purpose of the present paper is to explore the "renewed" interest of the Indian diaspora in popular Hindi or Bollywood films in the last decade of the twentieth century. I use the term "renewed" because the films have caught the fancy of not only the original immigrants, but also of second-generation and third-generation Indians. Films like *Kuch Kuch Hota Hai* (1998) and *Taal* (1999) created a record of sorts by climbing into the US/Canada top-twenty and UK top-ten charts, as well as playing to packed halls in the United Arab Emirates, Singapore, Mauritius, and South Africa. The "overseas market is huge for glossy, glamourous and up-market musicals . . . for this genre sky is the limit."[1] The spadework for this unprecedented success was accomplished by movies such as *Dilwale Dulhaniya Le Jayenge* (1996), which drew the Indian diaspora to the movie halls in a big way. The success of *Kuch Kuch Hota Hai*, among others, helped sustain the euphoria through themes designed for the NRI community, based specifically on family values, moral superiority, true (unpolluted) love, the sacrifice of individual desires for the greater good of the family or community, and the struggle and victory of the Indian diaspora in preserving their cultural universe through Indian rites of passage in an alien environment.

Popular Hindi cinema has not only recently gained a foothold in the South Asian diaspora, but it has been brought out of the closet from home video shows to public screenings, making it an event to be celebrated and flaunted. This trend is not restricted to films alone but is noticeable in art forms as well.

Is there any explanation for this renewed ownership of popular culture? The suggestions that the South Asian diaspora is patronizing new art forms out of nostalgia, and the Hindi film producers have finally perfected the formula to make NRIs buy cinema tickets are too simplistic.

Theoretical Considerations

It is important to define the terms like "popular films," or "popular culture," considering the strong opinions that keep alive the popular versus classical debate.[2] The cultural theorist often laments the debasement of cultural forms through mindless mass productions. This approach, coupled with the watertight categorizations of art, folk and popular, of simplistic and elitist. Popular culture is an urban phenomenon that articulates the concerns and issues of an industrialized people. And one cannot but agree that the factors of demand, supply, and profitability guide the culture production. But to term both the producers and the audience as intellectually and morally bankrupt is akin to the subscription of "cultural patriarchy," where only the ones located at the high end are capable of deciding what is good for everyone else.

Misgivings towards popular culture also arise when it is delinked from the dynamic processes of state and society formation. Popular cinema, like all other cultural forms, neither exists for a self-gratifying purpose, nor has an autonomous project. It deals with narratives that emerge from socio-political transformations with an acute emphasis on commercial factors. Popular cinema not only influences society, it effectuates a "reciprocal-influence" where the society presents the raw stock to be woven into film narratives. The history episodes/beliefs of a nation, community, or individual finds reflection in such narratives. These reflections can be understood as the 'symbolic representations' of society; not of how it is, but how it would like to represent itself.[3] But how does society like to see itself? In a medium such as film, with its strong urban–industrial–commercial overtones, who decides what the audience views? The standard answer of commercial filmmakers is: "we produce what audiences want." Film critics, on the other hand, lament the recycling of themes and the stereotypical characterization. But neither of these views explain why only a handful of movies succeed while most, including the so-called "formula films," fail to make an impact.

In an attempt to understand the "what" and "how" of the film content, I shall employ the 'dialogical approach' first used by Martin Barker to analyze comics. He suggested that there exists a 'contract' between the reader and the text involving an agreement that the text will talk to us in ways we recognize.[4] Film narratives emerge from a 'minimal consensus' between filmmakers and the audience, although the media are only capable of exerting power over audiences to the extent that there is a 'contract.'[5] But Barker stops short of fully exploring the transformation of an abstract contract into reality.

One needs to recognize that commercial film production is not merely a cultural project of anonymous technicians and profiteers but also an urban–industrial cultural form practised by individuals and groups with personal experiences and beliefs. The dominant issues and themes therein are articulated in commonly recognizable forms and are inclusive of the personal biases and interpretations of the individuals involved. The final product remains subject to acceptance or rejection by the audience, whose tastes and preferences keep changing in response to the changing realities. Also, the contract between the audience and the producer is not based on an equal partnership, as the latter is actively engaged in production while the former can only express its opinion by choosing to patronize or not. Nevertheless, the producer and the audience tend to be in constant negotiation, in search of a "dynamic minimal consensus." Moreover, there cannot be a unique format of the contract, as films are targeted for diverse groups. For example, although a producer may attempt to articulate dominant public opinion, it is seldom possible to address an audience as diverse as exists in India. Therefore, there must exist multiple contracts. Finally, the dialectics between the audience and the producer are subject to intervention by censorship bodies acting as arbiters. The emerging picture is that of a commonly recognizable cultural form that is constantly negotiated through multiple contracts, albeit on lopsided terms.

Does the final picture reflect reality? The Indian film historian M Madhava Prasad suggests the presence of "a pre-emptive force that defines it (Indian cinema) in advance as a *not-yet-cinema*, a bastard institution in which the mere ghost of a technology is employed for purposes inimical to its historical essence."[6] The form of Bollywood films itself is a subject of ridicule as they tend to be very long (often more than three hours), contain a number of wishful song sequences that happen from time to time with little correlation to the story, and use unrealistically colourful presentations, especially with regard to the female lead, who is glamourously made up in all circumstances.[7] As such, popular Hindi movies may be seen as diametrically opposed to "art" films.

However, I would suggest that these dichotomous comparisons of Indian films are misleading. This analysis of the Indian films, so far, has been dominated by Western film theories, which stem from the hegemonic alliance between advanced capitalism and cinematic institutions in the Euro-American cultures.[8] The presupposed kinship between cinema and Western culture leads one to search for a form that is exemplified by classical Hollywood cinema. It is not easy to avoid this pitfall as film technology was developed in Western capitalist centres and, therefore, brought along readymade categorizations and notions of acceptable forms. Yet, as Prasad points out, "the technology did not bring with it, readymade, a set of cultural possibilities which would be automatically realised through the mere act of employing it. At the same time, the technology is not neutral, so as to slide into pre-fabricated roles in any political-cultural fields, it has it's own unsettling, reorganizing effects on the field."[9] Although cinema arrived in India in the colonial setting, it soon became a *swadeshi* (homegrown) project with Indian images and narratives. I further propose that popular Indian films cannot be so neatly classified as "real" or "illusive," as they have developed a distinct form, with recognizable symbols and musical-style narratives. Nevertheless, the categories of art/authentic and commercial/unauthentic continue to be used by many Indian film critics.

Does anything called "authentic" actually exist? Are art films a more authentic representation of society than popular cinema? Pierre Bourdieu suggests that distinctions in culture are a significant aspect of the struggle between dominant and subordinate groups in society, and the illusion of 'natural distinction'[10] is ultimately based on the former's ability to impose, by their very existence, a definition of excellence that is nothing other than their own way of existing.

The ability to recognize pure art grows from the acquisition of "cultural capital"[11] through education and upbringing. Thus, argues Bourdieu, the choice of art (text, or way of life) corresponds to the social class one belongs to. Furthermore, the "ideology of natural taste,"[12] which insists that good taste comes instinctively or naturally to a gifted minority, is designed to legitimize this cultural hierarchy, which in turn helps sustain the universe of high culture to which only a few possess the golden key. The patronization of certain cultural practices locates one within the social space and the related class dispositions: "The social subjects classified by their classifications, distinguish themselves by the distinctions they make, between the beautiful and the ugly, the distinguished and the vulgar, in which their position in the objective classifications is expressed or betrayed."[13] This separation between authentic and the popular/nouveau art secures for the elite what Bourdieu calls the "profits of distinction"[14] earned through unequal distribution of cultural capital.

For example, in the context of the South African Indian community, new Indian films have emerged as much-needed 'identity markers'[15] in post-Apartheid society. The films serve distinct purposes for both this Indian diaspora as well as Indians in South Asia. The celebration of slick, modern-looking Hindi-language films by the diaspora is a way of flaunting the traditional-yet-modern, prosperous, conflict-free image of India to the host community where they struggle to move beyond the stereotypes of immigrants. Within India, the patronage of "quality" movies serves as a class marker, as discussed above. Even within the upper classes, there is a constant need to separate oneself from the upstart newly rich sections of society. This desire can be fulfilled by one's liking of art films, the appreciation of which needs qualities associated with the "cultural nobility."[16]

A Thematic Shift to a Celluloid Occident

Since the advent of Bollywood cinema, the choice of film subject tends to convey prevailing socio-political concerns. The emphasis on religious and nationalist themes in the earliest phase gave way to a genre of films in 1950s and 1960s that dwelt on rural-to-urban migration, feudal oppression, and class conflicts. *Do Bigha Zameen* (1953), for example, narrates the story of a small peasant family forced to migrate to the city in an unsuccessful attempt to save its little piece of land from the local landlord. A number of films during this period narrate the search for a lost one in the cities, and the loss of rural innocence in the uncaring urban landscape. Such narratives reflect a phase in Indian history that focused on industrial development and scientific advancement and largely ignored the rural sector. The acquisition of agricultural land for industrial purposes, which led to the uprooting of many communities and to conflicts with local capitalist interests, was a common story in many parts of India. The focus on industry, coupled with feudal oppression, led to large-scale rural-to-urban migrations. Consequently, film narratives turned their attention to urban slums, the exploitation of the industrial working class by factory owners, and the subsequent organization of trade unions. These themes were most popularly explored in the 1970s in the Amitabh Bachchan movies, which articulated the social anger of deprived classes. A significant development was the portrayal of an increasingly dishonest, complex, and oppressive social system that had to be fought, mostly by a lone crusader. In *Zanzeer* (1973) and *Deewar* (1974), Amitabh enacted memorable roles of this lone individual who fought the criminals and the state agencies simultaneously for justice. The 1980s, on the other hand, contended with violence and corruption in society. At the same time, middle-class cinema very successfully brought forward the pathos of urban life.

The decade of the 1990s marked the unveiling of free-market reforms in the Indian economy popularly known as economic liberalization. The Nehruvian model of a mixed economy with its strong socialist overtones was given up in favour of a liberal capitalism. The government emphasized disinvestments in the public sector, withdrawal of subsidies, and sustained seduction of Foreign Direct Investment, and it removed numerous restrictions on imports and foreign exchange to encourage international traffic. These measures not only increased the inflow of foreign visitors, but also encouraged Indians to travel abroad.[17] Economic liberalization saw the emergence of a globalized Indian middle class. Their conspicuous consumption patterns revealed a highly materialistic and uninhibited urban lifestyle, constantly fuelled by growing capitalist ambitions and the new challenges of the global economic order. This middle class has been joined by the newly rich technocrats of the "information revolution" with consumption patterns typical of their counterparts in developed countries, who include both "turn of the century" migrants and more recent arrivals having greater interactivity with their homeland. The influence of this connectivity is best illustrated in the sudden appearance of weekly celebrity chat shows on television and high society columns in newspapers and popular magazines[18] that celebrate the international lifestyle of the newly rich, urban Indians.

India's economic upturn was complemented by the nuclear tests of May 1998. These gave rise to the ambitions of the urban middle class to be on a par with the developed world, and were wholeheartedly supported and celebrated in the urban centres. The Indian diaspora also celebrated. The association with India could now be recalled, as the motherland seemed to be in tune with rest of the world. The shame, guilt, and low self-esteem associated with the poverty, corruption, and caste oppression in their home country, were replaced with military and economic success stories.

Thus, in the 1990s, films narrated stories of the upper-classes. Main characters are often returning graduates from foreign universities, and the complex issues they face include how to reconcile their experiences abroad with life back home. Themes concerning class and caste oppression, workers rights, and internal migration have been tucked away in the closet. Population movements now relate to international emigration of the qualified professional class, although the traditional immigrants like taxi drivers and shopkeepers still constitute the peripheral background. For example, *Aa Ab Laut Chalen* (1998) is the story of Rohan, an unemployed professional young man who emigrates to the United States. His adventures in the Big Apple are similar to the ones narrated in the films of the 1950s of the village bumpkin who arrives in big, bad Mumbai or Kolkata. Rohan's arrival in New York introduces the audience to well-known stereotypes: his acquaintance from the village is now married to an aggressive, rude, and foul-mouthed American woman who has total control over him. No longer warm and hospitable—the traditional Indian qualities—he turns the new arrival away. His moral corruption, greed, and selfishness are evident, as we see his parents being exploited as unpaid labour. Almost as compensation, Rohan is taken home by a kind Pakistani taxi driver who, by this act, demonstrates the South Asian tradition of hospitality.

Similarly, *Pardes* (1997) traces a young woman's journey from Punjab to the United States to be with her fiancé before their marriage is solemnized. Through her, the audience is once again confronted with the "good NRI" and the "bad NRI." Her fiancé, to her shock, falls into the latter category, as he displays his moral bankruptcy in his alcohol consumption, promiscuous sex life, love for smoke-filled night clubs, lack of respect for his elders, and absence of spirituality, all of which are understood to be a by-product of his Western upbringing. On the other hand, the heroine is also confronted with the good NRI who has not forgotten his Indian tradition and values, exemplified by his commitment to true love, his respect for elders, his visits to the temple, his abstention from drinking and smoking, and not having American girlfriends. In the end, she breaks her engagement against her family's wishes and marries the more traditional NRI.

The portrayal of "authentic" Indian values in the Hindi films reveals, however unintentionally, the long-held stereotypes of the West and constructs a celluloid Occident. Earlier, although white, Euro-American characters were not unknown on the screen, they were restricted to the roles of British colonial officers, international gangsters, or skimpily clad women who were no more than distant objects of desire. Globalization has brought foreigners closer to home in the films. Now they play roles of rude, aggressive wives, seductresses, crafty businessmen, hostile bus drivers, or greedy doctors who refuse to treat the patient until they get paid. The audience is given to conclude that in the West everything is valued in terms of money, and people are as cold as their icy native climate. The Indian diaspora is also judged according to the extent of its interaction with the local society. The less "polluted" it is with Western influences, the more Indian it is in its values. For instance, the Indian men married to or living with white women are essentially robbed of their values. Their redemption comes only after they have realized the hollowness of Western society and returned to their authentic roots. For Jonathan Spencer, the sharp contrast in the behaviour of Indians at home and abroad serves as the "rhetoric of authenticity where the West is used as rhetorical counter, which guarantees the . . . real understanding of the non-West."[19] The emerging images of the Occident, adds James Carrier, "include the history of colonial rule and, more broadly, the vast imbalance of power between nations. Such a West impinges upon the Orient in various ways and so helps define it."[20]

While it is emphasized repeatedly by Indian political parties and popular opinion-makers that the country's values are contradictory to a Western lifestyle, there is no single opinion about what these values are. Nevertheless, they are used to mark the definitive space of a consolidated group identity. The dominating values are further reinforced in the form of agendas followed by the celluloid Occident. For example, Sudipta Kaviraj finds a consistent linkage in Indian films with nationalism, where the imaginative universe of the former constantly represents the Nehruvian ideal of nationalism and democracy. He suggests that Jawaharlal Nehru's ideal of Indian nationalism—secular, reformist, mildly egalitarian, cosmopolitan—acquired a historical dominance carried forward by the typical Bollywood film: "both its narratives and musical repertoires were interpreted to give a . . . democratic view of social reality; the central ideological strand of these popular films was the deployment through stories of the twin principles of political and social equality that one associates with democracy."[21]

Conclusion

The recent restoration of pride in the motherland is reflected in the renewed patronage of Indian culture, particularly Bollywood movies. Representations of India no longer seem to be limited to folk dancers in exotic costumes or the sophisticated postures of classical danseuse at the "Festivals of India" abroad. Hindi films also bring relief from the genre of art movies replete with visuals of abject poverty, conflict, and misery that Satyajit Ray was often accused of producing for the sake of Western audiences. In contrast, the 1990s movies are generally located in prosperous surroundings and the characters are able to transport themselves to the much-sought-after northern hemisphere without any struggle or conflict. The plots are far removed from the clichés that a developing country like India is associated with. Rather, the emphasis is on Indian tradition and family values, where the young Westernized characters keep returning to roots located in a traditional-yet-modern India.

The super hit of 1998, *Kuch Kuch Hota Hai*, which drew the Indian diaspora to cinema halls as never before, was largely based on the return of a young, foreign-educated girl who gives up her superficial Western lifestyle to reveal her Indian values beneath. The only constant features in the movie are designer labels, expensive recreations, and rich locales. The movie was lapped up by the Indian communities abroad and was reviewed by an American on-line magazine as a

> . . . new Bombay musical that flaunts hip-hop dancing, *Grease*-like singing, drop dead edible beautiful people and an extravaganza of colour, romance and moral dilemmas the likes of which haven't been seen in American cinema for a long, long time. If you have never indulged in a bit of Bollywood, this is a delicious way to experience this contemporary form that mixes the insane optimism and giddy morality of old American musicals and the sensual excesses of MTV.[22]

Many, however, saw *Kuch Kuch Hota Hai* as a Hollywood clone, except that the actors were Indians.[23]

The Indian diaspora is particularly, prone to rosy pictures of Indian society. The new Bollywood films are definitely not about what India is, but do reflect the reality of a resurgent urban middle class far removed from the woes of the rest of India. Both privileged Indians at home and the diaspora abroad who had grown tired of routine stories of callous deaths, mishaps, drought, or famine in India as reported in the international media are keen to devour a cultural product that brings them no shame. Indeed, they can claim moral superiority over their Western counterparts by emphasizing family values, commitment, and traditional Oriental warmth. The belief that popular Indian cinema is removed from reality is misplaced. It may not depict the actual reality, but the new films of the 1990s quite effectively bring home the reality of the urban middle class and its distance from the rest of India.

Notes

1. Karan Johar, director of *Kuch Kuch Hota Hai*, comments during a live chat event on www.indiatimes.com/chatevents/kjohar.htm, accessed 28/08/00.

2. A vast amount of literature exists on this subject. See, for instance, D Strinati, *An Introduction to the Theories of Popular Culture* (New York: Routledge, 1995); J Storey (ed), *Cultural Theory and Popular Culture* (Georgia: University of Georgia Press, 1998); C Mukerji and M Schudson (eds), *Rethinking Popular Culture: Contemporary Perspectives in Cultural Studies* (Berkeley: University of California,

1991); and A A Berger, *Popular Culture and Genres: Theories and Texts* (California: Sage, 1992).

3. The feminist analysis of the 'reflective hypothesis' of film narratives can be used beyond the representation of women for which the term was originally used by G Tuchman in 'The symbolic annihilation of women by mass media,' in S Cohen and J Youngs (eds), *The Manufacture of News* (California: Sage, 1973).

4. M Barker, *Comics: Ideology, Power and the Critics* (Manchester: University of Manchester, 1989), p 261.

5. *Ibid*, p 261.

6. M Madhava Prasad, *Ideology of Hindi Film: A Historical Construction* (Delhi: Oxford University Press, 1998), p 2.

7. Film heroines are considered to be the bright spots in a Bollywood movie and they shine in death, childbirth, and poverty; appear in skimpy clothes on the icy mountain cliffs; and never forget to apply their latest imported cosmetics even while playing virginal village characters.

8. Madhava Prasad, *op cit*, Ref 7, p 2.

9. *Ibid*, p 2.

10. P Bourdieu, *Distinctions: A Social Critique of the Judgement of Taste* (London: Routledge, 1984), pp 1–7.

11. *Ibid*, p 80.

12. *Ibid*, p 68.

13. *Ibid*, p 5.

14. *Ibid*, p 86.

15. TB Hansen, 'Something happened in Durban: re ections on . lm and identity among Indians in South Africa,' paper presented at a seminar on State, Violence and Mobility, Copenhagen, 22–24 May 2000.

16. Bourdieu, *op cit*, Ref 11, p 2.

17. A small measure like raising the limit of foreign exchange issued for travel abroad from US$500 to US$2000 p.a. served as an incentive for many Indians to travel.

18. See, for instance, 'Metroscape,' *India Today*, 'Hi-Society in city section,' *The Times of India*, 'Lifestyle,' *The Hindustan Times*, and 'Roving eye,' *The Indian Express*.

19. J Spencer, 'Occidentalism in the East: the uses of the West in the politics and anthropology of South Asia,' in JG Carrier (ed), *Occidentalism: Images of the West* (Oxford: Claredon Press, 1996), p 234.

20. J Carrier, 'Introduction,' *ibid*, p 25.

21. S Kaviraj, 'The culture of representative democracy,' in P Chatterjee (ed), *Wages of Freedom: Fifty Years of the Indian Nation-State* (Delhi: Oxford University Press, 1998), p 151.

22. Reviewed by Carol Llyod, http://www.salonmagazine.com.

23. Hansen, *op cit*, Ref 17.

Tempting Sights and Seven Seas: The Diasporic Self, Bollywood and the Gendered Politics of National Longing

USAMAH ANSARI

Introduction

In a heated debate between the queen and the prince in Asif's epic classic, *Mughal-e-Azam* (1960), Queen Jodhabai proclaims, "*Humara Hindustan koi tumhara dil nahee hai, laundi jiski malika bane*" (our India is not your heart, one ruled by some whore). Prince Salim replies, "*To mera dil bhee aapka Hindustan nahee hai, jispe aap hukumat kare*" (my heart is indeed not your India, over which you can rule). This dialogue introduces India as an embattled site, in terms of both who can rule it and whose heart has a right to claim association with it. The very meaning of India as a nation, then, is being contested on screen. In the project of nation-building in post-independence India, films such as *Mughal-e-Azam* have played a vital role in providing a currency for imagining—and therefore discursively bringing to life—the contested nation-space of India (Deshpande 2000:169; Anderson 1983: 15; Chakravarty 1993:4). As a diasporic person, my relationship to this imagined nation-space has been lived through a sense of physical and symbolic separation from the geographic space of India. Moreover, as a descendant of Urdu-speaking North Indian Muslims, my relationship is further problematized by the existence of Pakistan—the state claiming to be our "new homeland" while Hindu nationalists attempt to erase our historic and contemporary presence in India (Devji 1992; Deshpande 2000). The search for a point of ancestral origin is therefore not a simple home-abroad dichotomy (Cieko 2001:140). With this noted, I cannot deny that the longing to know a diasporic "home," whatever that constitutes, continues (Moorti 2003:356; Lavie and Swedenburg 1996:1).

In what follows, I argue that Bollywood cinema mediates this longing by providing contested visual signifiers through which the diasporic subject imagines a "homeland." This discussion therefore attempts to know the diasporic self and reveal the gendered, classed, and ethnicized ways that diasporic subjectivity is embedded within the scheme of (post)colonialism, transnationalism, migration, and mass media. My argument will be articulated through three major sections. First, I will outline popular trends in visual anthropology for a methodological approach that appreciates complex audience-signifier relations, identities, and meaning creation. Secondly, I aim to outline Bollywood as an apparatus of cultural production and consumption both in South Asia and around the world, while highlighting how Bollywood's representational strategies construct and produce the nation and national subjects in particular, gendered ways. My final section will explore diaspora subjectivity and how Bollywood plays a role in managing and negotiating the diasporic self and its longing for an "originary-space" (Desai 2004:19–20). This will reveal how the national project is not fixed but, in a transnational framework, continues to enlist and be challenged by a global audience. My thesis thus echoes Cieko's (2001:140) claim that Bollywood continues "to invite [its] diasporic audiences, their imagined communities, to collaborate in nation-building across boundaries."

The Visual, the Anthropological, and the Audience: Methodological Propositions

The following is structured and organized around myself as a diasporic subject of Bollywood. It is thus a reflexive account that opens wider discussions on the different processes that traverse my positioning (Gergen and Gergen 2003:579). Though my approach is multidisciplinary and incorporates film theory and cultural studies, it is primarily influenced by visual anthropological discourse. As Willeman (1995:26) posits, film theory is generally ethnocentrically biased towards Western media terms and does not interrogate how national specificity expresses particular national identities, subjects and discourses. Cultural studies, on the other hand, provides a more nuanced lens with which to examine relationships with visual culture. Hall (1997:28), influenced by Foucault and Saussure, claims that meaning does not simply exist, but is produced "by the 'work' of representation" and constructed through signifying practices. Moreover, a cultural turn in the social sciences has emphasized signifying processes, enriching semiotics by viewing how particular power-laden contexts provide the "conditions of existence" for any meaning over a visual sign (Hall and Evens 1999:2–3). Hall and Evens (1992:4) thus claim that meaning is not in the visual sign itself and not inherently in the identity of the audience either; rather, meanings are "articulations between viewer and viewed, between the power of the image to signify and the viewer's capacity to interpret meaning" (*ibid*, 4).

Hall and Evens (1999) thus acknowledge the presence of agency in interpreting meaning from visual signifiers but do not ignore how these signifiers are themselves part of larger strategies of power. Althusser's (1999) discussion on ideology is an illuminating way to understand this. He claims that though representations are not "real," they allude to reality and are thus interpreted to reveal realities of the world; "ideology is a 'representation' of the imaginary relationship of individuals to their real conditions of existence" (*ibid*, 317). This is part of Althusser's general theoretical framework where ideology exists in practices, including the practice of (visual) aesthetics that make subjects through multiple interpellations (Hietala 1996:178). As Hall (1997:29) notes, however, that individuals must possess codes that can turn these power-laden signs into meaningful concepts. Foucault's concept of discourse as a regime of representation that provides the language to make sense of things reveals how strategies of power imbue the decoding of signifiers (Hall 1997:44).

I would argue, in agreement with Pink (2001), that though cultural studies rightly illustrates how practices of representation in visual culture involve both the interpretation of images and the social relations that produce meanings and signs, ethnographic and anthropological devices can enrich inquiry by potentially identifying the connections of images to daily lives and identities. Banks and Morphy (1997:21) also claim that, at base, visual anthropology aims to understand how the visual is integrated within social processes and thus affects larger structures. They further argue that visual inquiry can itself enrich the anthropological project, because studying visual systems exposes the complexities of social and political processes that signs are embedded in, many of which may not be identifiable through nonvisual methods (*ibid*, 1; MacDougall 1997).

Approaching Bollywood from a visual or media perspective positions individuals and their social relations at the centre of theoretical and methodological issues, while analyzing media itself as a social form (Ginsburg 1994). This addresses "current Foucauldian fashions in media studies which point to discourses of power as causative, but fail to locate them concretely in the lives of motivated social actors and the processes of every day life" (*ibid*, 13). Echoing Ginsburg, Drotner (1996:30) claims that media ethnography stems form the desire to decode mass-communication by stressing "viewing, listening, and reading as active processes of meaning-making." Instead of focusing solely on relations of production in media industries, this approach can also highlight the sociopolitical effects of media consumption and how media reception is itself mediated along many personal, local, and global axes (Drotner 1996:34; Crawford and Hafsteinsson 1996:2; Rothenbuhler and Coman 2005; Griffiths 1996:50–1). Visual anthropological approaches thus provide a way to map the subjective effects of a large-scale transnational producer like Bollywood.

Behkee Nigahe (Tempting Sights): Understanding Bollywood and the Nation

Dwyer and Pinny (2001) argue that the idea of popular culture, as so often discussed in cultural studies literature, is inadequate in the context of global modernity as specifically experienced in South Asia. The term "public culture" is better suited to conceptualize Bollywood as the space between private life and the strategies of the nation-state; it is thus involved in "mass-mediated forms of negotiated identity" (Dwyer and Pinny 2001:7; Desai 2004:9). Applying this notion of mediated, though negotiated, identities to Bollywood also acknowledges the presence of "cultural agency" in spectatorship by viewing the interventions of politics and aesthetics into the world through film-watching (*ibid*, 18). Public culture can also be considered a "zone of cultural debate" within the context of globalization and contested meanings of national culture (Breckenridge and Appadurai 1995:5). As Breckenridge and Appadurai (1995:14–6) note, analyzing Bollywood through this lens allows one to move beyond notions of pristine culture to conceptions of "national negotiations between history and Globality." Furthermore, experience of modernity is locally grounded, though the local is itself a contested and constructed site (see Comaroff and Comaroff 2003). Ultimately, then, Bollywood actively configures mass notions of community, national identity, and public-private life in a global context.

While keeping this notion of "public culture" in mind, it is plainly evident that Bollywood has played an instrumental role in constructing the nation space. Before analyzing this relationship, however, I wish to underline Anderson's (1983) conceptualization of nations as "imagined communities." He claims that "regardless of the actual inequality and exploitation that may prevail in each, the nation is always conceived as a deep, horizontal comradership," and that even though no member of the nation will ever know all others, they will have an image of communion in their minds (*ibid*, 15, 17). Imagining this community requires mass communication to transmit notions of national fraternity. Though Anderson examines how print media facilitated the historic construction of nationhood in Europe, film is perhaps more relevant in transmitting national consciousness in a setting where literacy rates remain relatively low (Virdi 2003:7, 32; Nandy 1992).

Indeed, producing imagined communities is never a uniform process. I thus wish to locate certain particularities of the Indian nation-building project itself, and specifically highlight its gendered and Hindu-centred biases. Indian nation-building can be seen, generally, as contradictorally a modernizing and traditionalist project: to bring India into the industrial and secular world while valorizing the image of folk traditions, the village, and the domestic sphere. Though this project has been constructed as a "triumph of secularism," the existence of communal strife and the state of Pakistan clearly problematize this notion and in a way represent its failure (Arora 1995:63). Moreover, as Deshpande (2000) and Mufti (2000) discuss, Nehruvian Congress-thinking implicitly appeals to Hindu-specific discourses. Baber (1998:27–8) further notes that even if secularism is the goal, it is doomed to fail, as it is in itself a Western construct. Communalism is thus not a failure of secularism, but is rooted in the inadequacy of the concept of "secularism" itself, the problematics of the national project, and the more general malaise of modernity.

In analyzing communalism in reference to nationalism, one risks overriding "the similarities between communal violence and other types of sectarian ethnic conflict" in South Asia (Baber 1998:27). With that said, it is important to see how the national project is fractured along religious lines, as it is along gendered ones. Indeed Mufti's (2000) analysis of nationalist writing exposes how these two interact: if the "home" is the gendered centre for organizing the nation, it is also a Hindu house, and Muslims are relegated outside the home, symbolized by the popular image of the Muslim brothel in film and fiction. Muslim positioning in the national space is thus problematized as belonging in Pakistan, bearing guilt for Partition, and generally producing strife within the nation (Devji 1992). This is tied to Anderson's (1983:16) discussion of how the nation is always imagined as limited by the Other—the non-national—who in this context of post-independence nation-building can be symbolized by the Muslim.

In this vein, Sarkar (2001) explores how nationalist discourse uses women as sites for the articulation of new national mores by constructing them as pure locations that, unlike men, have not been tainted by the very public colonial apparatus. Mondal (2002:916) furthers Partha Chatterjee's claim that nationalist discourse constructs the home as "true" Indian culture, by applying the notion of "emblematics" to illustrate how women have been disembodied from "women" in Indian national discourse and embody the postcolonial Indian national subjectivity. She also discusses how Gandhi specifically constructed women as the ultimate embodiments of nonviolent courage, but only if they renounce their sexuality. She links this to Gandhi's fear of Western forms of modernity, but I would extend this gendered discourse to how women are constructed as sites for Hindu coherency untouched by the non-national Other. Even within the context of Gandhian Hindu reformation, women are collective representations expressing the supremacy of "national traditions"; the gendered home, again, is called on to be the site for the national imaginary (Srinivasan 1994:7; Sethi 1991:73; Patel 2000:294).

The above outline runs the risk of obscuring how current trends in nationalism continue to develop around religious and gendered signifiers. Hindutvaism is an illuminating example. Banerjee (2005) argues that this movement, which proliferated in the 1980s, is tied to a larger neoliberal agenda to open India's economic markets. She also argues that this current spate of Hindu nationalism is also gendered, though she identifies it as a masculinized process mediated by the image of the Hindu soldier and warrior-monk (*ibid*, 2). Indeed the growth of Hindutvaism is also an alteration of the nation-space by explicitly identifying it is as a Hindu space and reorganizing popular interpretations of national history. Since this new national imaginary has to be communicated (Deshpande 2000:183), it is no surprise that mass media, and Bollywood as the industry with the largest audience (Ganti 2004:2), plays an important role.

The media generally functions to give a widespread identification with national space and helps produce shared notions of borders between national self and non-national Other—both in terms of geographical space and culture (Schlesinger 2000:22). This echoes Smith's (2000:45) claim that in film "we can see how the historicist vision of the nation, and its ethnic fund myths, memories, symbols, and traditions is unfolded." One of the objectives of national media apparatuses like Bollywood is thus to convince a designated audience that it is their nation that is represented (Smith 2000:47) and of course to legitimize systemic inequalities therein. The sheer size of Bollywood and its ability to reach large proportions of the urban working and middle classes in India gives its imagining of the nation special currency (Virdi 2003). One could argue that "a major part of 'India' derives from its movies," which create "influential paradigms for notions of 'Indianness,' 'collectivity,' and key terms of reference for the prevailing cultural hegemony" (Rajadhyaksha and Willemen 1999:10). Bollywood is thus not simply involved in representing India-as-a-nation but also is a meaning-creating apparatus that constructs it. I wish to explore this relationship, starting with a discussion of Bollywood's transmission of the dominant ideology.

Prasad's (1999:9) approach to Bollywood and ideology highlights how public culture codes the political economic reality of the state through the "dominant textual form of popular cinema." In other words, he understands cinema as serving dominant capitalist interests by furthering the legitimization of the state's unequal structuring while concurrently serving as a model for a "modern aesthetic" that reproduces developmentalist logic (*ibid*, 2–3). Bollywood is thus a part of the ideological apparatus (Althusser 1999) that formalizes national identity and interpolates people as subjects. Prasad (1999:5) criticizes anthropological and ethnographic discourse on Bollywood as focusing on the supposed tenacity of "traditional" Indian forms in movies. This has essentialized the audience as a group uncomfortable with modernity and whose "cultural needs" are satisfied by films (*ibid*). He rightly criticizes this as ignoring the complex and negotiated tensions around modernity and folk traditions—which are themselves constructed categories—and how market forces produce films as strategies to facilitate and legitimize the interests of capital (*ibid*, 16). Though it is important to note these market forces, Prasad obscures the presence of agency for audiences to challenge and subvert representations.

Chakravarty's (1993) seminal work on Bollywood cinema and nationalism has highlighted nation-building as a performative strategy that is mapped out on film, and especially films made in the Nehruvian period. She uses the idea of "imperso-nation" to illustrate the struggle between different conceptions of a popular national culture that are performed on screen (*ibid*, 4–5). Her principal focus is to highlight how the goal of Indian national unity is subject to the work of culturally elaborating "Indianness" through the visual tactics of cinema (*ibid*, 9, 13). Virdi's (2003) discussion follows the logic of Chakravarty's, using the idea of "ImagiNation" instead of "imperso-nation." She argues that Bollywood attempts to imagine a unified nation through collapsing contradictions and inequality, while constructing the consciousness of nationhood through specific gendered cultural referents (Virdi 2003:1, 7, 13). She also discusses the politics of language and how the attempt to foster Hindi as a pan-national language has mirrored the decline of proper Urdu in film dialogue (*ibid*, 20).[1] Both Chakravarty (1993) and Virdi (2003) discuss how this politics of language is one aspect of how the national project has increasingly become a Hindutva project mediated and sometimes furthered by Bollywood cinema. Though, as Virdi (2003:36–7) points out, films have also been instrumental in furthering the idea of secularism. Neither Hindutva nor secularism, however, sufficiently interrogate the dynamics of class, gender, and ethnicity.

Mishra's (2002) analysis of Bollywood similarly engages with how Bollywood has articulated the notion of a shared community so central to Anderson's (1983) discussion of the nation. He allegorizes Bollywood as "temples of desire" to illustrate how this shared community is constructed as pan-Indian though it actually constitutes a North Indian, Hindi-speaking male subject (Mishra 2002:1–3). Though Mishra tends to downplay the influence of Hindutva interests in the production and representational projects of South Asian media (see for example Menkekar 1999; Ganti 2004:51; Rajgopal 2001:31), he aptly addresses how cinematic signs are not monolithic and agency exists in interpreting and positioning meaning. Though films can be used for ideological purposes, their modes "of reception are fragmented enough to destabilize the seeming unity therein" and thus Bollywood can be a conduit for dominant Hindu nationalist ideology, but it can also "carry deconstructive or transgressive moments" (Mishra 2002:33).

Ganti's (2004) anthropological approach to Bollywood is methodologically distinct from those outlined above, as it is rooted in fieldwork within the industry. She provides an outline of Bollywood's history and discusses how cinema has played important roles in discourses of development, modernity and post-independence, "especially negotiating Gandhian moralism and naturalism" with Nehru's secularism and modernism (*ibid*, 47). She also considers the BJP's (the political wing of the Hindutva movement) role in the production and financing of Bollywood; her research finds a close tie between BJP influence and the predominance, in the turbulent 1990s, of films focusing on wealthy families, Hindu rituals, and weddings, which produce nostalgia for "Indian culture" and "family values" (*ibid*, 50) that are at the heart of the neoliberal and cultural project of the BJP (Rajagopal 2001:34). Ganti's work, however, rarely engages with audience response to the industry, though she does examine, and contextualizes, the workings of the industry itself.

Ultimately, then, Bollywood has played a role in the gendered national project, obscuring inequality, and providing a platform for representations of contemporary formulations Hindutvaism. Beyond this, Bollywood has also been involved in transnational projects, including visually coding ideas about the decadent West and formulating middle-class subjectivities in the context of a liberalized Indian economy (Kaur 2002:205; Gillespie and Cheesman 2002; Niranjana 2000:138–9). Bollywood thus plays political and cultural roles in mediating the nation both within India and globally. The idea of *behkee nigahe* (tempting sights) articulates how the temptation for a coherent postcolonial Indian nation is mediated by the visual and intricately tied to the hegemony of the visual media in India. As a member of the diasporic audience, I wish to explore how these tempting sights produce nostalgic attachments to signifiers of a national "home."

Sat Samandar (Seven Seas): Bollywood and Diasporic Longing

With widespread transnational linkages that problematize the notion of coherent, closed, national entities (Basch et al 1994), it may seem almost unnecessary to discuss nationalism or nation-building. However, given how the local and the global are connected and mutually constitutive (see also Comaroff and Comaroff 2003), Bollywood constructions of the nation still have important weight, both in the popular imagery within South Asia and across the world, and in the production of national subjects for the operation of transnational projects (Brodkin 2000). This section, first outlines some issues relevant to the diasporic condition and subjectivity. I will then attempt to deconstruct Bollywood's role in mediating diasporic longing by providing signifiers of the idea of an originary space. Perhaps Appadurai (1991:196) best articulates the purpose of this section: "The terms of the negotiation between imagined lives and deteritorialized worlds are complex . . . the task of ethnography now becomes the unraveling of a conundrum: what is the nature of loyalty, as a lived experience, in a globalized, deterritorialize world."

The South Asian diaspora includes people from any of the South Asian countries. Mishra (2001:235) outlines two major movements, the first that of South Asians to different centres within the colonial empire, and the second, which began in the 1960s. Lavie and Swedenburg (1996:1) argue that diasporic groups, which increasingly maintain ties with ancestral homelands, problematize the notion that specific places ground culture and identity. Diasporic subjectivity has often been identified as a condition of "hybridity," which complicates the disjuncture between "identity-as-essence" and "identity-as-conjecture" through the idea of a diasporic third space which is at once grounded to specific places, or ideas of places, while also existing in translocal flows (Lavie and Swedenburg 1996:13–4; Moorti 2003:355; Desai 2004:viii).

The diasporic subject thus maintains a double relation of loyalty to places imagined as "back home" while existing in other places (Lavie and Swedenburg 1996:14; Desai 2004:19). Frankenburg and Mani (1996) link this diasporic positionality to the postcolonial condition. They argue that postmodern conjecturalism, which attempts to counter simple correlations of identity to particular places, ignores the complex and shifting relations between subjects and (post)colonial history (*ibid*, 290). I am not positing the essentialist notion that specific ancestral places ground identities forever; rather, I aim to articulate how the "imagined community" of a national space extends beyond specific boundaries, and, with the proliferation of transnational media, can be mediated by certain representational apparatuses such as Bollywood cinema.

Before exploring this relationship, it is important to interrogate my own diasporic subject position. My parents emigrated from North India to Canada during the second wave of migration and were nestled into a middle-class, professional position mediated within a racialized landscape. Being Urdu-speaking Muslims has complicated my family's association with India, which, as outlined earlier, has been constructed as a Hindu homeland (Singh 2003:3–4); Urdu and Muslims have been imagined outside this space, usually in Pakistan. There is thus a transnational quality to my identity it has not lost ties with India, but it does not isolate this nation-state as representing a concrete or closed point of origin (Basch, et al 1994). Furthermore, the racialized political economy of the Canadian state, including the consumption-based notion of "multiculturalism," has always made me feel like an outsider (see, for example, Oberoi 2003; Mishra 2002:237; Yee 1990). A diasporic yearning for an accepting place, or a "homeland"—as essentialist as that may sound—continues to accompany my sense of self (Aftab 2002:93; Boym 2001:251). Bollywood movies have always provided me with the nostalgia of "home." This nostalgia has never been satisfied by stays in India. Bollywood thus offers the diasporic imaginary (Moorti 2003:355) something beyond the bound nation-state—the possibility of a point of departure, an originary home that may not exist in geographic terms. As Boym (2001) notes, this diasporic longing is often a visually mediated phenomenon. "Visual media products" enable diasporas to articulate a community as a "phenomenology of experience" and thus expresses how transnational flows shape ideas about home and abroad through the "diasporic optic" (Moorti 2003:358–62).

My relationship to Bollywood movies is not unique and it has to be interrogated in relation to the aforementioned gendered and Hindu-oriented nationalist agenda Bollywood has espoused. Mishra (2002) argues that for an ethnically and religiously fractured diaspora, cinema offers a "homeland" across differences; it "brings the Global into the local, presenting people in Main Street, Vancouver, as well as Southall, London, with shared 'structures of feeling' that produce transnational solidarity" (*ibid*, 238). Though he does note that diasporas enact voyeuristic pleasure from watching Bollywood cinema because they are removed from the lived politics of the nation state, he does not engage with the effects of diasporic watching when the "homeland" that Bollywood represents is gendered and sometimes serves Hindu nationalist interests (see, Ganti 2004:47–50). Nor does he engage with the role Bollywood plays in fermenting middle-class global subjectivities (Kaur 2002) while obscuring the diaspora's implication in the unequal structuring of South Asian and global political economies.

Chakravarty (1993:3) more critically engages with diasporic spectatorship by outlining how it evokes problematic essentialist "originary desire" that she relates to the motivations of state and capital strategies. It is this "originary desire," indeed, that motivates much support for Hindutva ideals of a pure, Hindu homeland. With this noted, however, I argue that given the agency of spectators to construct meaning around visual signs, the clinging to an "orignary desire" has a more ambiguous and contradictory presence. For example, my own spectatorship always frames Bollywood representations within the context of India and Pakistan; though I do not share the Islamist vision of Pakistan as the home for South Asian Muslims, my diasporic longing is not grounded by the nation-state of India in which Muslim identity is othered. This sense of double disjuncture is articulated by Fazila-Yaboobali's (2002) discussion on *muhajir* (Indian immigrants to Pakistan) positionality through John Matthan's film, *Sarfarosh* (1999). She argues that though Muslim identity is excluded from the national home of India, *muhajirs* are still labeled immigrants within Pakistan. Instead of strengthening the nation as an essential homeland, this film can indeed problematize the notion that particular states ground cultural or religious identities. Or, as Desai (2004:5) discusses, the hybrid, heterogenous, and fractured nature of the South Asian diaspora is often able to express social identity without grounding it within particular national boundaries.

Another film that explores the awkward positioning of Muslims in South Asia, torn between the fallacy of secular-based Indian nationhood and the myth of a Muslim Pakistan, is MS Sathyu's *Garam Hawa* (1973). After the Partition of India and Pakistan in 1947, the film's Muslim protagonists in the Indian city of Agra are left in an awkward and vulnerable position; they become non-national others, forced to reevaluate their ancestral homes and where, in the postcolonial moment, they belong. Ultimately, they refuse—unlike many of their kith and kin—to migrate to the newly created Pakistan. For the Indian Muslim diasporic, then, this film can illustrate how the longed-for "homeland" is not a concrete locale in either nation-state but a discursive construct that, not unlike the nation itself, is imagined. It is a space lying beyond any border, existing instead in the realm of ideas. My diasporic subjectivity is thus fractured along similar lines, which necessarily mediates my interpretations of Bollywood representational practices and does not lead to the essentializing of a nation-state as the ultimate target for "originary desire" (Chakravarty 1993:3).

Indeed, Moorti (2003:355–6) argues that although Bollywood can facilitate patriotic movements organized around a mythical national past, visual culture can also provide a way to form nonchauvinistic identifications with notions of a shared non-Western culture for diasporic audiences. This therefore provides a way to construct a community in the context of alienation from dominant Western societies. As has been extensively outlined in the previous section, however, one must also remain suspicious as Bollywood's constructions of the nation.

To explore this conflicted articulation of a visual currency for the imagining of preemigration identifications by diasporic audiences, I wish to provide a filmic example.

The "running-in-the-field" song sequence occurs in many Bollywood movies. This sequence usually involves the male protagonist (hero) pursuing the female protagonist (heroine) through local and, increasingly, international pastoral scenes. Though diverse in their specificities, the heroine eventually gives in to the hero's advances, and indeed sometimes becomes the pursuer. On other occasions it is a vampish heroine who initiates the ensemble in the first place. A common element is also that of the heroine's *sari anchal* or *dupatta*[2] either getting caught on a feature of the physical landscape or grasped by the pursuing hero.

For the diasporic subject, these song sequences may have special meaning. For one thing, the pastoral scenes communicate a sense of "rural purity" or "simplicity" that contrasts with the visual landscape of modernity: the cityscape. Moreover, the hero-heroine chase connotes, in gendered terms, an eternal search similar to diasporic longing. Sometimes there is no hero-heroine hunt and just one character singing and frolicking. The song *Piyar Hua Hain Chup Ke Se* (Love Happened Quietly) in Vinod Chopra's anticolonial epic, *1942 A Love Story* (1993), is one such example. The heroine is seen gaily singing, swinging, and dashing across the hilly rural setting; her *dupatta* gets caught on a piece of wood, so she stops to carefully free it, then throws it in the air. This scene, I argue, has special currency for diasporic audiences—the constantly caught *dupatta* can be conceptualized as a stubborn linkage to the idea of an originary space, and the throwing of it in the wind is perhaps the realization of the futility of this desire. There is also a gendered component to this: given the *dupatta*'s connotation of modesty and propriety, it being caught on the landscape can also represent the stubbornness of gendered notions of "originary traditions" that have particular currency for women in the diaspora (Moorti 2003:357). The tossing of it could subsequently reveal the renouncing of certain of these accepted mores, and thus exemplify that "films help foreground how women as gendered subjects negotiate and participate in transnational discourses enabled by the flow of global capital" (*ibid*, 372).

There is a risk in romanticizing these signatures of Bollywood cinematography and missing their use in dominant national discourses. As Sethi (1991:73–5) has argued, the valorizing of village life as the location of true "Indianness" as opposed to the colonially corrupted city has been a constant feature in Gandhian thinking. This rural/urban binary echoes the separation of the home from the public in nationalist thinking. Feminist subaltern historiography has long problemetized the way this has coded women and their guarded sexuality as the sites for the operation of national discourses on morality, community, and cohesion (Sarkar 2001; Mondal 2002). The song sequence in *1942 A Love Story* (1993) is thus worked into the film's more general nationalizing mission that explicitly conceptualizes the British Raj as a force that disrupts not only a nation but also the tenderness of heteronormative love. Moreover, the heroine is violated by being forced into the public realm and engaging in the struggle for independence instead of occupying the designated site of purity: the pastoral home. Bollywood, then, provides the images to visualize the diasporic longing for a homeland, but it does so within its own gendered project of nation-building. Given the "diasporic third space," however, there is a potential for spectators to problematize these signifiers by relating their own out-of-state status to fracture the idea of cohesion espoused by these filmic manifestations of nation-building. There is thus potential to disrupt the notion of a nation as a concrete site grounding essential culture and identity (Lavie and Swedenburg 1996:1, 13–4; Moorti 2003:355).

Conclusion

The idea of *behkee nigahe* (tempting sights) and *sat samander* (seven seas) thus provide an intriguing exit: the tempting sights of nationhood mediated by the tantalizingly tempting visions produced by Bollywood have implications across the world in a globalized context. Bollywood cinema mediates diasporic longing by providing contested visual signifiers through which the notion of a homeland is imagined. The national project itself is not fixed but continues to be undertaken, and challenged, by a transnational audience. Perhaps Bollywood itself provides a way to conceptualize this diasporic location: the courtesan Umrao Jaan (in Muzzafar Ali's *Umrao Jaan* [1981]) sings, "*justju jiski thi usko to na paaya humne/ is bahaane magar dekh li duniya hum ne*" (that for which I have been searching was never beheld, but by its excuse I saw the whole world).

Notes

1. Urdu, drawing heavily from a Persian lexicon, is the sole official national language of Pakistan and one of the many official languages of India. Though still an integral part of Bollywood dialogue, its position is more tenuous in India as Hindu-nationalists have constructed it as part of Muslim invaders culture that needs to be erased from any official literary or governmental status (Ahmad 2000). Others have linked the demise of Urdu from the very inception of India as a modern state, linking Gandhi's desire for a pan-Indian Hindi as ultimately alienating Urdu (Rahbar 2003).

2. A sari *anchal* (or pallu) is the long part of a sari that is thrown over the left shoulder in the style worn by women in North India. A *dupatta* is a piece of cloth that accessorizes various clothes, and is usually worn around the neck. These items have special meaning in that they sometimes represent modesty, especially when used to cover hair. Salman Rusdhie ingeniously articulates the conviction of the *dupatta* in popular imagination through his novel Shame (1983): Bilquìs Kemal is subjected to

a bomb-blast during the rioting in Delhi following Partition in 1947. The bomb blast seers off all her clothes, leaving her naked and feeling shamed in a public space. She then, however, "felt around her neck the remnants of a length of muslin. The *dupatta* of modesty had stuck to her body, fixed there by the congealed blood of the many cuts and scratches" (61). After being married and living with her powerful mother-in-law, Bariamma, Bilquìs was one evening forced to recount the story of "her nudity in the Delhi streets. 'Nevermind,' bariamma pronounced approvingly . . . , 'at least you managed to keep your *dupatta* on'" (*ibid*, 74).

References

Aftab, K. "Brown: The New Black! Bollywood in Britain." *Critical Quarterly*, Vol. 44, 2002. 88–98.

Anderson, Benedict. *Imaginged Communities: Reflections on the Origins and Spread of Nationalism*. New York: Verso, 1983.

Ahmad, Aijaz. *Lineages of the Present: Ideology and Politics in Contemporary South Asia*. New York: Verso, 2000.

Althusser, Louis. "Ideology and Ideological State Apparatuses." In Hall, Stuart and Jessica Evens, eds. *Visual Culture: The Reader*. London: Sage, 1999. 317–23.

Appadurai, Arjun. "Global Ethnoscapes: Notes and Queries for a Transnational Anthropology." In R Fox, ed. *Recapturing Anthropology: Working in the Present*. Santa Fe, New Mexico: School of American Research Press, 1991.

Arora, Poonam. "Sanctioned and Proscribed Narrative in Postcolonial India: A Bicultural Reading of the Courtesan Film." In Kostas Myrsiades and Jerry McGuire, eds. *Order and Partialities: Theory, Pedagogy, and the "Postcolonial."* Albany: State University of New York Press, 1995

Baber, Z. "Communal Conflict and the Nostalgic Imagination in India." *Journal of Contemporary Asia*, Vol. 28(1), 1998. 27–44.

Banerjee, Sikata. *Make Me A Man!: Masculinity, Hinduism and Nationalism in India*. Albany, New York: State University of New York Press, 2005.

Banks, Marcus and Howard Morphy. "Introduction." In Marcus Banks and Howard Morphy (eds.), *Rethinking Visual Anthropology*. New Haven: Yale University Press, 1997.

Basch, Linda, Nina Schiller, and Cristina Szanton Blanc. *Nations Unbound: Transnational Projects, Postcolonial Predicaments, and Deterritorialized Nation-States*. Langhorne, Pennsylvania: Gordon and Breach, 1994.

Boym, Sayetlana. *The Future of Nostalgia*. New York: Basic Books, 2001.

Breckenridge, Carrol and Arjun Appadurai. "Public Modernity in India." In Breckenridge, Carol, ed. *Consuming Modernity: Public Culture in a South Asian World*. Minneapolis: University of Minnesota Press, 1995. 1–20.

Brodkin, Karen. "Global Capitalism: What's Race Got to Do With It?" *American Ethnologist*, Vol. 27(2), 2000.

Chakravarty, Sumita. *National identity in Indian Popular Cinema, 1947–1987*. Austin: University of Texas Press, 1993.

Cieko, A. "Superhit Hunk Heroes for Sale: Globalization and Bollywood's Gender

Politics." *Asian Journal of Communication*, Vol. 11, 2001. 121–143.

Comaroff, Jean and John Comaroff. "Ethnography on an Awkward Scale: Postcolonial Anthropology and the Violence of Abstraction." *Ethnography*, Vol. 4(2), 2003. 147–179.

Crawford, Peter and Sigurjon Baldur Hafsteinsson. "Introduction." In Crawford, Peter and Sigurjon Baldur Hafsteinsson, eds. *The Construction of the Viewer: Media Ethnography and the Anthropology of Audiences.* Denmark: Intervention Press, 1996.

Desai, Jigna. *Beyond Bollwyood: The Cultural Politics of South Asian Diasporic Film.* New York: Routledge, 2004.

Deshapande, Satish. "Hegemonic Spatial Strategies: The Nation-Space and Hindu Communalism in Twentieth-Century India." In Chatterjee, Partha and Pradeep Jeganathan (eds.), *Subaltern Studies Conference: Community, Gender and Violence.* New York: Columbia University Press, 2000.

Devji, Faisal. "Hindu/Muslim/Indian." *Public Culture*, Vol. 5(1), 1992.

Drotner, Kirsten. "Media Ethnography and its Limits." In Crawford, Peter and Sigurjon Baldur Hafsteinsson, eds. *The Construction of the Viewer: Media Ethnography and the Anthropology of Audiences.* Denmark: Intervention Press, 1996. 28–46.

Durham, Meenakshi. "Constructing the 'New Ethnicities': Media, Sexuality, and Diaspora Identity in the Lives of South Asian Immigrant Girls." *Critical Studies in Media Communication.* Vol. 21(2), 2004. 140–61.

Dwyer, Rachel and Christopher Pinney. "Introduction." In Dwyer, Rachel and Christopher Pinney, eds. *Pleasure and the Nation: The History, Politics and Consumption of Public Culture in India.* New Delhi: Oxford University Press, 2001.

Fazila-Yacoobali, Vazira. "Yeh Mulk Hamara Ghar: The 'National Order of Things' and Muslim Identity in John Mathew Mattan's Sarfaroosh." *Contemporary South Asia*, Vol. 11(2), 2002. 183–98.

Frankenburg, Ruth and Lata Mani. "Cross Current, Crosstalk: Race, 'Postmodernity' and the Politics of Location." In Lavie, Smader and Ted Swedenburg, eds. *Displacement, Diaspora, and Geographies of Identity.* Durham, North Carolina: Duke University Press, 1996.

Ganti, Tejaswini. *Bollywood : A Guidebook to Popular Hindi Cinema.* New York: Routledge, 2004.

Gergen, Mary and Kenneth Gergen. "Qualitative Inquiry: Tensions and Transformations." In Denzin, Norman and Yvonna Lincoln, eds. *The Landscape of Qualitative Research: Theories and Issues.* California: Sage, 2003.

Gillespie, M and T Cheesman. "Media Cultures in India and the South Asian Diaspora." *Contemporary South Asia*, Vol. 11(2), 2002.

Ginsburg, Faye. "Culture/Media: A (Mild) Polemic." *Anthropology Today*, Vol. 10(2), 1994.

Ginsburg, Faye. "Mediating Culture: Indigenous Media, Ethnographic film and the Production of identity." In Devereux, Leslie and Roger Hillman, eds. *Fields of Vision: Essays in Film Studies, Visual Anthropology, and Photography.* Berkeley: University of California Press, 1995. 256–292.

Griffiths, Alison. "Ethnography and the Politics of Audience Research." In Crawford, Peter and Sigurjon Baldur Hafsteinsson (eds.), The *Construction of the Viewer:*

Media Ethnography and the Anthropology of Audiences. Denmark: Intervention Press, 1996. 47–65.

Hall, Stuart. *Representation: Cultural Representations and Signifying Practices*. London: Sage, 1997.

Hall, Stuart and Jessica Evens. "Introduction." In Hall, Stuart and Jessica Evens, eds. *Visual Culture: The Reader*. London: Sage, 1999. 1–7.

Hietala, Veijo. "Meanings, Texts, Contexts: Tracing the Spectacular in Post-Structuralist Film Theory." In Crawford, Peter and Sigurjon Baldur Hafsteinsson, eds. *The Construction of the Viewer: Media Ethnography and the Anthropology of Audiences*. Denmark: Intervention Press, 1996. 177–90.

Kaur, Ravinder. "Viewing the West through Bollywood: A Celluloid Occident in the Making." *Contemporary South Asia*, Vol. 11(2), 2002.

Kesavan, Makul. "Urdu, Awadh and the Ṭawaif: the Islamicate Roots of Hindi Cinema." In Zoya Hasan, ed. *Forging Identities: Gender, Communities and the State*. New Delhi: Kali for Women Press, 1994.

Lavie, Smader and Ted Swedenburg. "Introduction." In Lavie, Smader and Ted Swedenburg, eds. *Displacement, Diaspora, and Geographies of Identity*. Durham, North Carolina: Duke University Press, 1996.

MacDougall, Donald. "The Visual in Anthropology." In Marcus Banks and Howard Morphy, eds. *Rethinking Visual Anthropology*. New Haven: Yale University Press, 1997.

Menkekar, Purnima. *Screening Culture, Viewing Politics: An Ethnography of Television, Womanhood, and Nation Postcolonial India*. Durham, North Carolina: Duke University Press, 1999.

Moorti, Sujata. "Desperately Seeking an Identity: Diasporic Cinema and the Articulation of Transnational Kinship." *International Journal of Cultural Studies*, Vol. 6(3), 2003. 355–76.

Mishra, Vijay. *Bollywood Cinema: Temples of Desire*. New York: Routledge. 2002.

Mufti, Aamir. "A Greater Story Than God: Genre, Gender and Minority in Late Colonial India." In Chatterjee, Partha and Pradeep Jeganathan (eds.), *Subaltern Studies Conference: Community, Gender and Violence*. New York: Columbia University Press, 2000. 2–36.

Nandy, Ashis. "An Intelligent Critic's Guide to Indian Cinema." In Singh, KS, ed. *Visual Anthropology and India*. Calcutta: Anthropological Survey of India, 1992. 43–78.

Niranjana, Tejaswini. "Nationalism Refigured." In Chatterjee, Partha and Pradeep Jeganathan (eds.), *Subaltern Studies Conference: Community, Gender and Violence*. New York: Columbia University Press, 2000. 138–66.

Oberoi, Harjot. "Imagining Indian Diasporas in Canada: An Epic Without a Text?" In Parekh, Bhiku, Gurharpal Singh and Steven Vertovec (eds.), *Culture and Economy in the Indian Diaspora*. London: Routledge. 2003.

Patel, Divia and Rachel Dwyer. *Cinema India: The Visual Culture of Hindi Film*. London: Reaktion Books, 2002.

Patel, Sujata. "The Construction and Reconstruction of Women in Gandhi." In Thorner, Alice and Maitreyi Krishnaraj (eds.), *Ideals, Images and Real Lives: Women in Literature and History*. Mumbai: Orient Longman, 2000. 288–321.

Pink, Sara. *Doing Visual Ethnography: Images, Media and Representation in Research*.

London: Sage, 2001.

Prasad, M Madhava. *Ideology of the Hindi film: A Historical Construction*. Delhi: Oxford University Press, 1998.

Rahbar, Daud. "Gandhi and the Hindi-Urdu Question." In Harold Coward,ed. *Indian Critiques of Gandhi*. Albany: State University of New York Press, 2003. 217–238.

Rajadhyaksha, Ashish and Willemen, Paul. *Encyclopaedia of Indian Cinema* (New Revised Edition). New Delhi: Oxford University Press, 1999.

Rajgopal, Arvind. *Politics After Television: Religious Nationalism*. Cambridge: Cambridge University Press, 2001.

Rosaldo, Renato. *Culture and Truth: The Remaking Of Social Analysis*. Boston: Beacon Press, 1993.

Rothenbuhler, Eric and Mihai Coman, eds. *Media Anthropology*. California: Sage,2005.

Rushdie, Salman. *Shame: A Novel*. Toronto: Random House of Canada, 1983

Sarkar, Tanika. *Hindu Wife, Hindu Nation: Community, Religion and Cultural Nationalism*. Indianapolis, Indiana: Indiana University Press, 2001.

Schlesinger, Philip. "The Sociological Scope of 'National Cinema.'" In Hjort,Mett (ed), *Cinema and the Nation*. London: Routledge, 2000. 19–31.

Sethi, Rumina. *Myths of the Nation: National Identity and Literary Representation*. New York: Clarendon Press. 1999.

Singh, Gurharpal. "Introduction." In Parekh, Bhiku, Gurharpal Singh and Steven Vertovec (eds.), *Culture and Economy in the Indian Diaspora*. London: Routledge, 2003.

Singh, KS. "Cultural Policy, Cultural Pluralism and Anthropology: An Indian Perspective." In Singh, KS, ed. *Visual Anthropology and India*. Calcutta: Anthropological Survey of India, 1992. 7–15.

Smith, Anthony. "Images of the Nation: Cinema, Art and National Identity. In Hjort, Mett (ed), *Cinema and the Nation*. London: Routledge, 2000. 45–87.

Srinisavan, Amrit. "Women and Reform of Indian Tradition: Gandhian Alternative to Liberalism." In Kasturi, Leela and Vina Mazamudar (eds.), *Women and Indian Nationalism*. New Delhi: Vikas Publishing House, 1994.

Virdi, Jjotika. *The Cinematic Imagination: Indian Popular film as Social History*. NJ: Rutgers University Press, 2003.

Willeman, Paul. "The Nation." In Devereux, Leslie and Roger Hillman (eds.), *Fields of Vision: Essays in Film Studies, Visual Anthropology, and Photography*. Berkeley: University of California Press, 1995. 21–35.

Yee, May. "Finding the Way Home Through Issues of Gender Race and Class." In Bannerji, Himani, ed. *Returning the Gaze: Essays on Racism, Feminism and Politics*. Toronto: Sister Vision Press, 1993. 3–44.

The Trials of a Faithful Brahmin Wife, or How I Learned to Stop Worrying and Love *Roja*[1]

SONIA BENJAMIN

> January 1993. A cinema hall in Hyderabad. The Telugu version of Maniratnam's *Roja* is being shown. Every show displays the "house full" board, and every seat in the theatre is occupied. From the opening minutes of the film, the morning show audience (mostly male, middle and lower-middle class, possibly college going) indulges in loud cheering and shouting, their slogans calculated to strike a special chord after the destruction of the Babri masjid just a few weeks previously: Jai Sri Ram, Pakistan Murdabad. Bharat Mata ki Jai. (Niranjana 1994:79)

Released to wide commercial and critical acclaim in 1992 and the subject of much academic discussion since then, *Roja* was the film that brought accomplished South Indian director Mani Ratnam to the attention of the wider Indian audience. Dealing with complex contemporary issues of separatism in Kashmir and wider notions of Indian nationalism, It juxtaposes the personal story of a young Tamil cryptologist kidnapped by Kashmiri militants, and his wife's desperate struggle to free him, with the burning and basic political questions that India faced in the 1990s: Who is an Indian? What is the state of the Indian nation?

This essay aims to analyze *Roja*'s often simplistic responses to these queries. In order to understand these responses, I will look at how this film depicts Kashmir and Tamil Nadu, the portrayal of Hinduism and Islam, the depiction of the Indian state as represented by the Indian army, the characterization of Rishi, Roja, and Liaquat Khan, and Rishi's loyalty to the Indian state, which veers between a brand of nationalism and outright jingoism, versus Roja's loyalty to her husband above all else. I am also interested in exploring the differences between the dubbed

Hindi version and the original Tamil version. It is my contention that the mere act of dubbing robs *Roja* of the regional context so critical to understanding the film. When viewed through a regional lens, *Roja* provides subtly different answers to the questions it raises, though these answers continue to be both confusing and contradictory. For the purpose of this essay, I will refer mainly to the original, Tamil-language version and mention the dubbed Hindi version only to compare the two.

Roja begins with a cacophony of sounds: the whirring of helicopters, the barking of dogs, and the tramping of boots are coupled with the sounds of the forest and a muted *azaan*, the Muslim call to prayer, before the screen clears to reveal soldiers of the Indian army engaged in some sort of military operation. Within a few minutes the audience is drawn into a tense gun battle between the army and a group of men the film soon identifies as Kashmiri militants. One man, clearly of some importance, named Wasim Khan, is captured before the scene shifts to the pastoral allure of rural Tamil Nadu and the film's titular heroine prances onto the screen singing its most famous song, "Chinna Chinna Asai" (Small Desires of the Heart).

Thus, from the very beginning, Ratnam establishes the vivid differences between the northernmost and southernmost states in India. Kashmir, a land of legendary beauty and the primary location of the film, is a space inhabited by the Indian army and terrorists, who disrupt with their heavy boots and automatic weapons its very essence. Tamil Nadu, home to the director, his actors, and his original target audience, is a place whose normalcy is warm and inviting. Its fields are occupied by industrious women in colourful saris and its forests by impish heroines who steal fruits, unlike the Kashmiri forests that are the sites of war and weapons. Sundarpandipuram in the Tirunelveli district of Mani Ratnam's Tamil Nadu is not just miles away from the Srinagar of Ratnam's Kashmir, it is also worlds away. *Roja*'s "two beginnings" (Niranjana 1994:80) make clear its point of view—Kashmir in its current state is clearly the other.

It follows that those who live in this Kashmir are also part of the other. Since the film depicts no Kashmiris other than one Kashmiri Muslim newspaper boy, a few Kashmiri Muslim militants, and many, pretty Kashmiri women and children dressed in Kashmiri Muslim ethnic wear and used as props in songs, one is forced to conclude that this other is Kashmiri Muslim. In an influential essay that skewers *Roja*'s purported nationalism, Niranjana contends that *Roja* deifies a new middle-class that is distinctly Hindu at heart with Hindutva in its soul and does so by consistently othering Muslims. Its background score, editing choices, use of light, etc., all normalize "Hindu ethnicity" on one hand while demonizing "Muslim ethnicity" on the other. She posits that the rustic ethnicity of Rishi and Roja's wedding is in direct contrast to the blatant display of Muslim ethnicity seen through the dress of the Kashmiri militants and their constant praying. ". . . their (Muslim) ethnicity reveals them as anti-modern (therefore anti-national or anti-Indian), intolerant and fundamentalist, while Hindu ethnicity as displayed by the chief protagonists is merely part of the complexity of being Indian," (Niranjana 1994:80).

Rustam Bharucha picks up on Niranjana's overarching theme of othering the Muslim while ruminating on *Roja*'s links to fascism. He writes, "Here there are no villains in the earlier sense, but the enemy figures who are specifically marked as 'Kashmiri' and 'Muslim'" (Bharucha 1994:1391). Also troubling for Bharucha is the degree of realism that Mani Ratnam uses to depict these militants. The fact that "their representation is almost low-key, even 'realistic' by commercial film standards" and that "they are played in the context of verisimilitude" underlines Ratnam's darker purposes and undermines "the danger of its representation of the 'enemy'" for the audience (1391).

If Rishi, with his modern education and outlook, symbolizes the ordinary, middle-class Hindu male on whom the Indian nation must now rely on for protection and Roja, his high-spirited but still traditional Hindu wife, signifies why it must be protected, then Liaquat Khan denotes the danger that separation from the actual Indian state holds for the imagined Indian nation. In order to preserve that imagined nation which is unquestionably Hindu, this separation must be prevented and those who champion it recognized for who they really are, enemies of the state and the nation, and Muslim.

Parallel to this overwhelmingly negative representation of the Muslim militants is an unabashedly positive representation of the Indian army. Though scholars remain divided on the role and representation of the state in *Roja*, the representation of the prominence, power, and prowess of the army resounds in their varied arguments. According to S V Srinivas, contemporary Indian films have long denied the Indian politician the legitimacy to speak for the Indian state, so "the army alone is being projected as the authentic voice of the state" (Srinivas 1994:1226) and *Roja* is no different. In not questioning the army's stand on Kashmiri militants, for not investigating why Kashmiri militants are fighting for separation, by allowing General Royappa to castigate Roja for securing the release of her husband by appealing to the minister, *Roja* not only "slickly packages state propaganda" (1226) but also "helps to legitimise army activities such as search operations, the interrogation of 'terrorists' and the shooting of them" (Velicheti, in Srinivas 1994:1226).

Roja, thus, when viewed through these eyes is not merely difficult but extremely dangerous. Its insidious ideology, its often jingoistic tenor, its Hindu Brahmin, middle-class hero and heroine, even its sweeping cinematography and catchy music are all symptomatic of a time in Indian politics and society when the Hindu Right achieved an unparalleled hold on the imagination of India. Indian commercial cinema in its single-minded devotion to please audiences was quick to pick up on their new mood and efficient in catering to their new command, making sure, as always, to sugar-coat the pill with peppy music, perfect locales, and pleasant leads. *Roja*'s move from a regional film to a national one, its being dubbed into several languages including Hindi, its subsequent popularity with audiences all over India and to add insult to injury, its Presidential Award for National Integration, are all signs of this unholy nexus between Indian cinema, Indian audiences, and Hindutva politics that so typified the India of the 1990s.

It is possible therefore to read the politics of *Roja* as the politics of division, communalism, and majoritarianism. It is plausible to theorize that *Roja* denigrates Nehruvian ideals of secularism and rationalism while supporting the extremist ideas of Hindu fundamentalism. *Roja* certainly invites such an analysis with its infamous flag-burning sequence, its clever use of the poems of nationalist poet Subramanya Bharati and other patriotic punctuations like Rishi's repeated 'Jai Hind's. Roja's barbs about the reel-life treatment accorded to her kidnapped husband's case, the ordinary Hindu citizen, and the real-life treatment of the kidnapped minister's daughter's case, who was Muslim, raises eyebrows. Rishi's provocative question regarding the plight of the Hindus who have fled the Kashmir Valley while disregarding the miserable situation of the Muslims of the Valley raises not just eyebrows but also red flags. Niranjana, Bharucha, and Srinivas, among others, certainly make credible cases for such a reading.

Nevertheless, it is possible for *Roja* to be read differently, as a film of loss and mourning—the loss of beloved ideals and the mourning of lost humanity, the loss of opportunity and the mourning of the lack of responsibility. *Roja* indirectly chronicles a decisive shift in the idea of the Indian nation and is not necessarily sympathetic to that shift. *Roja*'s support of an idea of the Indian nation, and it does have a very definite notion of this nation, should not inevitably be read as support of the

Hindutva idea of the Indian nation. To maul Shakespeare, a rose by any other name need not smell as sweet or, in this case, need not reek of Hindutva.

In most critiques of *Roja*, despite the title of the film, Rishi is cast as the central character. He is the urbane technocrat, the ordinary citizen, the cosmopolitan city-dweller and above all, the middle-class but high-caste Hindu. Niranjana, Bharucha, and Srinivas all use his class and caste identity as the starting point for their diverse arguments. The film, however, never seems to emphasise his religion. Yes, he is Hindu, his name gives that away; he is married according to Hindu rites and enjoys it enough to dance at the end of it, but this is all incidental to understanding Rishi's character in the film. Unlike Roja, he is never shown in a temple other than at the time of his wedding ceremony and is never shown praying, not even in his darkest hour of captivity. Despite the religious connotations of his name, his identity seems to be defined by his career, his city, and his citizenship.

The film consistently frames Rishi as a man of science. It also emphasizes his urbanity seen through his consistent use of English, which seems to go part and parcel with his technical education. He works with computers and codes and mouths words in English like "cryptology" and "clearance." Rishi's affectionate but derisive moniker for Roja is *Pettikaadu* or "the villager or rustic." When Rishi takes Roja to meet his supervisor, his boss in a conversation with Roja is critical of Rishi's Tamil, which he dismisses as "Madras Tamil." In a Tamil-language film which is primarily a love story, Rishi's most important emotional interactions with Roja are in English. When he apologizes to her, he does so in English, spelling out the word "sorry." When he tells her he loves her for the first time, he does so in English, first checking if she knows enough of the language to understand his naughty, nonchalant "I love you." Rishi's other primary partner in the film is his main captor, Liaquat Khan, with whom he has many conversations about the motives of the militants. In a particularly heated exchange about what Liaquat terms his "jihad," Rishi retaliates with a disgusted "You're all misguided" in English.

The other marker of Rishi's identity is his nationality as an Indian. As Chakravarthy and Pandian remark, "He is not an arrogant Tamilian but an arrogant Indian" (Chakravarthy and Pandian 1994:642). His patriotism, which often devolves into jingoism, is a key facet of who he is and that is made very clear from his first remarks about Kashmir being an integral part of India. However, in my view, it is not drawn from an understanding of Hindu superiority but an intolerance of any form of communalism and communitarianism. His Tamil identity is closely bound to his Indian identity, but there is no doubt about which takes precedence. In this understanding of Rishi as being defined by science, rationality, modernity, and secularism, he is not a representative of the educated, middle-class, new Hindu male but a representative of the educated, middle-class, old-school, secular male. He seems more like a disciple of Nehru than an acolyte of Advani. His captors certainly seem to see him that way, since he is kidnapped not because he is an average Hindu but because he is an average Indian scientist.

The scene where Rishi throws himself on a burning Indian flag is one of *Roja*'s best remembered scenes. Intercut as it is with shots of Liaquat Khan serenely saying the namaz, it seems to suggest that the Muslim prays, while India burns. Often forgotten is that it is Roja's act of going unaccompanied to a temple that leads directly to Rishi's kidnapping. When put together, both Roja's and Liaquat's religious activities seem to be equally dangerous for Rishi and equally anti-national because it causes harm to the ideal citizen. The film seems to suggest that any religious activity has the potential for manipulation, and though it should be treated with respect, caution must also be exercised. Nehru once stated, this ". . . communalism which is only another name for groupism dividing mankind on some primitive notions and faiths, has no place at a time where science has placed truth at our door step" (Perumal 1992:163), which sounds suspiciously like a quote Rishi might have framed in his office.

If Rishi is a secular, rational man in the model of Nehru and a perfect Nehruvian citizen, then Roja is the constant challenge to that model. If Rishi represents the abstract ideals of the Nehruvian nation then Roja represents the problems with practicing those ideals in the current Indian state. Roja constantly questions the idea that one must be loyal to one's state and nation at all costs. Roja's loyalties and politics are personal because her loss is personal. Words like "jihad" and "*Jai Hind*" hold little meaning for her and she prizes emotionality above rationality. In a place where no one understands her language, she uses primordial human emotions to communicate what her tongue cannot.

In one scene in particular, where she faces the minister at the parade grounds, her Tamil words are initially translated by a conveniently placed aide. As her frustration grows at the minister's willingness to placate her but not take her plea seriously, the translation stops and the minister continues to hear an alien language, but finally listens to the emotion that laces it. The scene ends with the minister assuring her that he will take her case to Delhi. Roja's is a battle against a remote state and a suggestion that its problems are caused not by its secular nature but by its impersonal one. In prizing borders and barbed wires, this state has forgotten its citizens and has therefore forgotten its ideals. Like Rishi, who appeals to the humanity of the militants, Roja appeals to the humanity of the state. The appeal to humanize politics is not just a familiar theme for Mani Ratnam but also seems to be his solution to political problems.

One of Roja's most important dialogues clarifies the gendered politics that inform this problematization. When asked by General Royappa, after yet another futile attempt to find Rishi, where she will go, what she will do on her own, she says she will go from house to house asking about Rishi, appealing to the women of the houses, women like her. In one sense, *Roja* also represents Ratnam's request to his audience to understand that India's public problems have private consequences. The plight of a lone Tamil woman in Kashmir is not very different from the plight of many Kashmiri women, Hindu and Muslim, and also not very different from the plight of Sikh women at the height of the Khalistan movement.

If Rishi is the ideal citizen and Roja rebels against that definition by querying the state's methods, then Liaquat should represent the failure of the state but does not and this is *Roja*'s greatest misstep. Like Rishi, Liaquat is educated in the sciences; he possesses a B.Sc. in agriculture from Coimbatore, which explains his fluent Tamil and signals a time when he thought this country offered him opportunities as a citizen. He is now a militant persuaded by radical Islam and Pakistani rhetoric that those opportunities no longer exist for him. He battles the state of which he was a citizen, preferring to abandon the freedom he once had to a different kind of freedom. *Roja* suggests, as part of its Nehruvian point of view, that the replacement of Liaquat's secularism with fundamentalism has made him less human. Yet, making Liaquat's lack of humanism his defining characteristic is no less awkward than making, as some have suggested, his religion his central characteristic. This is when *Roja* moves into dangerous territory, because in making Liaquat less than human, it places the onus of secularism solely on the individual and not on the state.

In not questioning why an educated graduate would take up arms, *Roja* fails to understand the state's role in Liaquat's evolution or devolution. In the case of Kashmir in particular, where the Indian state has been involved since 1947, not always in very admirable ways, this lack of questioning is inexcusable. *Roja*'s jingoism, so obvious in many ways, also takes these more subtle forms, which is when it becomes most challenging. It is not enough to point fingers at Pakistan or depict Kashmir's loss of innocence, it is important to understand why that loss occurred. It is important to note both the state's role and its responsibilities in that loss. In prizing a Nehruvian idea of an imagined Indian nation, one united by its differences, *Roja* does not document the failures of the Indian state, Nehruvian and otherwise.

By making Roja and Liaquat servile to Rishi in its climax, *Roja* makes every question, concern and issue they stand for servile to Rishi's pure patriotism. It thus propagates an idealistic vision for India that evokes nostalgia but does not offer any concrete solutions to its many problems. *Roja*'s biggest failure, therefore, is that while it mourns the loss of secular values and humanity of some individuals, pleads for the state to investigate other means of settling conflict, and appeals to its citizens to take more responsibility in India's future, it concludes that all this is secondary to Rishi's Nehruvian ideals. It puts forward the notion that with the right kind of patriotism and nationalism, India will thrive. *Roja* extols Rishi's victory, even allowing General Royappa to glance happily at the happy, hugging couple, but never comprehends that the victory is Pyrrhic. Ratnam ends with Rishi and Roja united but we never know what happens to Liaquat. Thus, while *Roja* is a well-made film with good intentions, the shadow of Liaquat looms over its intentions, making them suspect and open to interpretations not as favourable as mine. It may be argued that to expect any different from a commercial Indian film is to not to understand commercial Indian filmmaking, but perhaps the answer lies not in the logic of commercial cinema but in the logic of contemporary Tamil cinema and politics.

Roja is, first and foremost, a Tamil-language film made for a Tamil audience. Its subject may have been national but its audience was regional. It was also made in 1992, at a time when Tamil Nadu politics was in a state of turmoil, as Nicholas B Dirks points out in an essay that is perhaps most kind to Roja's inconsistent ideologies:

> . . . We must recall that the film was made shortly after the political horror of the assassination of Rajiv Gandhi . . . by a suicide bomber, an act of terrorism performed by Sri Lankan Tamil terrorists . . . In this context, a Tamil hero sacrificing himself for the Indian nation in Kashmir readily displaces the guilt by association for the death of

> an Indian national hero on Tamil soil, even as it dramatically enacts the sudden change in Tamil political relations with the national state; after 1991, the Tamil Tigers were designated as enemies of all Indian Tamils and Jayalalitha's government associated itself more comfortably with mainline Indian nationalism . . . (Dirks 2001: 161–162)

Roja, thus, resonates very differently with its Tamil audience. To them, Rishi's and Roja's primary identities are those of Indian Tamils. Their religion is but a small, negligible part of this identity, as is Liaquat's. Liaquat Khan's primary identity is that he is not Tamil and is a threat to the Indian state. Everything else, his religion and dress included, can fall under the category of Ratnam's idea of Kashmiri exotica. He could be easily replaced by a Khalistani militant, an Assamese separatist or even a Bal Thackeray look-alike. They could and would all represent the same other. However, the Kashmir conflict was a contemporary issue and a part of India with which Indian cinema shares a very special relationship . Hence it was the softest target for Ratnam on which to locate his discourse of Tamil and Indian identity, while giving him the opportunity to showcase his style.

What best suggests that *Roja* is a film primarily about Tamil identity in the aftermath of the assassination of Rajiv Gandhi, and a paean to lost Nehruvian values just after the violent death of Nehru's grandson, is the lyrics of its most moving song, *Tamizha Tamizha* (O Tamil!). Originally a poem by Subramanya Bharati, it plays during Rishi's rescue of the blazing Indian flag and when the final credits roll over the frozen frame of Rishi and Roja, reunited on the bridge.

For Rishi's flag heroics, the song lyrics begin midway through the original, referring to the oneness of virtue regardless of the difference of community, the oneness of the land regardless of the difference of place, the oneness of the voice regardless of the difference of language, the oneness of the flag despite its various occurrences, until it finally ends in a lilting chorus, "*Namm India adh ondra tha*" (Our India is one and only one). As Rishi continues to fight, it goes on to talk of a common, modern India whose fundamental ethos is diversity, created after a long, hard struggle, a strong India that should never be separated, finally calling on all people to rise up and defend this land. Here in plain view are Ratnam's Nehruvian buzzwords on which the film is built, "modern," "unity," "diversity," and "human." Interestingly, the lyrics also contain a single word in English—"India."

The entire song then plays over the film's final credits beginning with the reassuring words that tomorrow and the nation both belong to the Tamil and that while Mother Tamil Nadu is the house, one must be firm in one's Indian identity. It then asks the Tamil not to cry, not to be distressed, because tomorrow will dawn. Finally asking rhetorical questions such as whether or not Indian blood flows in Tamil veins, and if it does, then united India will protect the Tamil. Again there are only two non-Tamil word and both are in English—"India" and "Indian."

This song is fundamental to understanding the film. It invokes not the "Hindustan" of the Kashmiri militant or the "*Bharat*" of the Hindutva rank and file but the India of Nehru and of Ratnam. This is not the India of fundamentalist manifestoes but of secular tracts like Nehru's *A Discovery of India*. It addresses not only the Tamil who makes Tamil Nadu his physical home but also the Tamil who makes India his spiritual abode. The dubbed version of this song is the basis for much of the misunderstanding of this film. Its Hindi equivalent begins with "Bharat humko jaan se pyara hai" (India is dearer to us than our life itself) before going on to talk of "*janamabhumi*" (birth place) and clichés of "*mandir*" (temple) and "*masjid*" (mosque). *Roja*'s regional recipe for Indian nationalism is subsumed in the dubbed version by the nationalist rhetoric that can be and has been interpreted as overpoweringly Hindu. It is also worth noting that in the Hindi version, new words enter the lexicon of *Roja*'s vocabulary. Words like "*deshpremi*" or "patriot" are bandied about more freely and the emotional sucker-punch that is Roja's lack of Hindi language skills suddenly does not factor into the equation. With each Tamil word that is erased, a greater depth of meaning is lost and another, almost alien layer is added.

The fact that many of Roja's academic critics, especially those writing in the *Economic and Political Weekly* debate of 1994, refer solely to its dubbed Hindi version to substantiate their arguments does not necessarily make their arguments less potent but it does make them lack some context. Those who do refer to the Tamil original often make minor mistakes such as Bharucha's reference to Roja's village as "Sundar Perumal Puram" (Bharucha 1994:1392). Their arguments are also as much a product of the time they wrote in as the periodin which it was made. Ravi S Vasudevan theorizes along these lines in the sole academic article of the 1994 period that attempted to provide another interpretation of *Roja*'s nationalism. He argues:

> . . . the complication of a certain agenda [emerges] in the radical

> critique of popular cinema. Of late this criticism has been particularly concerned with the way in which cinematic narratives reproduce nationalist ideologies which legitimate oppressive communal and caste perceptions. This approach reflects an impassioned protest against the figuration of the nation in majoritarian Hindu terms, and it has yielded many fresh insights. Yet this body of work may have begun to impose a priori framework of political perception, in the process sidelining the specificity of the cinema, and the complexity of narrative processes. The end result is univocal, with the various narrative elements drawn together in coherent demonology. (Vasudevan 1994:43)

In other words, the valid worries of the secular academics in the aftermath of the demolition of the Babri Masjid and the communal rioting in many parts of the country are as central to their argument as Tamil identity after the death of Rajiv Gandhi is to *Roja*. Just as *Roja*'s reel world refers constantly to the politics of real India, so do these arguments. Their fears while substantiated are not always *Roja*'s fears, their ideology while convincing when viewed in a certain light are not necessarily *Roja*'s. Similarly, the audience response in different parts of India, painful though some of it may be to stomach, cannot always be read back to *Roja*'s intended messages.

Roja is not Mani Ratnam's best film. It is not his only film that deals with politics, it is not the only one that won many state and national awards and is not the only one that is controversial. It is as flawed and fulfilling as many of Ratnam's other, better films. It is as ambiguous and paradoxical and as simplistic and superficial as his other classics. Yet, it is his most successful film to date and his only true all-India success. *Roja* lives on in video stores and film festival retrospectives, on television movie channels and music channels. Its many interpretations allow it to live in many imaginations. It can take on many forms, champion many causes, some more sinister than others, and can still be overanalysed in many an essay, this one included. Though many might roundly disagree, for me the perfect red rose of its title will always signify the Indian man on whose lapel it most famously rested, the film itself signifying an imperfect representation of everything he stood for.

Notes

1. *roja* is a Tamil word meaning 'a rose.'

References

Bharucha, Rustam. "On the Border of Fascism: Manufacture of Consent in *Roja*." *Economic and Political Weekly*. 4 June, 1994. 1389–1395.

Chakravarthy, Venkatesh and Pandian, MSS. "More on *Roja*." *Economic and Political Weekly*. 12 March, 1994. 642–645.

Dirks, Nicholas B. "The Home and the Nation: Consuming Culture and Politics in *Roja*." *Pleasure and the Nation: The History, Politics and Consumption of Public Culture in India*. Rachel Dwyer and Christopher Pinney, eds. Oxford University Press: New Delhi, 2001. 161–185.

Niranjana, Tejaswini. "Integrating Whose Nation? Tourists and Terrorists in '*Roja*.'" *Economic and Political Weekly*. January 15, 1994. 79–82.

Perumal, CA. "Nehru and Secularism." *Explorations of Nehruvian Thought*. VT Patil, ed. Inter-India Publications: Delhi, 1992. 158–166.

Srinivas, SV. "Roja in 'Law and Order' State." *Economic and Political Weekly*. 14 May, 1994. 1225–1226.

Vasudevan, Ravi S. "Other Voices: Roja Against the Grain." *Seminar* 423..November, 1994. 43–48.

Roja. Dir. - Mani Ratnam. Perf. - Arvind, Madhubala, Pankaj Kapoor and Nasser. Prod. - K Balachander and Mani Ratnam (in Tamil) and Babubhai Shah, Fatehchand Shah and Nitin Shah (in Hindi). Music Dir. - A R Rahman. Lyrics - Vairamuthu (in Tamil) and P K Mishra (in Hindi). Story, Screenplay and Dialogues - Mani Ratnam. Cinematography - Santosh Sivan. Editor - Suresh Urs. Madras Talkies (in Tamil) and Hansa Pictures Pvt. Ltd. (in Hindi), 1992.

Power and Representation in Modern Indian Cinema: Case Studies from the Toronto Film Festival (1994)

AHMAD SAIDULLAH

I. Film, and the Failure of the Democratization of Culture

This article aims to establish that *Roja*, *Vidheyan*, and *Pitr, Putr aur Dharmayudh*, screened at the Toronto International Film Festival in the fall of 1994, use various textual strategies to write minorities out of history, while the narratives and subtexts of other Indian films, such as *Ilayum Mullum*, *Hifazat*, and *Bandit Queen*, on the other hand, create interstices for the voices of the marginalized, oppressed communities to emerge, with varying success, in the public sphere.

Cinemathèque Ontario's Noah Cowan and fellow programmer David Overbey spent months in India "seeing a couple of hundred films" before choosing films for the India Now showcase at the Toronto International Film Festival in 1994. "There were over 800-900 films made this year in India," said Uma da Cunha, who helped with the showcase. "Selecting 25–30 films out of that was not an easy task." The programmers selected mostly Bengali, Hindi, Tamil, and Malayalam films from different parts of India.

In a country as culturally diverse as India with its highly politicized mass media, one would expect the presence of a plurality of voices in works of art, but minority filmmakers from India were poorly represented at the festival. In fact, representation did not concern the programmers. "We were concerned with quality primarily," said Cowan. Genre was the key factor in selection. "The goal of the programme was to give a general snapshot of the various genres operating in Indian cinema today with extra weight put on what would appeal to festival goers," said Cowan. Documentary filmmaker Anand Patwardan concurred. "The spectrum of Indian cinema is more than just a sample. They are the best films in the country." Included were commercial cinema, *ciné-romans*, *medium metrage*, and quite a few "socials" in forms that date back to Bombay Talkies days and to later influences of De Sica, Rossellini, and Italian neorealists and Warner Brothers' social-problem films. Best exemplified in the basti films of Gautam Ghose and Sudhir Mishra, the "socials," which dealt with the problems of daily living faced by ordinary people in India, got a lukewarm reception. Patwardan blamed the post-cold war climate which "sees the left point of view expressed in most Indian films screened here as being boring, pedantic and opposed to art."

Maniratnam: Populism and Puppetry

In modern critical practice, the aura of the work of art has not so much been lost in the infinite reproducibility of film in the mechanical age of production, as Walter Benjamin alleged,[1] or transferred to the film star, as it has been displaced to the auteur. Traces of the cult of the auteur still persist in the way Indian cinema is presented to North American audiences (witness the Maniratnam retrospective at the festival) which are, by and large, ignorant of developments in films from the subcontinent. Cinemathèque, which helps to host the festival, usually ignores the products of the most prolific film-producing country in the world in favour of a repertoire of mostly European directors. The prevailing taste of North American festival-goers is for self-reflexive auteurs such as Quentin Tarantino, obsessed with filmness, with fronting techniques, and devices of disruption and discontinuity that encourage a multiplicity of interpretations.

According to Cowan, the Maniratnam retrospective at the Toronto film festival represented "a synthesis of what is interesting in Indian cinema. He has an art sensibility incorporating rich cinematic traditions with genre representation. His cinematic language is unlike other films in India. He is able to create an epic scope in cinema which Hollywood has lost."

A commerce graduate from Madras University and an MBA from Bajaj Institute of Management in Bombay, Maniratnam made his directorial debut in 1983 with a Kannada film, *Pallavi Anupallavi*, which earned him the Karnataka State Award for best screenplay. Since then, most of his work has won official recognition. *Mouna Ragam* (Tamil, 1986) took the national award for best regional film; *Nayakan* (Tamil, 1987) the national awards for cinematography, acting, and art direction;

Gitanjali (Telegu, 1989) the national award for "best picture providing wholesome entertainment"; *Anjali* (Tamil, 1990), nominated for an Oscar, won national awards for best regional film, audiography, and child artistes; while his hugely popular *Roja* (Tamil, 1992), swept awards across the country, playing to full houses in India, Pakistan, and Sri Lanka, and spawned a lot of imitations.

Roja opens with Indian soldiers in a forest hunting down Kashmiri separatists. The leader Wasim Khan is captured. The rest of the film tells a seemingly simple story of Rishi, a cryptologist in Madras, about to be married to a village girl but who, through necessity, weds his bride's spirited sister Roja (played with energy and charm by Madhubala). After a few misunderstandings are cleared up, Rishi is sent to Kashmir to decode messages to separatists intercepted from a foreign source. However, he is kidnapped by another separatist, Liaquat, determined to get his leader Wasim Khan released. Rishi is punished in captivity after he is caught trying to escape. When a separatist burns the Indian flag after hearing that the Indian government will not trade Wasim Khan for their captive, Rishi flings himself on the flag, smothering the flames. Despite mistreatment, Rishi refuses to accede to his captors' demands. In the meantime, Roja persuades the Indian government to release Wasim Khan in exchange for her husband. The swap misfires when Liaquat's men refuse to release Rishi. Eventually, Liaquat's sister helps Rishi escape. In the final confrontation, Rishi persuades Liaquat to "become human" and to give up violence. Roja and Rishi are reunited as Liaquat melts into the forest hunted by Indian soldiers.

Pudovkin's, Cherkasov's, and Eisenstein's beliefs that film was a tool for propaganda effected through the filmmaker's organization of reality left their mark on Indian cinema. The links between nationalist party politics and commercial films, so pronounced with the DMK in the south, have been well documented.[2] That *Roja* reclaims the nationalist Hindutva project for the contested terrain of Kashmir is well-attested,[3] although, at the Toronto press conference, Maniratnam was quick to distance state interests from the film. "This is a question that I have been asked a couple of times since I came here: whether it was propaganda. To be very honest with you, it was the very last thing intended in the film. This film was aimed to bring out the situation in India, and Kashmir was taken as one of the backdrops. It could have happened in Assam, it could have happened in Punjab. It could have happened in any other part of India which is going through this separatist tendency. The film was basically against a group of militants fighting for a separatist India and it was taken from the point of view of an average Indian citizen who didn't want his country to be split into a million pieces."

I do not wish to rehearse the readings unearthed in *Roja*'s text and subtexts that deal with the decoding of such motifs as the temple under military protection and textual signals such as "I'll go anywhere in India. Isn't Kashmir in India?" and "Can't even break a coconut in Kashmir" that are greeted in cinema halls by Hindutva supporters with applause or with "Pakistan Murdabad" and other slogans.[4] It is germane, however, to note that the cooperation of the ministry of defence is acknowledged in the opening credits of the film, that the Indian government went so far as to exempt the film from entertainment tax, and that *Roja* won the national integration award.

The influence of advertising on Maniratnam's work is not limited to jump cutting and other techniques. Through an orientalist-type of approach to its exotic attractions, Kashmir is commodified as the object of desire for tourists, patriots, and the film industry.[5] In *Roja*, he constructs and privileges the consumer as an "average Indian citizen": a middle-class, upper-caste Hindu urbanite male who is in love with the soil of the motherland and who marries a village girl. In ironing out the heterogeneity of the consumer, Maniratnam's films manipulate a view that marginalizes Indian women (Roja's "lovely shape excites the lust for procreation," in the lyrics of one particularly lewd A R Rahman number, and her raison d'être lies only in serving her husband) and Muslim men, inscribed as fanatics, terrorists, or smugglers. In fact, *Roja* erases the presence of Muslim Kashmiris in the act of rewriting history, silences them (Liaquat's sister is mute throughout the film) or disfigures their shadowy presences through stock representations that resonate with Western prejudices against Islam and Muslims. (Ironically, one programmer admitted that *Roja* contained "hot images" such as the flag-burning scene, but saw Maniratnam as a "liberal humanist" whose depictions of women and Muslims were "humane and complex.")

Maniratnam's skill in manipulating syntagmatically the available Hindutva iconographical resources, specifically the Muslim-as-enemy fetishism,[6] is exceeded only by his knack for parading Western art film techniques in Indian dress. With scant regard for its politics, Toronto critics gave *Roja* high marks as exotica. *Globe and Mail* (Toronto) columnist Robert Fulford wrote "no matter how dry and flat North American cinema goes, movies are vividly alive somewhere and are always ready to take us places otherwise unknowable. Ratnam's *Roja* does the job remarkably well. It is a painstakingly obvious piece of Indian propaganda and a musical featuring hypnotically lilting tunes. Imagine *The Sound of Music* combined with *The Killing Fields* scripted by a Stalinist hack. But I wouldn't have missed it for the world."

Although more has been written on Maniratnam's *Roja* than on any other Indian release in recent memory, critics have been reluctant to analyze masala movies as the quintessential Indian film genre.[7] Apologists for these Indian musical extravaganzas derive them from traditional Sanskrit theatre which had become degraded but arguably these spectacles are no more natural or indigenous to Indian culture than *chanchadas* are to Brazil. The technology of film enters India during the colonization period and, despite Dadasaheb Phalke's experiments in the Sanskritization of the idiom in his "indigenous mythologicals," it remains an instrument for the manufacture of consent for the state. Indian producers and financiers have refused to back alternative or serious productions over the years for several reasons. The commercial formula is profitable in distracting the public from dealing with class, caste, and other issues usually by presenting conventional solutions that reaffirm the existing social order. Maniratnam's *Nayakan* seemingly indicts police brutality, slum clearances, union busting, corruption, and the harassment of Tamils in Maharashtra. However, the depiction of these issues is not new or counterhegemonic. Scenes of police brutality and corruption are exploited so often for their shock value in Indian films that, in their repetition, they have become a mere narrative commonplace, tropes emptied of content, subordinated to spectacle and song.

In *Nayakan*, as in most popular Indian films, these social issues are resolved through formulae generic to song-and-dance melodramas that perpetuate the status quo by failing to engage the issues critically. All the loose ends and ethical dilemmas posed in *Nayakan* are recuperated into a coherent whole by the single action of a madman who shoots the anti-hero, or through Ilyarajah's "hypnotically lilting" spectacles that suspend the critical function. A similar dénouement is enacted in *Thalapathy* which "questions the values, customs and privileges of the Tamil elite at the same time as it confirms its appeal and success."[8] (To understand fully why serious cinema has failed to develop popular appeal in India, one would need a detailed critical study of commercial Indian cinema as an agency of state control of masses, which is beyond the scope of this essay.) Maniratnam's decision to make socially contextualized movies in the commercial genre confirms his status as a revisionist filmmaker with populist appeal and a traditional worldview committed to preserving old and imaginary pieties of class, caste, gender, and religion.

Vidheyan: Trembling at Existence

In the mid-1940s, many Christian farmers from the princely state of Travancore moved northwards from the Wynaad hills in British Malabar, where they had been lured by rumours of large tracts of cheap, virgin farmland, to South Karnataka where they were forced to encroach on forest land. Pauperized by social and economic privations in British Malabar, those Keralite emigrants who had not succumbed to malaria faced next the despotism of the Patels instituted by the British to collect taxes and enforce laws in South Karnataka, an arrangement that persisted after independence until the early sixties when land reform legislation brought in revenue "regulars" to replace these chiefs. Adoor Gopalakrishnan, often touted as Satyajit Ray's successor, claims his film *Vidheyan* (The Servile) "can very well stand up as an authentic social document of the life and times of the Keralite immigrants in the feudal setting of a neighbouring state, [but] the concerns of the film go beyond mere realistic portrayal." In his words, it "is a study of the psychology and structure of power—as also an attempt to examine what lies buried beneath an obsessive servility." He claims that "I have used the plot of the story to explore the subterranean landscape of the human mind. Here, terror—the oppressive form of power—joins hands with servility in a pathological alliance of interdependence. Each of them, oppressor and oppressed, is the source of sustenance of the other."

Vidheyan purports to be a parable on the human condition placed within a historical context of a master-slave dialectic. Despite this position, I aim to show that the discourse that dominates *Vidheyan* celebrates the repressive will-to-power, the rule of authority, and the need for oppression. It refuses to legitimize the oppositional discourse of subaltern despair. It excludes, distorts, and deforms the humanity of ordinary people and devalues the role of the oppressed in making history.

In the act of viewing *Vidheyan*, the audience is both witness and judge to a controlled experiment in the psychology of willpower realized in harshly lit interiors and open spaces. The last of the migrants Thommi and Omana, his young wife, cultivate illegally a few acres of forest land before Bhaskara Patelar (played with characteristic bravura by Malayali actor Mamooty), shorn of his legal powers but exercising authority through force, notices them. Patelar terrorizes Thommi, rapes Omana with whom he has an open affair, tries to dynamite the holy fish at the temple ghat at dawn and, while drunk, assaults the rich trader Yusoof Pichai and insults Kuttapparai's newly wed son and his bride, despite his wife Saroja's gentle remonstrations (a luminous performance by Tanvi Azmi). Rather than resist, Thommi's instinct for survival renders him mute and craven without the will to avenge his humiliation. He becomes Patelar's accomplice in these depredations and is made a bartender at a toddy shop. Although he silently protests Patelar's sacrilege at the ghat, Thommi's complicity in oppression is near complete when Patelar's plan to kill Saroja misfires and Thommi gets injured. The farmer's lack of will is demonstrated when Yusoof Pichai and Kuttapparai persuade Thommi to invite Patelar to dinner where they attempt to kill him. Patelar escapes with minor injuries.

Patelar finally kills Saroja but the attempt of the master and the slave to fake the murder as suicide misfires. Patelar runs away and Thommi shelters and feeds him before taking him to his nephew who refuses him refuge. Patelar is finally shot down in a manhunt in the forest. In the end, Thommi picks up his master's rifle and throws it into a waterfall and runs through the wilderness to Omana in a scene that is said to contain the seeds of resistance.

The parallel with the slave fleeing his captors in the final scene of resistance in Thomas Alea's *The Last Supper* is deliberate but spurious. In Vidheyan's construction of history, the ordinary man is trapped in his own destiny, which he is powerless to overcome. Change happens only through the death of Patelar, not through the human agency of resistance. Gopalakrishnan's portrayal does not allow us to identify with Thommi's collaboration and his lack of will to resist victimization. The oppressed Thommi, through his total failure to articulate a challenge to what is illegitimate authority, only evokes contempt. The filmmaker's plea to North American viewers "to pity a character who may be culturally different from you" is dishonest, predicating as it does at the same time our sympathies with Patelar, "a lovable villain" who is allowed a fuller humanity in the eyes of the audience even while raping, assaulting, and killing. One should recall Robert Armes's stricture on Satyajit Ray—"Indeed, part of the problem of the Calcutta `trilogy' lies in the fact that the characters who should be condemned for their actions are allowed to engage us as people."[9]

Pitr, Putr aur Dharmayudh: Sacred and Profane Violence

Pitr, Putr aur Dharmayudh (Father, Son, and Holy War), the last in Anand Patwardan's documentary trilogy on communal violence, explores the roots of male and religious violence in India. Opening with a disquisition on society and matriarchy, *Part One: Trial by Fire* traces the resurgence in sati and the Bombay riots following the destruction of the Babri Masjid in Ayodhya through some powerful footage. *Part Two: Hero Pharmacy* describes the construction of "male" identity in the context of religious strife as Hindus and Muslims assert their manhood through communal violence.

Patwardan's irritating voice-over on the brief historical treatment of ancient societies ruled by female and male principles proves Leni Riefenstahl's dictum that "commentary is the enemy of film art." His equation of violence with patriarchy is a simplistic *gewollt* that deforms the film. To see male violence as a reaction to colonial constructions of the "effeminate Indian" where defeat in political terms was equated with a sense of loss of manhood does not explain why the constructed "enemy" has to be someone of another religion as opposed to, say, someone of another caste. Originally conceived as an inquiry into the Bombay riots, *Pitr, Putr aur Dharmayudh* suffers from the ahistoricity of its approach in failing to explain why, out of the many patriarchal societies in the world, a movement towards fascism is developing in India at this period in history. While *Hero Pharmacy* blames the incursion of Western media in promoting Macho Man and Rambo as role models for boys, the collapse of the Soviet bloc and the concentration of capital as global factors in the emergence of ethnic and cultural nationalisms are glossed over. There is no analysis linking the rise in communal violence to the IMF economic liberalization policies endorsed by the BJP and its supporters, an emergent Hindu urban trader class. Most anticommunalism activists are also aware that communal riots are not the result of a spontaneous urge to assert male sexuality but are premeditated, carefully planned and executed pogroms with clear economic and political motivations. The analytical thrust of the film could have benefited from studies on the mass sex psychology of fascism (Reich's work comes to mind) but what *Pitr* ends up doing is mystifying the issue.

Patwardan studied communications at McGill before returning to India to make his trilogy. His strengths as a filmmaker up to now have been the catholicity of his voices and his control over all facets of film production. His superb *Ram ke Naam*, for example, examined the political exploitation of religion and the rise of Hindu fundamentalism, which led to the demolition of the Babri Masjid in Ayodhya. *Pitr* fails to understand that communalism is practised by the dominant majority community, which imposes its ideology of religious and cultural superiority over other minorities—for example, Hindus over Muslims in India and Muslims over Hindus in Bangladesh and Pakistan. The failure of *Pitr* is the failure of left-wing intellectual versions of secularism movements abroad which perpetuate only their class interests. As the film exemplifies, these auto-representatives of secularism do not always include an understanding of culture in their analysis of communalism, they do not speak for the public, and they do not accommodate the voices of the oppressed communities. This dominance of the secular space by the middle-class Hindu intellectual elite in India has now been countered by public alliances among ordinary working people (specifically between Muslims and Dalits), which are necessary to form a truly national Indian culture.

Pitr takes a feminist approach that is not comprehensive enough to overcome the middle-class intellectual origins of its maker. In the film, a working-class Rajasthani woman refuses to glorify sati, a movement that gained momentum after the 1987 burning of Roop Kanwar on her husband's funeral pyre. A Muslim woman fights against divorce and other discriminatory personal laws. In failing to debunk myths in order to prop its central argument, the film actually promotes the idea that Muslims are given special treatment and that Islam is, by definition, repressive. Besides, feminist views may not necessarily provide the deepest insights into religious violence at this time in India since these discourses have been used in the subcontinent by communalist forces to erode Muslims' rights. The Bharatiya Janata Party (BJP), RSS, and other Hindu fundamentalist groups that form the right-wing alliance known as the "sangh pariwar" welcomed for obvious reasons Taslima Nasreen's criticisms of the shari'a published by the right-wing *Anand Bazaar Patrika* in Calcutta. Also, in the global context, feminist positions on Islam in the "Middle East" have been used to legitimize American foreign policy, strengthen Zionist interests, and subjugate peoples struggling against imperialism. *Pitr* also skirts the importance of Uma Bharati, sadhvis, and other female ideologues in the sangh pariwar in promoting communal violence. Undoubtedly, there is an urgent need for reform within the Indian Muslim community, for which Muslim female and male community activists—Asghar Ali Engineer is one name that comes to mind[10]—are working hard, but a directive for change from the dominant society merely reinforces stereotypes and plays to existing paternalist sentiments in the West.

II. Cinéma Engagé

Ilayum Mullum (Leaves and Thorns)

Jawaharlal Nehru University graduate K P Sasi's feature debut *Ilayum Mullum* (Leaves and Thorns) on the victimization of women in Kerala is a good example of the "imperfect film" which uses amateurs to convey a strong message of the need for social reform. Despite a strong matrilineal tradition and gender parity in literacy and the labour force in Kerala, "eve-teasing" has become a growing social ill. "The culture of any society depends on the way it deals with its women," says Sasi, the son of K Damodharan, former Indian Communist party chief, and a film activist with Alcom (Alternate Communication Forum). In Kerala, he adds, women "are not brutally raped or killed as in the north, but are subtly and persistently exploited at every level, all the time."

Kerala has the highest rates of literacy and suicide in India. "The rising expectations created by universalizing education, and the pressures of unemployment and poverty are [proving] so traumatic that Kerala has the highest rate of suicides in the country, especially among the young."[11] The rise in consumerist culture has resulted in a number of dowry deaths. The father of Parvathy, one of the young women in the film who tries to escape an abusive marriage (the result of insufficient dowry) and later becomes a dowry statistic, tells her that "women should learn to tolerate anything, to lower yourself to earth and don't utter a word." Other saws to inure woman to her fate are: "A woman must suffer," and "If she jumps higher than the man's knee, she'll land in the frying pan." The Malayalam proverb "Whether a leaf falls on the thorn or the thorn falls on the leaf, it's the leaf that suffers," which becomes the title of the film, is reflected in the imagery of a severed leaf which "runs like a leitmotiv through the film symbolizing a woman's helpless, vulnerable situation."[12]

Relying on newspaper reports of certain incidents in Kerala, *Ilayum Mullum* traces the struggle of a group of friends against harassment, which ultimately leads to the deaths of three of the women. Sasi's commitment to making socially meaningful films has resulted in a powerful indictment of the patriarchal forces that shape society, not only preventing women from attaining true equality but also forcing them to take their own lives while blaming "them for their own victimization."[13] The story is told from the female point of view with very few concessions to male values and none to commercialism.

Shantha, Parvathy, Laxmi, and Sreedevi, four spirited young women ferried to work at a cottage-weaving centre across the river by their friend, boatman Krishnan, are constantly harassed by a gang of lumpens at the local toddy shop. Shantha's father, like most of the males in the film, spends his time at the toddy shop and takes out his frustrations over being a bad provider by beating his wife. Outraged at being inspected like cattle, Shantha insults a suitor and his uncle who have brought a marriage proposal. Parvathy, who has been married, writes long letters to Shantha explaining that her husband beats her over the remainder of the dowry. Parvathy dies and only Shantha realizes why.

On the bus, the local panchayat president paws Shantha, who fights back and exposes him. At home, the women are chided for having dared to insult such an important personage. In another incident, Shantha runs into a house when she hears someone following her in the dark. The man who helps her later misbehaves with her as he walks her back. Another day, Raghavan and other louts from the toddy shop taunt Shantha and her companions. When she slaps him, Raghavan pours toddy all over her. Soon the rumours circulate that the women drink and are promiscuous. This leads to more open harassment. Even Krishnan, the raisonneur in the film, refuses to speak to them. They lose their jobs. Unable to deal with the ostracism, Shantha and Lakshmi commit suicide by throwing themselves off the bridge at night. There is an uproar in the village. Raghavan is consumed with guilt. In a move that bodes change, his wife throws him out of the house.

The power of the film lies in its creation of space for the expression of female points of view on oppression. The filmmaking style is uneven and shaky but this adds to the film's authenticity and to the impact of its message. According to Sasi, "Male repression may be more physical and violent elsewhere in India, but the specificity of male violence in Kerala is that it takes a more psychological form and seems to be more subtle. Here's a situation where people can kill and yet not be labelled as murderers." Sasi's sensitive treatment of the subject and the mixture of styles, if not the lesser finesse in his technique, owes a large debt to Ingmar Bergman. The texture and symbolism are surprisingly dense. Sasi's ability to create a constricting atmosphere amid the vistas of rural Kerala is reminiscent of Visconti's mise-en-scène in *Death in Venice* and adds to the force of his vision.

Hifazat (In Custody)

Some time back, communal riots broke out in Bangalore in reaction to a new Urdu radio news service on Doordarshan. Made in a spirit of protest over the trauma of language,[14] Ismail Merchant's directorial feature debut *Hifazat* (In Custody) is a deft screen adaptation of Anita Desai's novel *In Custody* about Nur Shahjahanbadi, the last great Urdu poet. Better known for his "literary films" illustrating the English colonial experience in India, Merchant grew up in a milieu where Urdu, "gracious, grand, poetic and special," flourished. "The contributions of great poets like Ghalib, Meer, Dagh, Pandit Daya Shankar, Naseem, Faiz Ahmed Faiz, Iqbal, Raghupati Sahae, Firaq, and many others have given strength and beauty to our lives," says Merchant. He adds that "the Urdu language and milieu from which it sprang are fast disappearing. In India politicians of every party—themselves Hindi speaking—have undertaken the destruction of something precious which for centuries has contributed to the culture of the subcontinent. Or, to put it another way, they have stood by while an artistic heritage has been allowed to be wiped out."

Shashi Kapoor plays the poet Nur living out his days in Bhopal on biryani and rum in the company of hangers-on and jealous wives. Om Puri is Deven, an Urdu specialist who teaches Hindi at a local college, and who gets permission to record Nur's poetry readings. Deven gets caught in a tussle with the university authorities and negotiates a byzantine intrigue between Nur's second wife Imtiaz Begum, a dancing girl-cum-poetaster who plagiarizes her husband's poems in her bid to appropriate his lustre and to be recognized as an artist in her own right, and Nur's first wife, Safiya Begum. Deven finally manages to spirit Nur to a brothel where he reads his poetry away from the clutches of Imtiaz Begum. The recording is unsuccessful but before his death Nur sends a package to Deven containing some of his unpublished work.

Kapoor seems to have modelled his screen persona on Faiz Ahmed Faiz and Kaifi Azmi, whose form of declamation and physical presence seemed to dwarf any room he was in. Nur's readings (Merchant obtained permission to use Faiz's poetry in the film) provide moments of sublimity that Western audiences will find hard to appreciate. A revolutionary subtext lingers unresolved in Shabana Azmi's nuanced and complex interpretation of Imtiaz Begum's unlikeable character that captures the struggle against tradition and the assertion of female autonomy and individualism. Siddiqui, from the Urdu department, who wants to sell his old mansion and move to the city with his lover best embodies the film's idyll of Urdu as a thing of slowly decaying beauty. The film is steeped in nostalgia and its attempts to confront the new India of Hindutva demagogues may not be anything more than elegiac, dying calls to conserve the past in all its faded glory without engaging the present. The provenance of the film has been questioned; its motives for keeping language and culture in custody are documented in *In Ismail's Custody*, a film on the making of *In Custody*.

Bandit Queen

The hit of Cannes and a *cause célèbre* in India, Shekhar Kapur's film on the life of Phoolan Devi was surrounded by controversy even before it opened in Toronto. Piers Handling, director of the festival, received a letter from Phoolan threatening to sue if *Bandit Queen* was shown. The letter went on to say that the film could only have been made by a male and asked how anyone could show somebody else being raped on screen. Phoolan's anger also arose from the fact that the film had not been shown to her, despite repeated requests.

Commissioned by Channel Four (UK), *Bandit Queen* is a frank account of Phoolan Devi's life as dictated in her prison diaries to Mala Sen. Phoolan operated as an outlaw in the Chambal Valley area from 1978 to 1983 before she surrendered with her gang on her terms before a cheering crowd of ten thousand who saw her as the protector of the poor and the low castes and the scourge of the rich and high-caste thakurs. During her rule, myths had sprung up about the Queen of the Chambal. She was blue-eyed. She was built like an amazon. She was a raven-haired beauty. In reality, she turned out to be a short woman with no distinguishing features, who came from a low-caste Hindu household and had been sold, according to the film, to her husband Puttilal at the age of eleven for a cow and a bicycle. She ran away a few times from her husband who continued to molest her. Eventually, he remarried. Phoolan first got into trouble with the police over a dispute with her cousin Maiyadeen who is not mentioned in the film. She was raped while in custody. She was then taken into Baba Gujjar's gang of dacoits. (It is uncertain whether Gujjar raped her or if she was his lover.) Phoolan fell in love with Vikram Mallah and formed her own gang after Baba Gujjar's death. She was captured by Lala Sriram's men, mostly thakurs, and gang raped for twenty-three days. Phoolan later became notorious for the Behmai massacre in which she was alleged to have killed thirty thakurs. After her surrender, she was imprisoned for eleven years without trial.

During her stay in jail, doctors operated on her for a routine illness and allegedly removed her uterus to avoid "breeding others like her." She was released by special order of the Supreme Court in February 1994 by which time Shekhar Kapur had completed the film.

A critic called it "another film where the camera knows no decency" and resented "the direction that induces a sense of helpless complicity in an atrocity. Or repeated atrocities." Phoolan Devi herself denounced the film as a fake and called its recurring scenes of rape a vyapar ("business"). The Indian censor board, concerned about the content and language, ordered massive cuts to the film. It is doubtful if Channel Four and the director will agree to release the film in India under those conditions but should it survive uncut the bourgeois liberal mores of Manmohan Singh's India, *Bandit Queen* will spawn a genre of explicit exploitation films once endemic to the West. However, while the film observes the canons of Hollywood outlaw films, its depth of characterization and maturity of presentation, the direction and its subtexts on civilization, savagery, and the loss of innocence rescue it from being an ordinary actioner of the Bollywood variety.

For its defenders, what prevents *Bandit Queen* itself from being an exploitation film is that the story is told mostly from Phoolan's point of view (played with fortissimo by Seema Biswas) and in her own words. For them, *Bandit Queen* tells an unsentimental tale of caste and gender oppression in rural India, of resistance and victimization, betrayal and surrender, and tells it unflinchingly, but its crucial dilemmas lie outside the cinema hall in the courts over the individual's right to privacy. The film's claim to be "the true story of Phoolan Devi's life" is *sub judice* and will determine the future of the film.[15] In occupying the space of a living subject, the filmmaker is vulnerable in what he has done and in the nature of the truth he has succeeded in conveying rather than in what he had hoped to achieve. The rape scenes may not be exploitative but the camera's intrusions on the territoriality of a living subject and the overplays on the "artistic" imaginings of Phoolan's sexuality violate the subject as much as some of the more humiliating acts in the film, undertaken as they are with the assurance of foreign capital arrogating colonial resources, which led one viewer to call it "the most exploitative, most sickening and the most neo-colonial film I have ever seen." This male-constructed dynamic of female sexuality, this "look" which mirrors others in the dominant discourses on women as victims, transports *Bandit Queen* to the paternalist "symbolic order" of Indian and Western film traditions. Although the film lacks intellectual subtlety and its

Lacanian symbolism is contrived rather than organic—take the girl at the well at the Behmai massacre—its obvious sympathy for the subject makes it one of the more powerful expressions of resistance to oppression ever to reach the silver screen.

Notes

1. Walter Benjamin, "The Work of Art in the Age of Mechanical Reproduction," in *Illuminations*, ed. Hannah Arendt, tr. Harry Zohn (New York: Schoken, 1969) p.221ff and T W Adorno, Aesthetic Theory, p.309.

2. Erik Barnouw and S Krishnaswamy, *Indian Film* (New York and London: Columbia University Press, 1963) pp. 172–6.

3. Tejaswini Niranjana, "Integrating Whose Nation? Tourists and Terrorists in *Roja*," *Economic and Political Weekly* 15, January 1994, pp. 79–82; Venkatesh Chakravarty and M S S Pandian, "More on *Roja*," *Economic and Political Weekly* 12, March 1994, pp. 642-644; Tejaswini Niranjana, "*Roja* Revisited," *Economic and Political Weekly* 21, May 1994, p. 1299; and Rustom Bharucha, "On the Border of Fascism: Manufacture of Consent in *Roja*," *Economic and Political Weekly*, June 4, 1994, pp. 1389–1395.

4. Niranjana, "Integrating Whose Nation?" p. 79.

5. Niranjana, "Integrating Whose Nation?" pp. 80–81.

6. Sumit Sarkar, "The Fascism of the Sangh Parivar," *Economic and Political Weekly* 30, January 1993, pp. 164–5.

7. Robert Armes, *Third World Filmmaking and the West* (Berkeley and Los Angeles: University of California Press, 1987) pp. 25, 65.

8. Ravindran Vaitheeswaran and Kandasamy Illanko, "A Rose among Thorns," *Toronto South Asian Review*, Spring 1993, p. 92.

9. Armes, p. 241.

10. Asghar Ali Engineer, "Status of Muslim Women," *Economic and Political Weekly*, February 5, 1994, pp. 297-300 and "Social Change and Modernization," *Seminar* 416, April 1994, pp. 28–33.

11. Sheela Reddy, "Eve-teasers storm bastion of women's emancipation," *The Pioneer*, February 9, 1994.

12. Raj Kamini Mahadevan, "Chauvinism of a Subtler Kind," *The Telegraph* (Calcutta), n.d.

13. Reddy, "Eve-teasers storm bastion."

14. See Athar Farooqui, "Urdu Education in India: Four Representative States," *Economic and Political Weekly*, April 2, 1994 pp. 782 ff. for a discussion of the factors.

15. Madhu Jain, "*Bandit Queen*: The Truth on Trial," *India Today*, October 15, 1994, pp. 92–4.

References

Adorno, Theodor. *Aesthetic Theory*. Eds. Gretel Adorno and Rolf Tiedemann. Trans. C. Lenhardt. London and New York: Routledge and Kegan Paul, 1984. 309.

Phoolan Devi's Open Letter to the Director of the Toronto Film Festival

September 7, 1994

Dear Director Sahib,

My name is Phoolan Devi. I cannot read or write, so I am asking a friend to write this to you.

I have been told that at your festival you are showing a film called *Bandit Queen* that is supposed to be the story of my life.

I have never met the people who made the film, and I have not been shown this film. I have asked them to show it to me, they have refused. They have given everybody the impression that I am being contradictory and that I did not want to see it. This is totally untrue.

I have been told that the main theme of this film is about how I was raped. And how many times. I have never once spoken of my rape, to *anyone.*

I would like to ask you sir, you and your audience what you would feel if you knew that the most private and humiliating moments of your life were being screened for other people's entertainment. Without your permission, without you having been shown the film.

If this film had been about the rape and humiliation of your daughter, of your wife, your mother or your sister, however well made the film was, would you have shown it at your festival? Would you sell tickets for the show?

I think you must be a man. Just like the makers of this film are men. I cannot imagine that a woman would do this to another woman. Anything else, but not this.

My humiliation and my shame is not for sale. Not for any price.

While you watch this film about me, while you enjoy my misery, I want you to know that I will fight this for as long as I have breath in my body.

Tomorrow an Indian Judge at the Delhi High Court will hear my plea.

As soon as I can find the money to hire a lawyer abroad, I will sue you and your festival and everyone else that is party to this shameful exploitation.

I request the public of Toronto not to participate in my humiliation. *I* would not go and watch *you* being raped, if I knew that you didn't want me to. Please don't go and watch this film. At least not until I have seen it.

Please try and understand, that whatever I may have done, I am a human being. Not an animal. I have feelings. I have a family. I have spent eleven years in prison.

I am thirty-two years old, and have a life ahead of me.

Statement From the Director of the Toronto International Film Festival

September 9, 1994, 3 P.M.

Attached you will find a letter from Phoolan Devi. Her story was the source of the film *Bandit Queen* which we are showing at this year's festival. We are obviously concerned by the accusations she makes in her letter.

I have talked to the producers of the film, Film Four who are based in London, England, and the director of the film Shekhar Kapur. They have an arrangement with Phoolan Devi and she was paid a fee. The film is based on testimony which she gave to a prison warder. Mala Sen wrote a book based on this testimony. Her screenplay is based on her book. Phoolan Devi has publicly gone on record regarding her rape. She has also met the people who made the film. I have been reassured by them that the film attempted at all times to be faithful to her story. Indeed, it is a sympathetic treatment of her life which finally celebrates her release from prison. *Bandit Queen* has also been shown at two other major international film festivals.

The film has recently been banned in India for reasons of content. The nudity and language depicted exceed the codes established by the Indian censor board. They have asked the director, Shekhar Kapur, to make approximately ten substantial cuts to the film before they allow it to be passed.

We are very concerned about images which denigrate women, and indeed any images which can be construed as racist, homophobic or misogynist, or which celebrate needless violence. We do not feel that *Bandit Queen* condones any of the above.

We have therefore decided to screen the film as announced.

Piers Handling
Director, Toronto International Film Festival

Press Statement

8 September 1994

The film Bandit Queen is based on the prison diaries of Phoolan Devi. These diaries were dictated in Hindi to a prison warder and from them Mala Sen, the writer of Phoolan's biography pieced together the story. The script for the present film was written by Mala Sen based on that biography. The film which was financed by Channel 4, went into production in 1993, was produced by Bobby Bedi and directed by the well-known Indian director Shekhar Kapoor.

The film ends with a written statement on screen celebrating the fact that Phoolan Devi was released from jail in February this year.

Channel 4 very much regrets that Phoolan Devi has now seen fit to bring proceedings to prevent the exhibition of the film in India. This is especially so as she signed agreements which clearly state that the producers had permission to film the story and base it on her accounts and furthermore that she had no objection to the making, and distribution of the resulting film. The producers paid money to Phoolan Devi for her contribution to the film.

Channel 4 refute the allegations made by Phoolan Devi which we consider are both unwarranted and without merit and will be vigorously defending the proceedings now under way in India.

Defining the Truth: An Interview with Shekhar Kapur

AHMAD SAIDULLAH

(Shekhar Kapur is the director of *Bandit Queen.*)

AS: Bandit Queen *as a film is as far as you can get from* Satyajit Ray. *Some people think that you have not made an Indian film but a Western film on India. Would you like to comment on that?*

SK: Yes, very much. You see, even film develops its own grammar. It develops its own theories and the theories and grammar really depend on what someone has done and been successful at. There was grammar in the beginning. There was no theory in the beginning. I know a lot of people are taken aback by the film and although a huge number of people have come out in favour of the film, most people can not take it because they believe the camera should be confined into a gentlemanly frame like Mr Ray did . . .

I'm not a filmmaker like Mr Ray. I'm a more extroverted filmmaker. I like my audience not so much to think as to feel. There's a slight difference. Whereas he would like to go to the heart from the mind I want to go to the mind through the heart . . . I like to grab the audience emotionally and through that try to make them think. He likes to grab them intellectually and through that try to make them feel. It's a different approach. I got upset with that kind of filmmaking. Not because it is not brilliant—he's absolutely brilliant—but to me it's too dominated by what I call armchair filmmaking so that you are comfortably watching. You know, I've said this before and I'll tell you again. [The place] where all the film industry [people] live in India, you have to pass a little street which we call Shit Street to go to your studios because all the women from the slums come out and shit there in the morning and everybody passing in their cars there roll up their windows and turn up their air-conditioning and they don't look and all those women expose all their parts except they have little black umbrellas and they hide their faces. Now, of course, everybody notices it and you have a choice. You can put your camera inside the car. You can take a long shot which would be a gentlemanly, comfortable view. It's a nice way to make a film. Or you can take the camera right there and smell it and try and be with those women who have to do it. I chose to do that. I chose to do that because I am normally known for very nice family films that you can take your kids to see and have a great time and cry a little and laugh a little and come back. In this film I chose to take the other point of view, to make it not from the point of view of the sophisticated film-going viewer but make a film from the point of view of the women sitting there. So I made it from the point of view of an oppressed low-caste woman. It is a totally different kind of filmmaking. I'm trying to explain why. I'm not saying I'm more relevant than Mr Ray. Both kinds of cinema are totally relevant. That's why people say it's Western because Hollywood directors generally will go that way. This was not an attempt to copy Hollywood directors. In our commercial films in India we do the same in any case. It's quite possible that since my training has been in commercial cinema, I [also] have gone this way.

AS: *It's inaugurated a new grammar for Indian films all right. But tell me what kind of audience do you have in mind? I think nudity, gang-rape, child rape, things of that sort would not get past the censors in India and, from what I understand, Britain. The first line of the film is "Main hoon Phoolan Devi, behanchod [I am Phoolan Devi, sisterfuckers]." There's a problem with screen violence also.*

SK: No, it got through the censor in England. There's no problem. My primary market is India. All filmmakers are coming to me and saying "Make this a test case." The message that the censor board is giving now is: "Listen, you guys. Stick to making films about overgrown people running around trees and singing songs to each other." I don't believe the film is vulgar. I believe that I have presented everything in it fairly and I have a left a lot to the imagination. In the gang-rape scene, you don't see any skin at all and in the place where she walks naked, the shots—there is absolutely no sensuality there—long, unabashed, unashamed, humiliating shots. I just hope Channel Four backs me up.

AS: *Reception to your film has been quite polarized. Some have described it as a picaresque-politico like Francesco Rosi's* Salvatore Guiliano. *Others see it as sensationalistic, Sergio Leone kind of curry western that lacks subtlety and depth. Then, it's also been called the most important Indian film ever made. Somebody said that Indian cinema has finally come of age with*

Bandit Queen. *Where do you place your film in the context of these varying opinions?*

SK: I just went out to make a film very, very honestly but then every filmmaker says that . . . I had no reference points [for this] film [from films] made anywhere else in the world . . . I was dealing with many issues. I was dealing with a woman who was still alive. I was dealing with a story I could not change. I was dealing with a woman everybody knew. So it's not like I was making *Zapata* because Zapata was dead and it was not like making *Gandhi* because Gandhi is dead and passed into legend. This legend [of the Bandit Queen] is still alive, [it is] about my age and a woman who was in jail. A woman who the world had forgotten about at that time. What I am writing about is *sub judice* in court. She came out of jail after I had finished the film . . . I had to depend on nothing but my own instinct . . . What else is honesty if not instinct? Your instincts will give you a truth which is yours, maybe not other people's. So that your instinct is your truth. Intellectually, you have a hundred [truths]; instinctively, you have one. Let me go inside myself and dig it out of there. I went on a whole journey of self-discovery to make the film . . .

Looking back at it, I have discovered that if you see it a second or third time—I have never seen an Indian film [and] very few foreign films, that have so much subtext in them. And I think that I find *Bandit Queen* a good film because there's so much in it, so many messages, you can't take them all in at one time . . . When I see it, I discover myself again . . .

There is a whole body of subtext beyond the emotional responses that you have and I think that's what makes it such an important film in terms of cinema . . . There is that one scene when there's nothing—there's a man on a loudspeaker and there's a woman hidden. I mean the kind of trauma people go through in that scene in the end just before she gives up. We were talking about sexual oppression. What was that? Was it sexual? No, it's power. You can see it in that guy's face. You can see it in the words he says. It's power expressed through sexuality. In any case it's a film with a huge body of subtext . . .

AS: *Phoolan's reaction has been quite outspoken. She denounced the story as a "fake." Is there any kind of rapprochement or communication between you two?*

SK: No. I met her when she first came out of jail and then I came abroad. Then she got married. She married a thakur. She got so embroiled in the marriage and this and that. And when she came out she became a political star so I thought "let that die down and then I'll go and meet her again." By that time, the whole thing exploded. I was in England or someplace, Edinburgh. Suddenly the whole thing exploded. I haven't been back since this thing came out. I think it's a bit irresponsible of the Channel Four producer not to show her the film. I think that's irresponsible. Yes, I am partly responsible for the way I wanted it shown to her because it's traumatic for people who watch it so it'll be traumatic for her. Make sure she is surrounded by people she trusts and people who care about her, that's all. I don't know whether it's possible she can find people she can trust, people who care about her. India is a political place. It's a very complicated place. India is a place where, as you know, if a person has an accident there'll be thirty people watching and sitting there till the person dies and nobody will lift a finger. Just watching. You know that. So when somebody becomes a political star people just hang on. Tons of people telling her to do this, say this, do this do that, say that. So whose mind actually wrote that letter? It's not her language. It's obviously a person with a Western-type education. I'm sorry that this has happened.

The film is not a fake. That's absolutely obvious. All the major incidents happened. There's a record of them happening in her own words and in many cases in the police records, and [there are] witnesses and people who talked about it. My source has been all the press publishings plus Mala Sen's book . . . and everything that has been written about her. So, it's not a fake. Yes, the interpretation: did she and Vikram make love like that? That's interpretation. Did she go to the temple before she went to Behmai? Was this the way they walked, talked? This is artistic interpretation. But all art is interpretation. Even a documentary really is interpretive. A feature is even more interpretive. But of course she was married at eleven. Of course she was taken by a man called Puttilal at thirteen. These are her own words in the book that I've used. "*Kab badi ho gi? Arre, aa ja jaldi se* [When will you grow up? Come closer quickly]." He went and said to her "You are my little theether [partridge]." "He used to call me and fondle me all the time. I had no idea that this is what marriage was all about." That's in her own words. The fact that she and Vikram were lovers, that's true. Now if she comes across and says "Vikram and I never indulged in any sexuality," that's going to be hard to believe. The fact that Baba Gujjar raped her—I've heard many versions of that. She says he raped her. A lot of people tell me she was Baba Gujjar's lover before that. I hope and wish that all these people who are trying to dig a case out—

two filmmakers have done it—against me, ultimately [make it] a defamation case. In the ultimate analysis, if they really care about Phoolan Devi, what are we going to say in court? The whole thing is a film.

In the final analysis, does it come out in sympathy . . . with her or against her? I am absolutely sure, from my own reaction, and most people who have seen the film [believe], it comes up in sympathy with her and the plight of women like her. So why all this? I don't understand it. And you have to look at the film in its totality. Of course, you can come and say, "Oh, how can you be showing Phoolan Devi making love with Vikram Mallah? Take that out. How can you show Phoolan Devi cussing? Take that out. How can you show Phoolan Devi being raped? Take that out." What are you making? A film? They said "Cut out profane language from the film." I just hope Channel Four backs me up.

AS: *You mentioned the script, which is based on Mala Sen's account of Phoolan Devi's prison diaries. Some people have noted gaps in facts and omissions. From my point of view, I thought perhaps including the story of Kusman Nair who was rejected by Vikram Mallah, which may have led to his death at the hands of the Sriram gang which she joined out of pique, could have added another layer of dynamics and tensions to the film.*

SK: First, it's a two-hour film. Second, you don't want to confuse the audience. Either you have to tell the whole tale or tell a selected tale. When you tell a selected tale it has to have a context. The contexts are: violence through sex, oppression through sex and, as you said right at the beginning, the caste system . . . [The story of Kusman Nair] is relevant to the private story of Phoolan Devi. It's not relevant to the context [of the film] because then I would have to explain more. . . I would have had to show the whole backdrop—why Vikram was having an affair with Kusman Nair, what was the relationship between Phoolan and Vikram, if Kusman was involved. Another thing that I left out—a very major thing—I left out the way Chaturvedi eventually got her to surrender. The whole politics of what was happening in the outside world when Phoolan Devi was operating here is another story, a huge story. After Behmai, the whole UP government was brought down. It's a television serial then, because I can't just flash by it without explaining the context. So I decided to just stick to this one core.

AS: *There is a scene that is key in the logic of the film leading up to the Behmai massacre. Could you elaborate on that scene in which Phoolan Devi is stripped at the well in public view by Lala Sriram? What problems did Seema Biswas have in playing that scene?*

SK: Seema had a problem. She had a nervous breakdown when she tried to do it. Because by that time the line between actor and character had blurred. The characters had merged. So when she tried to do it, it was her walking naked. She had an absolute nervous breakdown. I thought I would cause her serious psychological problems if I made her do it then. But I am sure that's what Phoolan Devi must have felt. So I told her, "Just remember what you felt now and then let's not shoot it right now. Let's dissociate yourself from the character." So we took four months off by which time she gathered herself together, became Seema Biswas again and not Phoolan Devi, isolated herself from the character and could look at it objectively that she was playing somebody who was doing it and that it was not happening to her. That was essential. Four months later, we went back to shoot it. I promised her and I promised everybody in my unit who was very scared. I said, "None of the rape scenes will have any sensuality or any sexuality in them." And I said again, "In this scene nobody is going to whistle in India"—Indian audiences are famous for that. I had two trials in Bombay for my film friends. Their drivers came to see the film—you know, all young, star drivers like heroes. I saw them crying in that scene. I saw tears coming down their eyes. I know why. As filmmakers, we know why. There is no hint of embarrassment in shooting that. It is as unabashed as a person sitting there watching and you almost lower your eyes because you have a full view. There is never a close up of her body or anything. There's either a close up of her face or a very wide shot. And you see not the sexuality; you see in nakedness pity. Sexuality in film is always helped along by the filmmaker. Sometimes the filmmaker takes a neutral, long point of view, allowing the viewer himself or herself to take an attitude and this attitude will be dominated by what the subtext of the film is saying. That's what happens in that film. I have not taken an attitude except a very long shot. So, it is the previous scene confirming the attitudes with which the viewer is watching that scene.

AS: *I did not find the scene exploitative. In fact, it arouses pity. However, there are other sexual scenes. It is uncommon for female sexuality, especially aggressive female sexuality to be shown on the Indian screen. Some feminists see this as a film of resistance against male oppression. Social critics see it more as a fight against caste oppression. Do you find these readings simplistic?*

SK: No, I don't think they are simplistic at all. The context of the individual is only relevant in the context of the environment. To me the caste system, the caste war that is going on and the caste oppressions that have been there for many, many years is the context in which Phoolan Devi's story becomes relevant in a much larger sense. As well, it's not so much as fighting back male oppression to me. To me, there's another. A woman is the easiest prey and a low-caste woman is *the* easiest prey. What for? It's not sexual domination. It is when man feels the need to go out and dominate something and the easiest kind of person to dominate is woman. So I don't see rape or anything like that as a sexual act at all. It is one kind of human being which is woman being used by another kind of human being which is a man as a tool for his own insecurities in the ultimate analysis. You feel insecure inside so you feel the need to assert yourself. You need to kick butt, as they say... It's no different from skinheads walking around and finding an old man and kicking him. It's the same thing. That's what man does. So just because there's a rush of blood into your male organ at the time does not mean it's a sexual act at all. So [that's] what I've tried very hard to do in this film . . . to say it's a question of oppression, because man needs to oppress to overcome his own insecurities. For Phoolan Devi it destroyed her sexuality. Therefore she had problems in the first scene with Vikram Mallah and had to reassert herself. That is sexuality. That is why I am so surprised [at] all these people, all these women, who are writing these letters. They talk about it as rape. Phoolan Devi wrote—you must have heard about that—to the festival and said—the words were: "How would you feel if somebody showed the shame and humiliation of your daughter, your mother or your sister raped on screen?" For God's sake, who wrote this script? Who wrote these lines? Isn't that what the world is fighting against? Isn't that what the film is fighting against? Why should it be the daughter's or mother's shame? If an old man is being kicked to death, is it his shame? Or is it the shame of the people who do it? I expect this [sort of] letter from the rapists . . . Why is the shame of rape put upon the victim, and certainly somebody like Phoolan Devi should not feel that shame because she reacted so strongly to it in her own life.

AS: *It's interesting that you talk about sexuality in terms of power. Throughout the film, sexuality is linked with violence and death. Would you say that the central themes of your film are tensions created by betrayal and the loss of innocence and resistance and surrender?*

SK: No, I don't think that's it. I don't think there's that much difference between civilization and savagery. If you look at human behaviour, it's like an iceberg . . . The tip of the iceberg is what constitutes how we will behave towards people. So the difference between civilization and savagery exists just in the tip of the iceberg and it doesn't take very long to change from one to the other. I have an empathy even towards these thakurs because they also are victims. . . That's the reason that people have interpreted the child at the massacre in many, many ways. To me, it wasn't because Phoolan Devi was naked at the well, it was as if these people, the people who are killing, the people who are dying, the people who raped are not far away. So when you say "It's a loss of innocence," yes. The central theme in my film, in all films, is the loss of innocence and I don't think we are that far away from that child though. Innocence can be lost like that. And therefore if you looked at the massacre at Behmai that was the reason for all the top shots. That's what I'm saying. That in all these things they are all equal, in death, in oppression. Ultimately human beings are equal in one cauldron and there's one child standing up and that one child is representing to me the fact that "Where did we go wrong?" We just went wrong somewhere. We are not that far from that child but even "that far" creates all these divisions and oppressions.

AS: *You talked about the scene with Vikram Mallah where she has problems relating to him sexually. There's another scene where she's sitting on top of Vikram Mallah. Vikram Mallah's a very gentle romanticized figure and for Western audiences almost a Christ-like figure whereas Phoolan Devi has a kind of aggressive sexuality. Was that an interpretation?*

SK: Yes, that's an interpretation. I tried to shoot Phoolan Devi through her eyes. Everything she said in her book and everything that her mother said, everything that I've read about Vikram Mallah was totally different from what other people said about Vikram Mallah or told me about Vikram Mallah. But I selected her point of view. I understood that here was a woman who needed to remember one relationship in respected, romantic terms, so let me give that in the film. I understood that there is a female aspect in a man. We are all male and female. When that balance gets totally upset, you become too much of the oppressor. I tried to give him female characteristics so I selected an actor that had an ethereal kind of look—he wasn't macho-looking or musclebound—and who would give, and who did not need constantly to assert himself sexually and was the kind of person she needed at that time to be able to assert her own sexuality.

AS: *On the topic of politics and violence, Mulayam Singh Yadav got Phoolan released from jail. He used that occasion to justify the fact that a lot of people in his government had criminal records. He blamed that on thakur-police complicity. And now we hear that Phoolan Devi is being groomed for the Samajwadi party. Do you want to comment on that aspect of Indian politics?*

SK: I've never been of any doubt that she is being groomed for a political career. I am not sure whether she is going to be standing for elections directly or whether she'll be asked to support a candidate. My suspicion is that she is going to be asked to support a candidate. That's one of the reasons I've always had a doubt whether Phoolan Devi or anybody else, her supporters, would stand up for the film because in India to become a political leader means you have to have the respect of men. Men can only respect you once you've crossed menopause. You have to be Sita, the mother, the goddess, or a woman after menopause. The film reminds people of her being a woman, a sexually active woman. They didn't want that. That's part of the politics all over the world really. I keep saying India because that's where I live but I see this as part of politics all over. So I'm not surprised that everybody is harping on the sexuality of the film so much. Politics is in the ultimate analysis an attempt to gain power. I seem to have lost the faith to [believe in] an honest politician. There isn't one . . . It's not that power corrupts. You are already corrupted and therefore you want a lot of power.

Bollywood's Female Fantasies of Resistance: Online Fan Discourse and Modern Indian Identity

JENNIFER THOMAS

At the end of *Sholay*,[1] Hema Malini performs a dance that encapsulates the many paradoxical expectations forced onto female Bollywood stars. As her character Basanti dances barefoot over broken glass to save her lover's life, Malini is at once a modest and chaste daughter of a traditional Indian village, a modern independent career woman, a seductive courtesan performing to a crowd of lustful men, a future devoted wife, and a courageous self-sacrificing hero. Her performance in *Sholay*, one of the most popular films in the history of Hindi cinema, made Malini an extremely empowering role model for Indian women. According to a reception study of the film, women were attracted to her character for the ways she resisted patriarchal ideals of femininity: her talkative outgoing personality, and her active involvement with the exploits of the male leads, "two professional law-breakers."[2] The study also reveals that this identification with the character Basanti was bound up with gossip about Malini's personal life. She had had a well-publicized affair with her already married on-screen love interest from *Sholay*, Dharmendra, and she eventually married him in spite of some ruthless public scorn. For her fans, Malini's on-screen and off-screen personas synthesized to form a role model that was at once traditional and modern, and both exceptional and realistic.

A few decades prior, Nargis and her various on-screen personas provided a similar model for female identification. As Rosie Thomas has described in her study of *Mother India*,[3] Nargis's very modern star persona inflected her character Radha's very traditional virtues and way of life. Within the film, she was characterized as a virtuous, modest, and self-sacrificing mother with traditional values. But off-screen, Nargis's persona was riddled with scandal: rumours of her sexual exploitation by courtesans and the scandalous public knowledge of her adulterous affair with her long-time co-star, director, and producer, Raj Kapoor. After the success of *Mother India*, Nargis's off-screen persona was radically transformed. She married her co-star Sunil Dutt, and left the film industry for a traditional family life. Thomas argues that these off-screen details, and the elaborate stories that surrounded them, added nuance to Nargis's performance as Radha, and inflected her character's metaphoric signification of India as a nation, making *Mother India* "a site of extraordinary emotional potency and clear political effectivity . . . in the area of gender relations or the narrower forum of national politics" (29). As "Mother India," Nargis could be perceived as an emblem of the nation's purity and, at the same time, a symbol of a nation that had fallen from grace. Within her image, rebellion collided with motherhood, free love with sexual restraint, glamourous luxury with extreme poverty, and fame with modesty.

The persona of any given Bollywood star is determined through multiple layers of discourse. Seasoned Bollywood spectators often entwine characters with a star's personal life, his or her previous on-screen personas and multiple sources of fan gossip. Fans often infer romantic connections from on-screen chemistry between characters, and rumours about a star's personal life can both tarnish and enhance her or his on-screen performances. Thomas's study of Nargis and the case of Hema Malini reveals that this fan discourse worked to negotiate the personas of female stars in the classical period of Bollywood cinema. This function of fan discourse not only persists, it has also intensified. A greater polarity of expectations now binds contemporary female Bollywood stars. Indian nationalism still puts a great deal of stake in traditional representations of women's bodies. In Thomas's words, the female body "is used as a metaphor for purity, and hence the 'purity' of traditional values for an ideal society uncontaminated by colonial oppressors, and for India itself."[4] In the face of the processes of globalization, this need to preserve the "purity" of the nation has become more desperate. Yet the enhanced modernization of Indian society requires female stars to reflect the modern aspirations and lifestyles of their viewers. In order to remain viable role models, they need to align with the social realities that are now often in conflict with traditional mores. Consequently, as public models of ideal Indian womanhood, the personas of female stars must oscillate between the conflicting demands of traditional and modern values, and both nationalist and feminist agendas.

The dynamics of fan discourse have also intensified since the classical period with the introduction and popularization of the internet in India. Online forums have become a popular venue for public expression and social interaction amongst the youth in India. Within these communities, young web-savvy fans discuss at length celebrity style, characters, plots and casting choices, as well as cultivate rumours about Bollywood stars and their personal lives, in particular their off-screen romances.

While somewhat unconventional, the use of spectatorial responses like these discussion forums as points of research is not without precedent. For her 1991 essay "Feminine Fascinations: Forms of Identification in Star-Audience Relations," Jackie Stacey put out an open call to American female cinema goers for letters discussing the appeal of Hollywood stars of the 1940s and 1950s. While this approach to spectatorship had its methodological shortcomings,[5] by approaching audiences directly she was able to analyze those identification processes that women actively participate in. She writes that "identification does not simply involve the passive reproduction of existing femininities, but rather the active engagement and production of changing identities."[6] Here, I too am looking to the female spectator's active use of star personas in their identity construction, as well as the more general social spectator's active use of fan discourse to shape, control, and contain those star personas. The discussion forums are a venue for this discourse. Because they are anonymous, uninhibited, and not accountable to the authority of the film industry or government officials, fans can use the forums as a check on the industry's power to construct models of female identity. By making their own meaning out of a star's persona, and sharing that meaning within a public space, the online forum users negotiate their ideals of femininity and by association their collective identity and rapport with modernity.

Taking both Stacey's and Thomas's models as points of departure, in what follows, I analyze the discourse fostered on these fan forums in relation to cinematic texts that have shaped the personas of two prominent contemporary female Bollywood stars: Rani Mukherjee and Preity Zinta. By supplementing textual analysis of their on-screen performances with the passionate responses of Bollywood fans online, I demonstrate the multiple layers of discourse at work in negotiating these female stars' personas. Through this analysis, I show that Bollywood audiences actively work in relation to the films to contain and define female star personas in accordance with competing pressures of traditionalism and modernity.

My first example, actress Rani Mukherjee, has been constructed as an ideal model for traditional Indian femininity. Much of this construction relies on her adherence to traditional modes of dress in both films and public appearances. As one fan forum contributor describes:

> In parties, premiere shows or press meets, she is hardly seen in skimpy dresses. She loves to rock the sari though without showing mid-riff. All bold scenes she has done, have received high critical acclaims. Simply titillating audiences is not her way. Rani is truly a good girl in the tinsel town.[7]

Fans pay a great deal of attention to Rani's clothing, dedicating entire discussion board threads to her saris and her on-screen costumes.[8]

Rani is also known for having a very traditional family life and personal life. A recent article written for the *Times News Network*, which was widely circulated amongst fan forums, describes her as the devoted daughter of a close-knit family whose career ambition was driven mostly by a desire to support her parents.[9] Her love life has been downplayed for the most part. Compared to many of her rivals, few rumours circulate that link Rani romantically to other Bollywood stars. One rumour surfaced early on in her career that linked her to one of her recurrent co-stars, Govinda, who is twenty years her senior and married.[10] Yet Rani has publicly denied the affair, and it is generally viewed by fans as unfounded and maliciously fabricated.[11] In fact, Rani's traditional persona has managed to retrospectively taint her Govinda films for many devoted fans. Several fan forum contributors have identified those films as ones they wish she had not done, remarking that "she made too many films with Govinda . . . one is enough," and that those films allowed her "no scope to show her talent."[12] They seem to resent these films as a blemish on her record, which reveals their stake in her idealized persona and their awareness of the threat that negative fan discourse poses to it.

Other rumours have linked her to star Abhishek Bachchan, but these have also been unsubstantiated and short-lived. One story circulated that announced a clandestine marriage against Bachchan's parents' wishes,[13] but these were quickly quelled by news of his affair with another female star, Aishwarya Rai. For the most part, rumours of her affair with Bachchan served to promote Rani's virtues. For example, one story that announced Bachchan's engagement to Rai praised Rani for her religious devotion. It described her finding redemption and solace by "temple hopping," and seeking "shelter at Lord Krishna's feet."[14]

Rani is also known by her fans for being charitable. The release of her recent film, *Black*,[15] in which she played a deaf, mute, and blind character, marked her for fans as particularly sympathetic to the disabled. Their praise was complemented by rumours of Rani's charitable activities: one story in particular tells of Rani spending her birthday at the Helen Keller Institute for the Blind and Deaf.[16] The news media quickly picked up on this and responded enthusiastically: "Playing Michelle on-screen, Rani has become a source of inspiration for the deaf and blind students and restored a faith in their abilities."[17]

While Rani's virtues seem exaggerated, her fans and the press have been careful to present her as a model of Indian femininity that is attainable for young women. Many consider her to be unexceptional or plain when compared to other Bollywood stars, describing her as having a "girl-next-door" look,[18] or as the kind of girl one would want to introduce to their parents.[19] A fan site devoted to Rani emphasizes this in its biography of her:

> She defies all logic of being the number one actress of Bollywood. With 5' 2" height, ordinary vital stats, a simple face and an unusual, irritating (yes to many) voice, she might not come across as a typical Bollywood queen to an onlooker. Unlike most of the previous number one actresses in Hindi Cinema (the exceptionally beautiful Madhubala, dreamgirl Hema Malini, seductive Rekha, sensuous Sridevi, magnificent Madhuri Dixit or the lethal beauty Aishwarya), she has no extraordinary charms.[20]

Many fans also see her as a more "realistic" figure than other actresses.[21] One wrote: "What I love about her is her natural acting. She acts as if she resembles you or the person closest to you. No overacting or put-on acting."[22]

As opposed to an essential star quality, many fans attribute Rani's success to her modesty and strength of character. Much has been made about obstacles that she has overcome in her career. Her first two films were box office failures.[23] But she rose to fame by taking a role in *Kuch Kuch Hota Hai*,[24] which was reportedly dismissed by many other actresses for being too small.[25] She also overcame problems posed by her voice, which is considered too low by Bollywood standards "in an industry where heroines should squeak rather than scratch."[26] Rumours also speculate that her weight has been the cause of a constant personal struggle and abuse.[27] These characteristics were also picked up by her promoters as a point of interest on her website:

> Rani was a born fighter. Though she had full confidence in her acting abilities, she felt something was still missing. She then followed a rigorous diet regime, worked on her looks, took on the services of Manish Malhotra [a prominent stylist for Bollywood stars] and vowed not to sign movies rashly . . . The audience saw a completely transformed Rani, sexy yet with the innocence of the girl-next-door.[28]

Together with her idealized qualities, these minor flaws make Rani's model of femininity realistic and attainable for young Indian women, sending them the message that they too can achieve the feminine ideal with modesty, traditional values, and hard work.

Regardless of the stress put on the traditional aspects of her off-screen persona, the characters Rani performs are allowed to express a very modern disenchantment with rigid traditional practices. In *Kabhi Alvida Naa Kehna*,[29] for example, she plays Maya, a woman who is left unfulfilled by her marriage. She eventually has an adulterous affair with a married man, which results in both parties abandoning their respective spouses. Similarly, in the film *Paheli*,[30] she plays Lachchi, a traditional woman who becomes disappointed by an arranged marriage and transgresses moral codes to find love. In the beginning, Lachchi is shown excited in anticipation for her wedding night and first sexual relations. Yet the film troubles this excitement with several realizations that Lachchi has about the realities of the arrangement. First, her female family members and friends tell her that she must resist her husband's initial sexual advances. This suggestion reveals the tensions between standards of female modesty and the expectations of sexual relations with an unfamiliar individual that can accompany arranged marriages. Second, she expresses sorrow in her awareness that she must leave her family and friends behind to move in with her husband's family. Lachchi's excitement turns to despair shortly after the wedding when she realizes that her husband, played by Shah Rukh Khan, plans to abandon her for the first five years of their marriage. The film shows her miserable and alone, living amongst her husband's unfamiliar family, until she is presented with a solution. A spirit, also played by Khan, who had fallen in love with her prior to the wedding, magically takes the form of her husband. With her approval, the spirit takes the husband's place in the family, and Lachchi quickly falls in love with him. They have passionate sexual relations (never shown in explicit detail, of course), and Lachchi ends up giving birth to the spirit's child. The spirit also significantly allows Lachchi a great deal of power in their relationship, continuously asking her opinion and seeking her approval. Through this narrative, *Paheli* offers female viewers a model of a traditional Indian woman who is able to transcend rigid Indian traditions to gain control over her love life.

While *Paheli* can be read as remarkably empowering for Indian women, it is significant that it only offers women a model of sexual freedom under a very unrealistic pretense. For one, *Paheli* is set in an indeterminate distant past. Although Lachchi's world is undeniably premodern and preindustrial, it lacks any signifiers of a specific time period. Because of this lack of historical specificity, the film offers no indication that Indian society has evolved from that condition, or that the oppressive social circumstances Lachchi experiences have been overcome. The film also denies the viewer any coherent solutions to Lachchi's condition. For obvious reasons, finding love with a spirit is not a viable option for women who are faced with similarly grim arranged marriages. By setting the film's narrative in an unrealistic circumstance, *Paheli* denies the real feminist issues that its story raises. By confining Lachchi to the realm of unrealistic fantasy, the film denies Indian women any real identification with her transgressions of traditional moral codes, and in doing so contains the threat of her sexual power.

In contrast with Rani Mukherjee, actress Preity Zinta has been constructed as a model of modern Indian femininity. She most clearly transgresses traditional ideals through her mode of dress. Unlike Rani, Preity almost never dresses in traditional saris, on- or off-screen. Some of her fans have said that they would like to see her wear more Indian clothing out of fear that she looks too "Western" and is not properly representing herself as an "Indian" actress, but generally most fans feel that Western clothing suits her better.[31]

Preity has also been much more forthright about her personal relationships than Rani. She has had two very visible romantic relationships with prominent public figures, the first of which, John Abraham, is a model turned actor known for his overtly sexual poses, as well as rumours that he appears naked on-screen in Deepa Mehta's *Water*.[32] Rumours have often questioned Preity's virginity, which typically would be perceived as a threat to her reputation. Yet, for Preity fans, rumours of her sexual exploits are innocuous. The most widely circulated responses to the rumours stressed that she "never claims to be a virgin," an assertion that suggests that she disregards traditional codes of sexual conduct, and furthermore that for her fans sexual purity is not an important aspect of her persona.

This attitude is reflected in many of the roles selected by Preity, especially in films that address taboo social topics. She first came under the public eye when she starred in the film *Kya Kehna*,[33] in which she played an unwed pregnant teenager who chose to keep her child against social norms. In *Chori Chori Chupke Chupke*,[34] Preity plays a prostitute and surrogate mother who falls in love with the father of the child she's carrying. More recently, in *Salaam Namaste*,[35] she plays one half of an Indian couple who lives in "pre-matrimony" abroad in Australia. Her character again becomes pregnant out of wedlock and she chooses to keep the baby without getting married. By making visible the disparities between traditional moral codes and the realities of modern Indian women, these films have made Preity an unofficial spokesperson for social change. Entwined with her confident and defiant star persona, her model of femininity has become a powerful threat to traditional patriarchal gender ideals in India.

Preity's power is often downplayed by the industry, the media, and her fans who typically describe her with such words as "cute," "bubbly," and "innocent." Fans often have a hard time grappling with her age; for example, some fans have said that Preity is too young for some of Rani Mukherjee's roles,[36] even though Rani is four years her junior. Fans also tend to characterize Preity as young and almost prepubescent, such that her defiant sexual ideals are not really taken seriously. This is clear from fans' reactions to a recent transformation in Preity's looks. It is said that prior to filming *Salaam Namaste*, she lost a substantial amount of weight and had her eyebrows shaped and/or lifted. This transformation became a serious matter of contention on fan forums. For example, one fan felt that

> Preity did it purposefully to grow out of the cute 'n bubbly image that she was stuck with and always hated. She is really stupid to think so because that was her strength. If only she can change this "I'm not bubbly" attitude. I think this attitude is self destructive.[37]

Another wrote, "it was the cute bubbly Preity that caused me to become her fan and I just want THAT Preity back."[38] Comments like these suggest that Preity's popularity was contingent on her being "cute" and "bubbly." While these descriptors might seem complimentary for a thirty-two-year-old actress who has had a critically successful career, they seem condescending. They mark her as childlike and essentially sexually innocuous. Other fans took issue with the control she exercised over her own image; for example, one argued that, "She just can't 'be' sexy . . . because how she truly is, is cute and bubbly . . . that's her NATURAL own self . . . if she tries to be too sexy, its' too fake for her."[39] This remark was complemented by fans who said that she should wear only "necessary makeup,"[40] and who were content with her new look in *Salaam Namaste* so long as she never revealed too much skin.[41] With these comments, fans suggested that they disliked visible markers of her sexuality, or that they were uncomfortable with the power she had over her image. Her efforts marked her as a mature woman who could access and control the visible signifiers of her sexuality, and this power was inherently threatening for fans. In addition, thin eyebrows, excessive makeup, and a trimmer figure also point to a very Western model of ideal femininity, one that these fans appear to be wary of. Finally, their desire for her not to reveal her adult feminine body points to the threat her sexuality poses, a threat that has been drastically enhanced by her modern ideals.

Some rumours have speculated on Preity's true national identity, and some sources have claimed that her heritage is British and not Indian.[42] By marking her as foreign, and not authentically Indian, this gossip displaces the threat that her sexuality poses to the Indian nation, robbing it of its symbolic resonance. *Kal Ho Naa Ho*, in which Preity starred in 2003, enacts this defensive strategy, and in so doing works to contain some of the threatening aspects of her identity. Preity's character, Naina, is a second-generation member of the Indian diaspora, living in New York City. When we first meet Naina, she is miserable and overstressed, living with her dysfunctional family, with a negative attitude towards life. Against her grandmother's constant urging, she rejects the idea of arranged marriage (or marriage of any sort), deeming romance to be something beyond her sphere of interest. She consistently wears baggy, unflattering Western clothing and a very severe looking pair of glasses, and it is noted through dialogue in the film that she never smiles. Naina and Preity share a striking resemblance: they both lost their fathers at a young age, a detail that would not have been lost on avid Preity fans. This loss is emphasized in the film as a continuous source of torment for Naina. She cries often, walks the streets alone in the rain, and is repeatedly short with family and friends. Enter Shah Rukh Khan; his character,

Aman, who was born and raised in India, moves across the street from Naina and brings happiness to her life. In his first encounter with Naina, he serenades her from the street with a song that both embarrasses her and secretly perks her interest. A loose cover of the unmistakable American anthem "Oh, Pretty Woman,"[43] this song identifies Naina explicitly as an Americanized heroine. It also references the iconic American romantic comedy *Pretty Woman*[44] and its prostitute-turned-society-woman romantic heroine played by Julia Roberts. The musical number also neatly ties the film back to Preity's real life persona through an ironic translingual pun on her name. As the story continues, Aman infiltrates Naina's family with the Indian culture that they have lost. He brings traditional food back into their home and revives Naina's mother's downtrodden restaurant by giving it a traditional Indian theme. His presence also affects Naina, changing her disposition completely. She becomes friendlier, learns to smile, sheds her glasses, and starts to wear more feminine clothing. She eventually warms up to the idea of romantic love, and gets married in a traditional Hindu wedding.

Using Preity's public persona as a point of departure, *Kal Ho Naa Ho* prescribes Naina as an ideal model for the rehabilitation of modern Indian femininity. It represents Preity's modern ideals as undesirable and emotionally stifling, while offering a prescription for overcoming her modern disparities. At the same time, it emphasizes Preity's persona as non-Indian and distances her modern ideals as foreign, thereby again marking her sexuality as nonthreatening.

In her study, Stacey suggests that female audiences of 1940s and 1950s Hollywood films tended to identify most with stars whose personas resisted patriarchal constraints of ideal femininity. She identifies a "fantasy of resistance"[45] offered by stars who exhibited power and confidence, which could be pleasurably incorporated into the spectator's own identity. The personas of both Rani Mukherjee and Preity Zinta offer this kind of fantasy to their fans. This is more overt in the case of Preity, who resists patriarchal constraints through her modern lifestyle and the controversial roles she chooses. It is less obvious but still apparent in Rani's persona. While she may adhere to certain traditional standards for Indian femininity, the roles she chooses, and the modern points of view her characters express, also offer female audiences points of resistance. Rani's ability to be both ostensibly traditional, and still socially powerful, is perhaps more threatening than Preity's persona. Both the fan discourse and the films I have analyzed communicate an anxiety around the power that these female star personas exhibit, and both convey a desire to tame or inhibit the fantasies of resistance offered by these two women.

Although Rani and Preity are but two examples of female Bollywood star personas, they can help us to approach an understanding of the complex roles played by female stars in Indian society, as well as the authoritative power of fan discourse in mediating those roles. As Stacey argues, spectatorship should be read as part of a society's "cultural construction of identity."[46] In Indian society, where a star's personal life is consumed as avidly as her films, every characteristic of a female star, fictional or real, is woven into the country's fabric of collective identity. Between the competing demands of nationalism, traditionalism, modernity, gossip-mongering, sexuality, and the aspirations of young women, both Rani Mukherjee and Preity Zinta have contributed powerful models of Indian femininity that transgress traditional patriarchal codes. Yet the fantasies of resistance offered by these two stars have been limited. The forces that intervene to shape female personas are never obtrusive, coming in the forms of casual entertainment, like fan sites, gossip columns, and even the films themselves. Nevertheless, they force female star personas to oscillate between incompatible standards.

Notes

1. Sippy 1975
2. Dissanayake Sahai
3. Khan 1957
4. Thomas 20
5. For example, the spectators who willingly contributed letters to this study undoubtedly share a particular enthusiasm for Hollywood stars, which makes them a poor sample of the general public.
6. Stacey 208
7. Dazzlingdesi. "Good Girl: Rani." Online Posting. 11 Mar. 2006. India-Forums. 25 Mar 2006.
<http://www.india-forums.com/forum_posts.asp?TID=228652&KW=Rani>
8. For an example see
<http://ranimukerji.proboards25.com/index.cgi?board=chat>
9. Ronitfan. "Reign Woman – Rani Mukherjee." Online Posting. October 23, 2004. India-Forums. March 25, 2006.
<http://www.indiaforums.com/forum_posts.asp?TID=210579&KW=Rani>
10. They acted together in Hadh Kar Di Aapne (2000), Pyaar Diwana Hota Hai (2002), and Chalo Ishq Ladaaye (2002)
11. "Bollywood Celebs," Online Posting. 1 Jul. 2004. Entertainment i-Africa. 25 March 2006. <http://entertainment.iafrica.com/bollywood/profiles/324368.htm>

12. "Which movies you wished Rani hadn't acted in?" 24 Feb. 2006. Rani Mukerji Online. 25 Mar. 2006. <http://ranimukerji.proboards25.com/index.cgi?board=chat&action=display&thread=1140794640>

13. "Abhishek Marries Rani," Parinda.com 2005. 22 Mar. 2006. <http://www.parinda.com/bollywood_gossip/bollywood_gossip5.shtml>

14. Kidwai, Rasheed. "Rani at Lord's Feet," Telegraphinda.com. 13 Feb. 2004. 22 Mar. 2006. < telegraphindia.com>

15. Bhansali 2005

16. foreverfreind2. "Rani showed on her B-day - she has a golden heart." Online Posting. 22 Mar. 2006. Rani Mukerji Online. 25 Mar. 2006.<http://ranimukerji.proboards25.com>

17. Aaf. "Rani Mukerji latest news topic." Online Posting. 21 Mar. 2006. India-Forums. 25 Mar. 2006. < http://ranimukerji.proboards25.com/>

18. Bollywoodcrazed. "Aish and Abhi all set to marry!" Online Posting. 23 Feb. 2006. India-Forums. 25 Mar. 2006. <http://www.india-forums.com/forum>

19. Anand7. "Letters to Rani Mukerji." Online Posting. 24 Nov. 2005. Rani Mukerji Online. 25 Mar. 2006. <http://ranimukerji.proboards25.com/index.cgi?board=chat&action=display&thread=1130481011&page=1>

20. See <http://fansites.hollywood.com/~rani/bio.php>

21. Mona Ali. "Topic:Preity or Rani ?????" Online Posting. 13 Dec. 2005. India-Forums. 25 Mar. <http://www.indiaforums.com/forum_posts.asp?TID=150211&KW=+Preity+or+Rani%3F%3F%3F%3F%3F>

22. foreverfreind2. "Since when are you a Rani fan? Share it.." Online Posting. 12 Mar. 2006. Rani Mukerji Online. 25 Mar. 2006. <http://ranimukerji.proboards25.com/index.cgi?board=chat&action=display&thread=1130481011&page=1>

23. Raja Ki Ayegi Baraat (Gaekwad, 1997), Ghulam (Bhatt, 1998)

24. Johar 1998

25. "Rani Mukherjee Profile." Bollywhat.com. 22 Mar.2006. <http://www.bollywhat.com/Biographies/RANI_bio.html>

26. *ibid.*

27. *ibid.*

28. *ibid*

29. Johar 2006

30. Palekar 2005

31. Mani_d17. "Preity's Canteen." Online Posting. 03 Mar. 2006.
Preity Zinta Fan Club 22 Mar. 2006.
<http://www.hostingphpbb.com/forum/viewtopic.php?p=95535&highlight=saris&mforum=preityzinta#955>35

32. 2005

33. Shah 2000

34. Burmawalla and Burmawalla 2001

35. Anand 2005

36. John_abraham. Preity's Canteen. Online Posting. 18 Mar. 2006. Preity Zinta Fan Club. 22 Mar. 2006.

http://www.hostingphpbb.com/forum/viewtopic.php?t=2377&postdays=0&postorder=asc&start=255&mforum=preityzinta

37. Savika. "Cute Look or Sexy Look???" Online Posting. 30 Mar. 2006. Preity Zinta Fan Club. 30 Mar. 2006. http://www.hostingphpbb.com/forum/viewtopic.php?t=2661&mforum=preityzinta

38. Shivani. "Preity's Canteen. Online Posting. 26 Mar. 2006. Preity Zinta Fan Club. 22 Mar. 2006. <http://www.hostingphpbb.com/forum/viewtopic.php?t=2377&postdays=0&postorder=asc&start=255&mforum=preityzinta>

39. mani_d17. "Cute Look or Sexy Look???" Online Posting. 26 Mar. 2006. Preity Zinta Fan Club. 30 Mar. 2006. http://www.hostingphpbb.com/forum/viewtopic.php?t=2661&mforum=preityzinta

40. vicky116. "Preity's Canteen." Online Posting. 03 Mar. 2006. Preity Zinta Fan Club. 30 Mar. 2006. <http://www.hostingphpbb.com/forum/viewtopic.php?t=2661&mforum=preityz-inta>

41. Bgal. "Cute Look or Sexy Look???" Online Posting. 27 Mar. 2006.Preity Zinta Fan Club. 30 Mar. 2006. http://www.hostingphpbb.com/forum/viewtopic.php?t=2661&mforum=preityzinta

42. "Preity Zinta Bio." Bollywhat.com. <http://www.bollywhat.com/Biographies/PREITY_bio.html>

43. First recorded by Roy Orbison in 1964.

44. Marshall 1990

45. Stacey 201-202

46. Stacey 199.

References

Dissanayake, Wimal and Malti Sahai. *Sholay: A Cultural Reading*. New Delhi: Wiley Eastern Limited, 1992.

Thomas, Rosie. "Indian Cinema: Pleasures and Popularity," *Screen* 26: 3–4 (May–August), 1985. 116–131.

Stacey, Jackie. "Feminine Fascinations: Forms of Identification in Star-Audience Relations." *Feminist Film Theory: A Reader*. Sue Thornham, ed. New York: New York University Press, 1999. 197–209.

Nargis and Aurora Zogoiby: Imaging Mother and Nation in Mehboob Khan's *Mother India* and Salman Rushdie's *The Moor's Last Sigh*

FLORIAN STADTLER

In *The Moor's Last Sigh*, Rushdie strategically deploys Bombay cinema to explore issues of Mother and Nation, defeated love, and the dangers and destructive forces of corruption and religious fundamentalism. He focuses on specific cinematic intertexts to make his assessment of post-Ayodhya Bombay and closely links them to the portrayal of Aurora Zogoiby and her conceptualization of a secular India, reflected in her art and by extension Rushdie's writing. In particular, he uses the film *Mother India* (1957) as an intertext to construct his alternative version of Mother India. The South Indian Malabar Coast and the metropolis Bombay serve as the narrative's backdrop. The novel was written in the aftermath of the communal riots in December 1992 and January 1993 and the bombings in March 1993 in Bombay. Many commentators and intellectuals, including Rushdie, saw these events as the death of cosmopolitan Bombay.[1] Rushdie very firmly believes that for India secularism is not a matter of point of view but integral to its survival: "If what Indians call 'communalism,' sectarian religious politics, were to be allowed to take control of the polity, the results would be too horrifying to imagine." (Rushdie 1992:404). In *The Moor's Last Sigh*, Rushdie engages with the rise of an exclusionist nativist Hindu nationalism that threatens the Nehruvian vision of the Nation, which Nehru outlined in his "Tryst with Destiny" speech on the Eve of Independence as follows: "We have to build the noble mansion of free India where all her children may dwell." (Rushdie and West 1997:3)

In *The Moor's Last Sigh*, Rushdie imagines an epic family saga that begins on the periphery in the city of Cochin in the South Indian state of Kerala. Thematically, Rushdie reevaluates India's myth of the nation and in this respect the novel can be seen as a companion volume, if not a sequel, to *Midnight's Children*, extending the time frame by fifteen years. In the light of increasing communal tensions and Hindu fundamentalism, the rise of the right-wing extremist party Shiv Sena[2] in Bombay and Maharashtra and the destruction of the Babri Masjid in Ayodhya in 1992, Rushdie decided to write a family saga that is pluralistic and eclectic in cultural and religious terms. Rushdie explains his idea behind the novel in an interview with Alvaro Vargas Llosa in 1996:

> If there is this idea that only Hindu India is India, let me do the opposite of that and try to find the smallest minority group. The Indian Jewish community in South India is tiny, especially in Cochin. Then there are different types of Christianity, including the Church of South India, based on the legend of the apostle St Thomas's trip to India after the death of Christ. I took these two very small communities, and created an even smaller community by intermarriage (something that, in actuality, the South Indian Jewish community doesn't allow). I tried to show that, far from being a marginal or inauthentic experience, you could put this in the center and grow the whole of the country out of it. (Llosa 2001:211)

The result is a multilayered novel that challenges the reader to unpick the various narrative threads and to reexamine the historical palimpsest that makes up India as a nation and is linked through the history of colonialism to European history. Rushdie throws down the gauntlet, challenging the idea that "only Hindu India is India." The locale for this challenge is Bombay and the rise to power of the Shiv Sena in Bombay is central to the story. *The Moor's Last Sigh* highlights the impact of Hindu fundamentalism and the concept of *hindutva* and the damage it has done to the all-India idea.[3]

In the novel, Bombay serves as an example, a metaphor for modern India. In an age when nationalism is more and more dissociated from its secular roots, the effects of a new breed of religious nationalism can be observed meticulously in this multiethnic and multireligious city. In this context, Aurora and her art are set up as a counter-narrative that decentres "only one way of seeing" that Rushdie associates with any form of fundamentalism. In *The Moor's Last Sigh*, the role of Mother India is contested by the artist Aurora Zogoiby, fashioning herself into an urban version of Mother India in direct competition with Indira Gandhi and Nargis, the Bombay film superstar who became an icon through her performance in *Mother India*. Mother India is one of the defining myths of post-independence India and is closely linked to the independence struggle and India's birth as a nation. Hence, the representation of Mother India is of vital significance in an age when ideological conceptions about nation become more and more religiously invested and entrenched. Mehboob Khan's *Mother India* has become part of popular Indian mythology as it is translated for the masses by Bombay cinema, reiterating, drawing together, and creating a new myth for the newly independent nation. In *The Moor's Last Sigh*, Rushdie through his narrator provides an ironic commentary on the film and its concerns, useful in generating a wider argument about and social criticism of a national allegory that does not live up to reality in its idolization of peasant heroism, female suffering, and sacrifice, and its project of strengthening the nation state. In itself, Moraes's critique in *The Moor's Last Sigh* offers various ways of reading not only the film, but also his relationship with his mother. While on the surface the interest focuses on Aurora's love for gossip as proliferated by an abundance of film magazines, beneath that lies the assertion that mother-son relationships are summarily nothing more but "sublimation." Within this realm are a number of texts, penetrating not only the grand narrative of MOTHER, but also the nature of Bombay cinema, featured to a greater or lesser degree in many Rushdie novels.

Mother India makes a wider argument about a specifically Hindu female code of honour, while artificially constructing the figure of Mother India out of a complex, heterogeneous, religious, and social history. Like Rushdie's novels, *Mother India* is not a religious but a secular epic for the new modern India, despite the characters' resemblance to mythic parallels (Radha, Sita, Parvati) and mythic structural antecedents that are not lost on Rushdie as they are expressed in *The Moor's Last Sigh*. In its construction *Mother India* is a complex film. In the absence of the father figure the son Birju can never complete the Oedipal narrative of separation from the mother and identification with the father, since the mother has absorbed the father's patriarchal authority. This enables the film to concentrate fully on the mother-son binary, which is also of great concern in Rushdie's novel. Within this deconstruction of the patriarchally conditioned family Rushdie proliferates the figures of Mother India, from the self-fashioned urban version of Mother India Aurora to film-icon Nargis to Prime Minster Indira Gandhi. Nationalism is linked to the symbolic use of women in this context in the movement from regional to national in the modernizing process of postindependence India, as Woman becomes the testing ground for modernity and Mother

India becomes the site for mythic unity in the face of fragmentation.[4]

In flashback, *Mother India* narrates the plight of the peasant woman Radha and her family, who together with her husband and her children struggles to repay the moneylender for a loan to pay for their wedding. After losing both his arms in an accident, her husband abandons his family, leaving Radha to fend for her children on her own. She continues to repay the moneylender, while refusing his sexual advances. The village is destroyed in heavy floods, yet she decides to stay on with her family to rebuild their lives and continue farming the land. Because of her oppression, suffering, and sacrifices, the main character acquires a larger-than-life persona of high moral standing and spiritual strength. Sumita S Chakravarty asserts that *Mother India*'s enduring popularity has to do with the way it shapes a fundamental level of the Indian experience of suffering into the stuff of myth, investing the everyday with the heroic, allowing its audience to renew their most cherished cultural assumptions with regards to women (150). These assume, according to Chakravarty, woman's mythic strength and endurance, and "her ability to provide stability and continuity in Indian social life" (150). As Chakravarty points out, within the context of a patriarchal culture, the idealization of woman is closely intertwined with the role of woman for the guardianship of communal norms and values and a harnessing of female sexuality. Chakravarty further asserts that a celebration of woman in the role of wife and mother is aimed at offsetting the destructive and vengeful woman and the prostituting woman as it finds its expression in myth and folklore from which Mehboob drew for his message of service and devotion to the motherland (151). Furthermore, the picture offered by Mehboob is much more ambiguous. The Oedipal undertones between mother and son throw up an array of issues and while these might be overstated in discussions of the film through Western psychoanalytical discourse, they are undeniably there, especially when the characters of the film are seen as intertextual with the stars of the movie.[5]

The notion of Mother India takes much of its symbolism from the cult of the Mother Goddess, the Devi. However, many argue that Hindu mythology is devoid of one single mother figure. Rather, while these female goddesses are mothers, they are foregrounded more as wives and lovers. Still, as E O Cousins claims in *The Awakening of Indian Womanhood*, "the apotheosis of the mother has reached a greater height in India than anywhere else. No other religion of the present time worships goddesses, no other looks on the Mother as Divine" (Chakravarty 1993:152). Woman as mother allows her to rise above woman as mere woman, which is implied in Mehboob's title. Chakravarty asserts that the celebration of woman as mother in popular tradition and in social life is a key element and this symbolic force is transferred to the national level.[6] *Mother India*, then, can be regarded as Mehboob's attempt to articulate for mass consumption the values that should give guidance to the national life, using woman to mediate tensions and oppositions: Mother as life-giving and life-destroying, pitiable yet terrifying. In order to achieve this, his film fuses mythological references, cult worship, social tradition, and customs that allow him, as Chakravarty claims, "to elaborate codes of behavior in contemporary India" (152).

Mehboob's constant use of flashbacks, recuperating the past through memory, produces a cyclical narrative that immediately establishes the position of woman in his film. At the beginning, a heavily garlanded mother, dignified in her old age, conveying respect and distance, is persuaded by her son to inaugurate the irrigation project of the village. The entire opening is an ode to progress represented by bulldozers, power lines, and ultimately dams.[7] Within this imagery of progress, the elder mother marks stability and continuity in an age of progress, but also a realm of moral virtue that is still intact. As her life unfolds in flashback, Chakravarty argues, she is already established as a special role model: as a bride, she is of blinding beauty, as a wife she is devoted to her husband, as a woman she fulfils her biological and social role bearing her husband only sons, as a mother she fiercely protects and defends her children, and as a peasant she battles fire and flood for a rich harvest (154).

In *The Moor's Last Sigh*, the narrator Moraes Zogoiby stresses: "Motherness [. . .] is a big idea in India, maybe our biggest: the land as mother, the mother as land, as the firm ground beneath our feet. Ladies-O, gents-O: I'm talking major mother country" (Rushdie 1996:137). Rushdie's narrator creates a list of mother figures that have all been connected to the mythic figure of Mother India. Moraes, born ten years after Independence, in 1957, is quick to point out his connection with the film:

> The year I was born, Mehboob Productions' all-conquering movie *Mother India*—three years in the making, three hundred shooting days, in the top three all-time mega-grossing Bollywood flicks—hit the nation's screens. Nobody who saw it ever forgot that glutinous saga of peasant heroinism, that super-slushy ode to the uncrushability of village India made by the most cynical urbanites in the

> world. And as for its leading lady—O Nargis with your shovel over your shoulder and your strand of black hair tumbling forward over your brow!—she became, until Indira Mata supplanted her, the living mother-goddess of us all. (Rushdie 1996:137)

Moraes highlights the hold of Mother India over the popular imaginary and the film as one of the defining texts of Indian popular cinema as well as that of Nargis as the embodiment of the role. Furthermore, Rushdie's narrator emphasises references to the idea of "Mother" as it is defined and exploited in nationalist rhetoric to trigger the reader to make comparisons between the various mother figures in the novel.[8] Rushdie develops these connections most overtly in relation to the Mother India trope and provides the reader with a model that may help him to unpack a novel that is dense with historical and popular cultural allusions. Hence, the Mother India trope is developed into a thread that runs through the novel, which is not only significant as a plot device that sets up and parallels the Oedipal relationship between mother and son, but also helps to thread the narrative together. Throughout the novel, the Mother India idea is countered by Moraes's rewriting of the trope, which sets up his mother as an alternative urban version to Nargis's interpretation in Mehboob Khan's film:

> In *Mother India*, a piece of Hindu myth-making directed by a Muslim socialist, Mehboob Khan, the Indian peasant woman is idealised as bride, mother, and producer of sons; as long-suffering, stoical, loving, redemptive, and conservatively wedded to the maintenance of the social status quo. (Rushdie 1996:138–39)

This image of the benevolent, stoic, nurturing, and caring Mother India has been harnessed through the Indian epics, the *Mahabharata* and the *Ramayana*, but is given a new dimension in the film by stressing the connection between the land as mother and the mother as land, as well as India's progress ten years after Independence. In a wave of change that is sweeping the country, the Mother symbolises continuity in times of upheaval. This stoical image is countered and exploded by Rushdie's provocative, metropolitan version of an aggressive, treacherous, foul-mouthed, ruthless, exploitative calculative and cruel mother. Yet in the final rejection of her son, Aurora makes the same choice as Radha in the film, connecting her to the conservative values that the heroine mother in the film reiterates and embodies. So Aurora as Mother India is a complex, multilayered figure who on the one hand strives to break the patriarchally constructed image of Mother India and on the other hand ultimately adheres to her moral code, both divorced from and linked to the traditional mythical image. Rushdie pursues several strategies in the creation of Aurora. He sets her up as an iconic figure who embodies an eclectic, multiethnic, multireligious, tolerant secular India that he associates with the Bombay of the 1950s and 1960s. He also creates a subversion of the image of India as the mother goddess, which he has described in an interview with Michael Silverblatt: "I thought I'd like to invent a different sort of mother, . . . not rural, but urban. Not slushy but kind of gritty and sassy with a bad mouth on her." (199) Thus, while she still embodies India, she can also be read as a counter narrative to the traditional image of Mother India.

In his conception of the film, Mehboob has drawn from many popular tropes that not only arise from the Indian independence movement, but also from his earlier film version of the *Mother India* story *Aurat*, Hindi for "Woman." *Aurat* (1940) itself is very much indebted to Russian realist cinema, most notably Pudovski's adaptation of Maxim Gorky's *Mother* (1926), and MGM's *The Good Earth* (1937), based on Pearl S Buck's novel portraying Chinese peasant life (Mishra 2002:66). Rachel Dwyer notes in *All You Want Is Money, All You Need Is Love: Sex and Romance in Modern India*, the glorification of the woman as nation as self-sacrificing, benevolent Mother India "shows a continuity with earlier valorizations of women in non-sexual roles"—Radha in *Mother India* is first and foremost mother, not a wife, and is one of the few goddesses not to have a male consort (132). This can also be said of Aurora or Indira Gandhi, who both sidelined their husbands. While the reader is confronted by Aurora's promiscuity, even an alleged affair with Nehru, she throws herself into her work during the independence movement, portraying and documenting the struggle in her art. Her involvement allows her to lay claim to the title of an urban version of Mother India as she is mythologized by the narrator and her public. In this respect, the narrative bears a striking resemblance to the film. *Mother India* does not only portray rural village life under the strains of colonialism and feudalism, but, as Rachel Dwyer suggests, one of its main attractions is the film's aim to create a new mythology for the independent nation (132).

At the beginning of the film, Radha is presented as the village elder, mother of the whole village, but in tracing her journey, the film identifies her with other figures of Hindu mythology. She develops from daughter, to wife, daughter-in-law, and finally mother. Dwyer persuasively argues that she can be identified with other goddesses, such as the Sita-Savitri model of the steadfast wife, while her love for her husband clearly echoes that of her namesake Radha in Hindu mythology and her relationship with Krishna, a story which is often used as an intertext in Bombay cinema (133). In *Mother India*, her husband is even called Shamu, one of Krishna's names. The village moneylender, the greatest threat to Radha's honour, identifies her with the goddess of wealth, Lakshmi. Furthermore, her actions implicitly connect her with the goddess Kali, making her an ambivalent figure. In defence of the village girls' honour, she kills her own son, while she is also responsible for her husband losing both his arms when she persuades him to farm a barren piece of land full of boulders. Thus, the equation of Mother as Goddess seems contradictory in the film through its heterogeneity. Quite strikingly, Mishra points towards the fact that *Mother India*'s heroine is not named after Sita, Durga, Parvati, or Lakshmi, religio-epic examples of Motherhood and Land-as-Mother, but Radha, who is already marked by her strong will and longing for Krishna (77). This raises a vast array of problems, as the eroticism of Radha as woman creates the uncertainties within the film, especially in the mother-son relationship. In *Mother India*, the absence of the father leads to an identification with the mother. As she has to usurp the role of the father, she by default also has to absorb the threat of castration, normally associated with the father. In this respect, Mishra argues, the mother becomes a "subject that duplicates the father's aggressivity, but succumbs to a threat from precisely the object that it desires" (81). This comes across in the visually highly ambiguous narrative. Essentially, the son's problem is that he cannot accept his mother's position of power as he is unable to fulfil "the Oedipal narrative of separation from mother and identification with the father" (Mishra 2002:81). Mehboob resolves this dilemma unambiguously by stipulating that since Birju is a serious threat, bringing shame upon a village girl through the attempted abduction of the moneylender's daughter, the mother has to make the ultimate sacrifice. It sets up the mother as upholder of the law and at the same time casts her in the role of avenger and renouncer.

According to Dwyer, the depiction of Radha as a "bad mother" is unusual in traditional Indian mythology and she points to Sudhir Kakar's suggestion that images of the bad mother usually emerge when mother-son relationships are portrayed as too intense (133). This again highlights connections between Aurora and Moraes's mother-son relationship, but is also an implicit hint at Indira Gandhi's own intense relationship with her son Sanjay and Nargis's marriage to the actor Sunil Dutt, who played her son Birju in the film. Furthermore, Nargis, too, had a very intense relationship with her son the actor Sanjay Dutt, and his alleged involvement in the 1993 bombings did not escape Rushdie's attention. The film version of *Mother India* sublimates the Oedipal tensions in its powerful portrayal of a mother making the ultimate sacrifice by killing her own son to protect the honour of the village, though this seems like a shoddy resolution to the tensions built up throughout the film. Radha has to take on the role of avenger in the absence of the father. In psychoanalytic terms the film offers many possibilities of discussion and these observations are most crucially taken up by Moraes and Rushdie.[9]

Rushdie extends the analogy by linking three intense mother-son relationships with three women who all set themselves up as Mother India. These Oedipal tensions are not as easily resolved in *The Moor's Last Sigh*. The reconciliation between Moraes and Aurora never happens and is deferred to the showdown in Benengeli where Moraes dramatically reclaims the remains of his mother's artistic legacy. In *Mother India*, the Oedipal tensions are underlined by Birju's obsession in reinstating his mother's honour by reclaiming her wedding bangles from the moneylender, and Radha in her obsessive and possessive role as doting mother. This is further underlined by the fact that in name, too, Birju can replace his father, since they both have names associated with Krishna. This connection is further emphasized by Birju teasing the village girls and breaking their womby waterpots. Yet, unlike Krishna, Birju will not submit to the laws of society and this transgression pushes his mother to kill him to uphold the law of society, a role which normally the father fulfils (Dwyer 2000:135).

While an analysis in psychoanalytical terms has its limitations, considering that it is not a defining analytical text in Indian mythology, a reading in these terms was reinforced when Nargis fell in love on set with Sunil Dutt. After the film, Nargis reinvented herself as the ideal wife and mother. Before *Mother India*, Nargis presented herself as the modern woman, a secular Muslim, a working woman, who has chosen her own lovers. After her marriage, she became a bourgeois housewife and mother, leaving the seedy film world, re-emerging into public life as a politician (Dwyer 2000:136). Nargis's role in *Mother India* came soon after her split from Raj Kapoor. They were Bombay cinema's Golden Couple, since they epitomized a "modern" freedom and lack of inhibition, despite the fact that Kapoor was married with children. When the affair ended, Nargis was regarded on the one hand as a ruined woman and on the other as a figure of sympathy. *Mother India* in that respect salvaged her honour as she was "rescued" by Sunil Dutt through marriage. She settled down to family life, leaving the "seedy" film world. The association with Mother India and Nargis's devotion to her son and husband and her commitment to community charities allowed her to redeem herself in the public imagination. More significantly, she forged a close connection with Indira Gandhi and in 1980 joined the Rajya Sabha (The Upper House of the Indian Parliament). By that time, she was a national symbol of dignified glamour and respectability, the other First Lady of India—Indira Gandhi's alter ego.[10] In this respect, there seem to be obvious parallels with Aurora—her affair with Nehru, her clash with Nargis, and the conception of the figure of Aurora in the public imagination falling in and out of love with her, play mischievously with set conceptions of Indian womanhood, blurring the boundaries of public and private spheres, the nation, and the family unit. Aurora takes this up in her confrontation with Nargis, conflating real life events with the narrative of the film:

> "The first time I saw the picture," she confided to the famous movie star on the high terrace at *Elephanta*, "I took one look at your Bad Son, Birju, and I thought, O boy, what a handsome guy—too much sizzle, too much chilli, bring water. He may be a thief and a bounder, but that is some A-class loverboy goods. And now look—you have gone and marry-o'ed him! What sexy lives you movie people lead: to marry your own son, I swear, wowie."
>
> The film actor under discussion, Sunil Dutt, stood stiffly beside his wife and sipped lemonade, flushing. [. . .] "Auroraji, you're mixing truth and make-belief," he said pompously, as if it were a sin. "Birju and his mother Radha are fictions only, in two dimensions on the silver screen; but we are flesh and blood, available in full 3D—as guests in your fine home."[. . .]
>
> "Even in the picture, but," Aurora went relentlessly on, "I knew right off that bad Birju had the hots for his gorgeous ma."
>
> Nargis stood speechless, open-mouthed. Vasco Miranda, who could never resist a bit of trouble-making, saw the storm brewing and made haste to join in. "Sublimation," he offered, "of mutual parent-child-longings, is deep-rooted in the national psyche. The use of names in the picture makes the meaning clear. This 'Birju' moniker is also used by God Krishna, isn't it, and we know that

> milky 'Radha' is the blue chap's one true love. In the picture, Sunil, you are made up to look like the god, you even fool with all the girls, throwing your stones to break their womby water-pots; which, admit it, is Krishna-esque behaviour. In this interpretation," and here clowning Vasco attempted unsuccessfully to convey a certain scholarly *gravitas*, "*Mother India* is the dark side of the Radha-Krishna story with the subsidiary theme of forbidden love added on. But what the hell; Oedipus-schmoedipus! Have another chhota peg." (Rushdie 1996:137–138)

Here, Rushdie betrays his love for *filmi* gossip. There were concerns by the director and his production team that it might harm the film, if Nargis's romantic attachment to Sunil Dutt entered the public domain. Rushdie uses the Oedipal implications of the film to point out the analogies with his own cast of characters in the novel, especially the intense relationship between Aurora and Moraes, which he then intricately ties to a wider argument about nationhood.

Rushdie invites a metaphorical reading of Aurora, yet the mythic stature that he invests in his female characters is undercut and deconstructed through their own actions when they operate as characters within the narrative. Amidst the patriarchal male-dominated discourse and conception of Nation, Aurora encapsulates the various images of Mother India and acts these out either in her paintings or in real life, taking on the role of prophetic Cassandra and annihilating mother. This ultimately sets her up as an urban version of Mother India that can compete with the notion in the film *Mother India*, the star persona of Nargis, and the political figure Indira Gandhi.[11] It also underscores the intensive mother-son relationship that dominates the novel as much as the film. Bishnupriya Ghosh points out in 'An Invitation to Indian Postmodernity: Rushdie's English Vernacular as Situated Cultural Hybridity,' the witticism that 'the entire country has a mother-son problem' has more serious repercussions, suggesting that the mother-son symbiosis depicts the central political imaginary of the Indian nation, which is reaffirmed by cinema and popular culture (139). Mother and son form an eclectic secular unit. Aurora transforms her son into the prime subject of her paintings, the Moor series, functioning as a mirror through which the rise of communalism and the decline of pluralistic Bombay is viewed. Moraes in turn exposes himself as a Bombay movie fan, explicitly and implicitly connecting films such as *Mother India* to his story. The authorial reciprocal gaze of mother and son allows Moraes to paint his own portrait of his mother, albeit in words, and infused with the movie language of his city:

> This is what I saw: a tall woman in a paint-spattered, mid-calf-length homespun kurta worn over dark blue sailcloth slacks, barefoot, her white hair piled up on her head with brushes sticking out of it, giving her an eccentric Madame Butterfly look, Butterfly as Katherine Hepburn or—yes!—Nargis in some zany Indian cover version, *Titli Begum*, might have played her. (Rushdie 1996:219)

Moraes draws analogies to *Mother India* as he tries to explain the story of his immediate family and his relationship to Aurora through the filmic text. While Aurora transforms into the "image of an aggressive, treacherous, annihilating mother" who "haunts the fantasy life of Indian males," Moraes concedes that "I, too, know something of that image; have been cast as a Bad Son in my turn" and he goes on to extend the analogies between the film and his family:

> My Mother was no Nargis Dutt—she was the in-your-face type, not serene. Catch her hauling a shovel on her shoulder! *I am pleased to say that I have never seen a spade.* Aurora was a city girl, perhaps *the* city girl, as much the incarnation of the smartyboots metropolis as Mother India was village earth made flesh. In spite of this I have found it instructive to compare and contrast our families. Mother India's movie-husband was rendered impotent, his arms crushed by a rock; and ruined limbs play a central rôle in our saga, too. (You must judge for yourselves whether Abraham was a potent fellow or im—.) And as for Birju and Moor: dark skins and crookery were not all we had in common. (Rushdie 1996:139)

This section foreshadows Moraes's own fall from grace, his descent into the shadow world of crime and gangsterism of the city and the use of his ruined limb as a weapon as one of Raman Fielding's henchmen.[12] In turn, Moraes is trapped, impotent and powerless among the colliding personalities of Abraham, Aurora, Uma, Vasco Miranda, and Raman Fielding. Ghosh persuasively argues that by highlighting issues of imagination, narration, and representation, the social responsibilities of the artist and the historian, Rushdie "creates a novel about a national culture—its ramparts, possibilities, failures, and evolutions—rather than a nation!" (Ghosh 1999:139). Through *Mother India*, Bombay cinema provided the newly independent nation with a secular, inclusive way of imagining Woman in the role of Mother as Nation. The film reflects this by taking up the Nehruvian vision of the Nation, celebrating unity in diversity. It is such a perfect intertext for Rushdie not only because of the plot parallels, especially the Oedipal triangle, but also in its deployment of allegory in its reading of Indira Gandhi, Nargis, and Aurora Zogoiby as stand-ins or representatives of Mother India. In *The Moor's Last Sigh*, Rushdie constructs an urban version of *Mother India* that stands for tolerance to preserve India's unity in diversity. The intertextual relationship to one of the defining myths of post-Independence secular mythology, in the form of Mother India, and the palimpsestual relationship to India's smallest minorities enables Rushdie to write an epic novel that encapsulates this vision.

Notes

1. According to Jayant Lele, "the rise and fall of the Shiv Sena in the political events of Bombay-Mahrashtra has often been described in terms of waves of popularity and decline." However, the events of December–March 1992/1993 require to be treated not as just another communal riot (Lele 1996:186). According to Kalpana Sharma, the genesis of the two sets of communal riots in December 1992 and January 1993 could be traced back to a series of social political and economic developments going back at least three decades: "The communalisation of Bombay politics had been taking place throughout the 1980s, and particularly after the emergence of the Shiv Sena as a force in electoral politics" (Sharma 1996:269). Sharma further points out that the riots cannot be separated from the bombings in March 1993 when a series of powerful explosions ripped through Bombay's financial district, targeting amongst other buildings the Bombay Stock Exchange and the Air India Building. The riots and explosions have left behind a permanently altered city and has exposed its fragility. Sharma concludes that "in the past, a shared history, the nature of the economy of the city from which many benefited directly or indirectly, contributed to its stability. The riots revealed how overt and covert changes in the city's economy and political life that had been taking place eventually contributed to the collapse that was witnessed in those weeks" (Sharma 1996:286). In the aftermath of the bombings, it became increasingly evident that Bombay has become a divided city not only between Hindus and Muslims, but also between those who have gained from the changed economic environment and those who have been excluded. It is against this backdrop that Rushdie's narrative unfolds. For a full account of events that led up to the Bombay riots see Sharma, 268–286.

2. The Shiv Sena was launched in 1966 and initially only had a very limited constituency with a simple programme, mainly the reservation of jobs and new economic opportunities for Maharashtrians, specifically protesting against the influx of workers from South India, which had increased dramatically since Independence

and which was deemed to be responsible for a lack of jobs. Between 1960, the creation of the state of Maharashtra, and 1966, Bombay's economy underwent fundamental structural changes and the underside of state-sponsored private capitalist development started to emerge, an 'underworld' of extortion, smuggling, drug trafficking and contraband peddling. By the end of the 1960s, although the Sena publicly attacked the underworld, it managed to established strong ties, building up a strong following that gave the organisation its muscle and power and in return gave those in the underworld the benefit of its organisation and benefit. The Shiv Sena's founder Bal Thackeray structured the organisation around a concept borrowed from the Rashtriya Swayamsevak Sangh, a Hindu nationalist organisation of long standing, into *Shakas* (branches) in numerous neighbourhoods. For a detailed account of the Shiv Sena's genesis and politics see Lele 1996:185–212.

3. I use the term *Hindutva* not in its original sense, but in its more recent political meaning. *Hindutva* has become a term that describes a specific ideology of cultural nationalism that seeks to reorganise Indian society. Through, amongst others, the BJP, it is no longer used in religious terms, but has taken on more of a political meaning. It no longer stands for Hinduism, but for a distinctive world-view that, according to the BJP, seeks to reorganise cultural nationalism along the concept of one people, one culture, one nation. During the BJP's term in government, this became concrete, for example, when many history books were rewritten to align school syllabuses to this conceptualisation, one of the first things the new Congress government has reversed. The fascist implications of this line of thinking are also evident.

4. In *The Discovery of India*, Nehru describes the crowd's reaction to his question who and what *Bharat Mata*, Mother India, signified when they were shouting the slogan *Bharat Mata ki Jai* (Victory to Mother India). The response ranged from the good earth of India from their particular village patch to all the patches in the district and the province to the whole of India. Nehru extends this to the people who populate this vast land. 'Mother India was essentially these millions of people, and victory to her meant victory to these people.' (Nehru 2004:53) This consideration is important when reading the symbolism of the Mother India character in the film. In how far do we need to read her as an allegory, in how far does she operate as a character? This too is relevant when considering the heterogeneously accumulated image of Mother as Mother India that Rushdie deconstructs in his novel. For an interesting discussion of the role of women in the Indian nationalist movement and their role in public and private spheres see Chatterjee 2001:151–166.

5. For an interesting discussion of this theme see Thomas 1989:11–30.

6. After her successful campaign in the Bangladesh war in 1971, Indira Gandhi was invariably hailed as Bharat Mata. For an interesting discussion of Indira Gandhi in relation to gender constructions, leadership and representation see Sunder Rajan 1993:103–128.

7. In Nargis's attack on Satyajit Rai's films, she accuses him of only showing India's poverty, while she in her films strove to highlight the positive in Indian society, like dams.

8. In his interview with Michael Silverblatt, Rushdie describes the Mother India theme as 'the intellectual way into the book. The fact is that the idea of India as a mother, the idea of the mother goddess has always been the most central defining image of India.' (Silverblatt 2001:199)

9. For an interesting discussion of *Mother India* in psychoanalytical terms see Mishra 2002:61–88.

10. The example of Nargis provides various parallels that merit comment, especially since *Mother India* is Rushdie's chosen filmic intertext. Behroze Gandhy and Rosie Thomas in 'Three Indian Film Stars' have looked closely at the phenomenon of the subcontinental star cult. They argue that "the films and the subtext of gossip about stars are most usefully seen as debates around morality, in particular as negotiations about the role of 'tradition' in a modernising India" (Ghandy and Thomas 1991:108). This is interestingly negotiated in relation to Nargis as her film roles ranged from coy coquette to village damsel, from Westernized career woman to the resilient earth mother and champion of the oppressed peasantry (Ghandy and Thomas 1991:116), but always with a fundamental emphasis on purity and moral soundness. Gandhy and Thomas are concerned with the persona of Nargis as publicly constructed rumour, which is an interesting parallel to Aurora. See Gandhy and Thomas 1991:107–131.

11. There are deliberate parallels between the three, for instance the love letter Nehru writes to Aurora is actually taken from Nehru's letters to Indira. Aurora is linked to the Nehru family, she is alleged to be his lover and Moraes implies that he might be their illegitimate love child (Rushdie 1996:175). This implies not only the Nehru dynasty as a parallel, but also draws analogies between their relationships. Thus, the intense mother-son relationship of Aurora and Moraes is an explicit connection to that between Sanjay and Indira Gandhi. Furthermore, these legends contribute in setting up the family as dynasty, paralleled in South Asia's political life.

12. In the novel, the parallels between Raman Fielding and Bal Thackeray are more than evident. Before founding the Shiv Sena, Thackeray worked as a cartoonist for *The Free Press Journal*, an English-language daily, but left in 1960 to set up his own Marathi weekly journal, *Marmik*, featuring cartoons, political comment and humour. In *The Moor's Last Sigh*, he is nicknamed Gup Mainduck, which roughly translates as 'ugly toad,' reflecting Thackeray's unflattering facial features. Even before founding the Shiv Sena in 1966, Thackeray was politically active during the language riots that led to the partition of the former colonially defined Bombay province into the states of Maharashtra and Gujarat. Initially not pursuing a consistent political line, his journal severely criticised all practicing politicians and public figures that did not meet Thackeray's approval, which increased his popularity among the lower middle classes. During these years, his strong strain of Hindu nationalism emerged in his writing.

References

Chakravarty, Sumita S. *National Identity in Indian Popular Cinema, 1947–1987*. Austin: University of Texas Press, 1993.

Chatterjee, Partha. "The Nationalist Resolution of the Women's Question." *Postcolonial Discourses: An Anthology*. Gregory Castle, ed. Oxford: Blackwell, 2001. 151–166.

Dwyer, Rachel. *All You Want Is Money, All You Need Is Love: Sexuality and Romance in*

Modern India. London: Cassell, 2000.

Gandhy, Behroze and Rosie Thomas. "Three Indian Film Stars." *Stardom: Industry of Desire*. Christine Gledhill, ed. London: Routledge, 1991. 107–131.

Ghosh, Bishnupriya. "An Invitation to Indian Postmodernity: Rushdie's English Vernacular as Situated Cultural Hybridity." *Critical Essays on Salman Rushdie*. M Keith Booker, ed. New York: GK Hall & Co., 1999. 129–153.

Lele, Jayant. "Saffronization of the Shiv Sena: The Political Economy of City, State and Nation." *Bombay: Metaphor for Modern India*. Sujata Patel and Alice Thorner, eds. New Delhi: Oxford University Press, 1996. 185–212.

Llosa, Alvaro Vargas. "The Last Sigh of Diversity." *Salman Rushdie Interviews: A Sourcebook of his Ideas*. Pradyumna S Chauhan, ed. Westport, Connecticut: Greenwood Press, 2001. 209–212.

Mishra, Vijay. *Bollywood Cinema - Temples of Desire*. New York: Routledge, 2002.

Nehru, Jawaharlal. *The Discovery of India*. New Delhi: Penguin Books India, 2004.

Rajadhyaksha, Ashish and Paul Willemen. *Encyclopaedia of Indian Cinema*. 2nd edition. London: British Film Institute; New Delhi: Oxford University Press, 2002.

Rushdie, Salman. *Imaginary Homelands: Essays and Criticism 1981–1991*. 2nd edition. London: Granta/Penguin, 1992.

___. *Midnight's Children*. London: Vintage, 1995.

___. *The Moor's Last Sigh*. London: Vintage, 1996.

Rushdie, Salman, and Elizabeth West, eds. *The Vintage Book of Indian Writing 1947–1997*. London: Vintage, 1997.

Shahani, Roshan G. "Polyphonous Voices in the City: Bombay's Indian-English Fiction." *Bombay: Mosaic of Modern Culture*. Sujata Patel and Alice Thorner, eds. Bombay: Oxford University Press, 1995. 99–112.

Sharma, Kalpana. "Chronicle of a Riot Foretold." *Bombay: Metaphor for Modern India*. Sujata Patel and Alice Thorner, eds. New Delhi: Oxford University Press, 1996. 268–286.

Silverblatt, Michael. "Bookworm with Michael Silverblatt, Guest: Salman Rushdie." *Salman Rushdie Interviews: A Sourcebook of his Ideas*. Pradyumna S Chauhan, ed. Westport, Connecticut: Greenwood Press, 2001: 199–212.

Sunder Rajan, Rajeswari. "Gender, Leadership and Representation: the 'case' of Indira Gandhi." *Real and Imagined Women: Gender, Culture and Postcolonialism*. London: Routledge, 1993. 103–128.

Thomas, Rosie. "Sanctity and Scandal: The Mythologization of Mother India." *Quarterly Review of Film & Video* 11.2, 1989. 11–30.

Index

Acknowledgements

"Globalizing Bombay Cinema: Reproducing the Indian State and Family" by Monika Mehta first published in *Cultural Dynamics* Vol. 17, no. 135. 2005. Reproduced by permission from Author (©Sage Publications, 2005) by permission of Sage Publications Ltd.

"Gender, Nation, and Globalization in *Monsoon Wedding* and *Dilwale Dulhania Le Jayenge,*" by Jenny Sharpe first published in *Meridians: feminism, race, transnationalism* Vol. 6, no. 1. 2005. 58–81. Reprinted by permission of the publisher (Indiana University Press).

"Viewing the West through Bollywood: a Celluloid Occident in the Making" by Ravinder Kaur first published in *Contemporary South Asia*, Vol. 11, no. 2. 2002. 199–209. Reprinted by permission of the publisher (Taylor & Francis Ltd, http://www.informaworld.com).

"Power and Representation in Modern Indian Cinema: Case Studies from the Toronto Film Festival (1994)" by Ahmad Saidullah first published in *The Toronto Review of Contemporary Writing Abroad* Vol. 13, no. 2. 1995. 3–16. Reprinted by permission of the author.

"Phoolan Devi's Open Letter to the Director of the Toronto International Film Festival" by Phoolan Devi. Reproduced from *The Toronto Review of Contemporary Writing Abroad* Vol. 13, no. 2. 1995.

"Statement From the Director of the Toronto International Film Festival" by Piers Handling. 1994. Reproduced from *The Toronto Review of Contemporary Writing Abroad* Vol. 13, no. 2. 1995.

"Defining Truth: An Interview with Shekhar Kapur" by Ahmad Saidullah first published in *The Toronto Review of Contemporary Writing Abroad* Vol. 13, no. 2. 1995. 25–32. Reprinted by permission of the author.